Remembering the Personal Past

Remembering the Personal Past

Descriptions of Autobiographical Memory

Bruce M. Ross

The Catholic University of America
Washington, D.C.

New York   Oxford
OXFORD UNIVERSITY PRESS
1991

Oxford University Press

Oxford   New York   Toronto
Delhi   Bombay   Calcutta   Madras   Karachi
Petaling Jaya   Singapore   Hong Kong   Tokyo
Nairobi   Dar es Salaam   Cape Town
Melbourne   Auckland

and associated companies in
Berlin   Ibadan

Copyright © 1991 by Oxford University Press, Inc.

Published by Oxford University Press, Inc.,
200 Madison Avenue, New York, New York 10016

Oxford is a registered trademark of Oxford University Press

Library of Congress Cataloging-in-Publication Data
Ross, Bruce M.
Remembering the personal past:
descriptions of autobiographical memory Bruce M. Ross.
p. cm.   Includes bibliographical references and index.
ISBN 0-19-506894-7
1. Autobiographical memory.   I. Title.
BF378.A87R67 1991   153.1'3—dc20
91-4233

1 3 5 7 9 8 6 4 2

Printed in the United States of America
on acid-free paper

*To my parents for memory
and my sister for courage*

PREFACE

Rumor has it that the unexamined life is not worth living. But what from one's past can reasonably be known and subjected to examination? And there is a further troubling complication: what psychical baggage is retained from one's past with all identification lost? Every person possesses not only a waiting room of memories where old favorites are recalled but also a Lost and Found where recollections from the past appear without being recognized. Other less accessible memories are hidden in mental suitcases to which we have misplaced the keys; elsewhere suitcases are discovered empty that we thought were full. Piled in with the rest are convenient imitation packages of memories constructed out of dreams and fantasies that were never paid for with experience. Every baggage room of memories is open day and night, for no living traveler rides free of the burden of old luggage.

The major impetus for this book is the belief that a comprehensive description of the field of autobiographical memory, in both its form and its function, must be an eclectic, interdisciplinary endeavor. This attempt at providing a panoramic view goes directly against the spirit of the current age, which favors rigorously minimalist and reductive descriptions. But however one may wish it otherwise, an adequately fleshed-out description of human memory must consider such factors as motivations and emotions, whether one treats them as potentially retainable memory components or as part of an enabling ambience for recollection. Here theoretical opinions vary widely. Nonetheless, a purely cognitive memory must belong either to a robot or to an inert database.

Chapter organization, in the main, proceeds from consideration of memory attributes of the individual in relative isolation to retention in social groups and institutions; likewise, temporal durations extend from the fairly immediate to the very long term. The description of sensations and images found in laboratory-based retention studies is followed by ideas about memory recall in the dyadic relation of traditional psychotherapy, while later chapters deal with memory in social groups and across historical time spans. Multiple memory frameworks are required to represent the possibilities of autobiographical memory, since, as in love and war, every stratagem is permissible, with potential memory disclosures ranging from unconscious actions to public communications. The present work includes several instances in which, in spite of widely differing content, there has been considerable unacknowledged agreement across disparate disciplines.

At odds with much contemporary thinking about autobiographical retention is my emphasis on the old-fashioned problem of memory accuracy. Even when evaluation must be extremely problematic, accuracy would seem to be a determination that cannot altogether be ignored. Nevertheless many psycho-

therapists who otherwise disagree claim that worrying about the objective
truth of memories serves no useful purpose, since it is only the patient's
subjective belief in the truth of often error-prone and partially fabricated
memories that needs to be heeded.

A note on the same theme is struck by W.-J. T. Mitchell, an authority on
narrativity theory, an approach recently in ascendancy with regard to the
integration of life-history memories. Mitchell is altogether dismissive of truth-
verification discussion, adducing the peculiar reason that it is *not a theoretical
problem*. The argument runs:

> It is a commonplace of modern relativism, of course, that there are multiple
> versions of events and the stories about them and that there is something
> suspect about claims to having the "true" or "authorized" or "basic" version
> in one's possession. The real problem, however, is not the telling of true
> stories from false (this seems to be a practical rather than a theoretical
> problem) but the very value of narrativity as a mode of making sense of
> reality (whether the factual reality of actual events, or the moral, symbolic
> reality of fictions). (Mitchell, 1980, p. 2)

I argue, to the contrary, that to evaluate multiple versions of past happenings
for truth content is a necessary task. Memories cannot always be easily separated from fantasies, but approximate orderings can frequently be made. How
one goes about determining memory veridicality, whether performed by individuals themselves or by external evaluators, is a crucial, though undeveloped, theoretical category.

Very recent theoretical developments are not described in this book;
rather, emphasis is on interdisciplinary breadth and feasible approaches that
appear to have been neglected in current research. It is my self-serving con-
ceit, omissions notwithstanding, that in the recent spate of empirical studies
dealing with autobiographical memory few *theoretical* ideas of any generality
have emerged that have not been foreshadowed. This is not to deny the value
of experimental studies, but the necessity for administering common treatment procedures to a statistically adequate group of subjects has frequently so
narrowed the scope of group investigations that they are less theoretically
fruitful than extended single-case studies.

A word can be said about my treatment of psychoanalytic concepts, since
more space is devoted to them than to those of any other discipline. Uncertain
as verification is regarding many of these concepts, the fact remains that
Freud and later psychoanalysts put forward a greater number of ideas pertaining to autobiographical memory than theorists of any other persuasion. Even
for academic investigators skeptical of psychoanalysis, ideas concerning autobiographical memory stemming from psychoanalysis still furnish something of
a theoretical reservoir. Academic psychologists, however, typically relate to
psychoanalysis either by simplifying and testing single concepts or by rejecting
psychoanalytic contexts and then inventing presumably equivalent but more
quantifiable concepts on a functional, common-sense basis. Although many
older psychoanalytic concepts are still of interest and others have not been

fully exploited, a fundamental change in theoretical climate is under way. Owing to recent theoretical revisions in both the theory and the therapy of psychoanalysis, which I relate in some detail, the era during which psychoanalysis originated important new concepts relating to autobiographical memory now appears to be over.

A better bet for the future formulation of novel ideas might be those studies that deal with memory contexts in social frameworks—for example, sociology, anthropology, and folklore—which have been only fringe contributors to memory theory up to now. My sampling of theoretical concepts thus draws from those disciplines that concern themselves with the preservation of the temporal integrity of society as well as those that emphasize the continuity of the individual. Discussion of these disciplines is highly selective but is intended to be illustrative of future possibilities that could give a wider sweep to memory studies. In this regard, any field concerned with the retention and distortion of retained meanings in which human capability and limitation play a role can be envisaged as a potential contributor.

It can be further assumed as a general principle, if one acknowledges the inevitable social forging and shaping of personal memories, that it is somewhat arbitrary to limit influences that affect memory to the lifetime retention-span of a single individual and not also consider memories that are communicated between individuals and social institutions that transcend more than one generation. In one way or another, many of the humanities and social sciences other than psychology do possess such a historical dimension that touches on cross-generational remembering. Exceeding the boundaries of individual memory has the particular virtue of demonstrating conclusively that in the real world, autobiographical memory modeled on a rote memory paradigm—though not an indictable offense—comes close to being an unnatural act.

Readers of this text in several manuscript versions have pointed out that I have not in every case made optimal choices among memory theorists. I am sure they are right. Nor can I plead in my defense that any of the omitted theorists were excluded because they failed to meet some hypothetical criteria, since orienting landmarks often became clear to me only after I had obtained adequate acquaintance with rival alternatives. Some of my own early contenders in the end "failed to make the final cut" because their views overlapped too much with those of others or their ideas were those of common currency. In this regard, it is less the particular theorists who are of interest than specific ideas. In this quest I have not hesitated to extricate some older ideas about memory from their antique settings and suggest that they possess some stand-alone qualities that still deserve consideration. A potentially more serious deficiency is that in searching out relevant ideas from diverse disciplines I have sometimes gone astray by making faulty interpretations and bending concepts to fit my own biases. Concerning such mistakes, inevitably multiplied by the wide variety of academic fields with which I have consorted, I can only acknowledge my limitations in advance. I have attempted to present a unified viewpoint, though certainly this is not always quite attained, with theoretical possibilities and shortcomings found all round.

The various individuals and groups to whom I am indebted for assistance are in no way responsible for any errors of omission or commission. I would especially thank for early encouragement, manuscript reading, and source material recommendations Leslie Hicks, Catherine Kerst, Robert Ketterlinus, Nissim Levy, Ronald Shectman, and Samuel Weiner. Also I am grateful for interactions with the members of three graduate seminars that dealt with memory topics, the comments of two insightful readers on behalf of the Oxford University Press, and the helpfulness of the staffs of the Mullen Library and the Life Cycle Institute. In particular, for lengthy labors in word-processing many manuscript revisions I thank Marcia Annis and Cindy Schmid. The three people who worked with me most intensively in giving knowledgeable recommendations are my former graduate student, Thomas Granzow, and my two colleagues and friends for more than a quarter century, Hans Furth and James Youniss. Gratitude *in extenso*.

Washington, D.C.   B.M.R.
March 1991

CONTENTS

Remembering the Personal Past

1

Introduction

Now I am wiser: for I know there is not any memory with less satisfaction in it than the memory of some temptation we resisted.

JAMES BRANCH CABELL

What is patriotism but the love of the good things of our childhood?

LIN YUTANG

We are a people who do not want to keep much of the past in our heads. It is considered unhealthy in America to remember mistakes, neurotic to think about them, psychotic to dwell upon them.   LILLIAN HELLMAN

We each remember our past in the best amateur tradition without receiving any instruction or ever being offered lessons. In spite of many mistakes and confessions of inadequacy, we each become the ultimate insider and foremost expert on our own memories. How is this crucial task accomplished? The goal of this book is to collect and interpret theoretical ideas that pertain to autobiographical memory and that originate from a variety of diverse sources in the scientific literature. The present work assembles, comments critically, and to a degree integrates three general approaches to autobiographical memory: (1) the subjective or experiential dimensions of autobiographical memory, (2) the early development and later recall of childhood memories, and (3) social, historical, and folkloric perspectives on autobiographical retention.

Because memories of one's past thoughts and actions are pervasive and inescapable, the world has not waited on scientific investigations to draw conclusions about the nature of such memories. It has become a truism that poets know more about memories than psychologists do. Indeed, the quotations with which this chapter opens illustrate some shrewd assessments of autobiographical memory. However, a codification of literature insights, like these samples drawn from a novelist, an essayist, and a playwright turned memoirist, must wait for another forum. Though, to be even-handed, each of the perspectives to be considered—the subjective, developmental, and social-historical—is represented by an epigraph.

Instead of worldly wisdom regarding autobiographical memories, an interpretive survey is presented that includes the older psychology literature, emphasizing the introspective and developmental viewpoints; psychoanalytic theory, concentrating on Sigmund Freud's ideas, but also including the range

3

of modifications in memory concepts suggested by later analysts; and a sampling of concepts pertaining to autobiographical memory from history, oral history, sociology, folklore, and anthropology. Emphasis is placed not only on what are important perspectives but also on neglected areas of interest that are seldom related to the psychological study of autobiographical memory. Excluded from my theorizing are the extensive and recently well-reviewed literatures on the psychology of testimony and memory reminiscence in old age. The developmental emphasis is strictly on the initial period of life, from infancy to adulthood.

Considering the intrinsic interest that attaches to autobiographical memory and the considerable number of maxims, witticisms, and epigrams concerning it that have been produced by pundits of all persuasions, one must expect that autobiographical memory would be a flourishing, well-researched area of psychology. Surprisingly, this is not the case; academic psychology has largely ignored the explicit study of autobiographical memory. Recently, though, this situation has changed, with an increasing number of empirical studies and the publication of two pioneering edited books (David Rubin's *Autobiographical Memory* in 1986 and Ulric Neisser's *Memory Observed: Remembering in Natural Contexts* in 1982). These books exploit a diversity of data sources, apply ingenious experimental designs, and sample some unusual real-world testimony in regard to memory performance. Explanatory theories are somewhat limited, however, as they are generally closely tied to specific data-gathering procedures. Perhaps the time is favorable, then, "to refresh the memory" of autobiographical memory studies by presenting, within the three proposed categories, an interdisciplinary survey of past (and some present) theoretical ideas. Just as important as close consideration of one's own personal memories, is the attempt to determine how well older ideas and concepts stand up to current scrutiny. As to the ports of call in circumnavigation of the vast expanse of autobiographical memory, some consideration must be given to emotional and motivational retention. To limit oneself to cognitive considerations, as is often done, is to set an itinerary before embarking on the exploration.

How can autobiographical memory be differentiated from other forms of memory? This is a question better answered at the end of this survey, but it is appropriate to begin with some basic characteristics. My working definition is aligned with ordinary usage in that it addresses the possible or actual descriptions of past happenings that would be considered by most people as "part of one's personal history." In this regard, and unlike some other writers, I use the terms *autobiographical memory* and *personal memory* interchangeably. The contents of autobiographical memory, insofar as they are veridical, derive from happenings that are unrepeatable because they occurred at a specific point in time. In general, a specific event is the origin of personal memories, even though similar events tend to coalesce when recollected. Memorized material and factual information without personal reference are largely excluded. Of relevance here, though physiological considerations will not be pursued, is the recent claim that in neuropsychological terms "a strong case can be made for a distinction between a memory system that supports gradual or incremental learning and is involved in the acquisition of habits and a system that supports rapid one-trial learning and is necessary for forming memories that represent specific situations and episodes" (Sherry and Schacter, 1987). The latter description conforms to the present loose definition of autobiographical memory.[1]

There is a broad way and a narrow way to construe autobiographical memory. The narrow way is to allow only what can be remembered overtly to count as retained memory content. Using the narrow criterion, neat, well-designed empirical studies can be undertaken. Autobiographical memory experiments of either description are not easy, however, because of the problem of memory verification. The broader interpretation includes (memory) responses expressed in terms of symbolic expressions, repetitive activities, and emotional reinstatements that often are outside the awareness of the rememberer and that therefore cannot be recalled on demand.[2] To handle these situations theoretically, one first looks to psychoanalysis, for psychoanalysis and its derivatives offer the only theories that deal in any detail with the unconscious dimensions of memories, particularly in relation to long-term memories initiated in childhood. Psychoanalytic theory in this realm must nonetheless be assessed for its adequacy, since no analyst today accepts completely Freud's original memoric concepts, which were in fact presented over a long period of years and are somewhat contradictory.

A special emphasis given in my critique of psychoanalysis, Chapters 3 through 6, is the highlighting of Freud's stress on subjective memory imagery, a dimension almost completely omitted from contemporary psychoanalytic discussions. An emphasis on imagery is almost mandatory when discussing dreams, but Freud extends this emphasis to memories, sometimes giving priority to the interpretation of memory imagery over words. The analyst Erik Erikson remarks in an autobiographical note how attractive he found this emphasis on imagery when, as a young artist, he first became interested in psychoanalysis:

> I soon detected in Freud's writings vivid manifestations of an indomitable visual curiosity, which sent him hurrying to Italy and through her city squares whenever his work permitted. His descriptions of his patients' memories and dreams also reveal that he deeply empathized with their imagery before he entered what he had heard and seen into the context of verbal nomenclature. (1975, p. 30)

Chapters 5 and 6 in this book present in very condensed form the ideas of psychoanalysts and other theorists who have enlarged, revised, and in some cases discarded Freud's views on memory. My aim has been to present a representative sampling of ideas rather than to attempt completeness. One major area of disagreement is particularly noticeable between Freud and some later analysts. For Freud, who construed memory broadly, a partial memory or memory fragment, or even an incomplete symbolic representation of a past experience, counts as a memory. Later analysts have frequently set up strict criteria, demanding nearly complete retention of past happenings recalled as accurate verbal descriptions before a present experience could be classified as a memory experience. Naturally these analysts find that their patients have retained only a few memories, and the same analysts downplay both the possibility and the necessity for memory recovery in describing how therapeutic success can be achieved. No one formulates therapeutic theories predicated on achieving failure!

Consistent with the theoretical aims just outlined, an overview can be given of the topics central to each of the chapters that follow. The knowledge that can be obtained about memory through the analysis of subjective experience is the subject of Chapter 2. A number of problems that have been of historical interest to psychologists and philosophers of memory are described. In several instances I argue that these earlier theoretical issues could be of interest today and in the future (e.g., volitional, chronological, and definitional difficulties relating to personal memories). Although I start with the academic introspective psychologies of William James and Edward Bradford Titchener, I use introspection also in the ordinary, wider sense of self-examination of one's own mental life. How far is the human mind able to go in delineating the nature of human memory where the same individual is both subject and observer? With the obvious biases and prejudices that self-report methods entail, psychologists of widely varying allegiances would tend to agree—"not very far." Yet introspections give us the face of memories as we know them, and they are essential for determining which memories are autobiographical for the rememberer. Theories that do not account for the experiential dimensions of memory are incomplete.

In academic psychology there is little modern information revealing the experiential side of memory, although recent investigators have been less constrained in areas other than memory study. In the study of thinking processes, for example, reintroduction of subjective protocols occurred about 30 years ago, at the beginning of the adoption of the information-processing point of view. With few exceptions, recent memory researchers have been more conservative and have excluded descriptive subjective reports. (Perhaps a major unstated barrier is that since words are commonly the objects of memorization, it would contaminate performance to also require verbal subjective reports.)[3]

I would emphasize that easily differentiated subjective distinctions can be central to quite ordinary retention situations that appear objectively similar. Such subjective differences need not depend on emotional or dramatic content. As a simple example, suppose that you remember quite correctly that you have never before seen a particular object now present. There are a number of alternative experiences that can account for or accompany your accurate responding: for example, (1) you straightway recognize the specified object as *novel;* (2) you feel that, try as you will, you cannot remember the object, the experience is that of *uncertainty about knowing,* as occurs when you have forgotten something you once knew; or (3) you consider the context of the object and remember that it was *not there before.* Related to possibility

(3) is a less precise yet distinctive experience (4) in which there is a general class rather than specific object-related recognition of a change or difference. Arthur Koestler (1967) has given the example of noticing that something has been changed in a friend's room, but you cannot tell *what* has been changed, an outcome Koestler terms "negative recognition." Such trivial experiential differences might seem pedantic nitpicking, but in other than mundane perceptual contexts such distinctions can be important, even crucial. Results that lump all correct retentions together without experiential distinctions are inevitably incomplete and qualify as information *processed* rather than information *processing*.

Chapters 3 and 4 in this book present Freud's theory of autobiographical memory, beginning with such well-known fundamental concepts as screen memories and repression and continuing with less central concepts, such as ideational mimetics and Freud's early association model of memory. Although in his early theorizing Freud was more concerned with memory recovery than he was later, he continued to comment on the nature of human memory to the end of his life, and he exhibited an extraordinary confidence in the possibility of recovering early childhood memories. The full range of his memory theorizing is described, with occasional commentary about how other analysts construed some of his important concepts. My emphasis is on description and clarification of memory concepts without close assessment of empirical validity or concern with psychotherapeutic success rates when Freud's concepts are put into practice. Somewhat surprisingly, there appears to be no other extant summarizing review concerned with the entire range of Freud's memory conceptualizations. Possible virtues and disadvantages of Freud's concepts and potential linkages with nonpsychoanalytic ideas are discussed in later chapters.

Chapter 5 discusses some of the ways in which psychoanalysts after Freud have modified his ideas about memory. Greatest space is devoted to psychoanalytic ego psychology as represented by the theories of Ernst Kris and his theoretical colleagues, but a brief survey of more recent psychoanalytic ideas is also included. The range of these theories is wide, and some theorists are highly skeptical of Freud's ideas. Critics who are outside psychoanalytic circles often ignore this literature. Even for many psychologists interested in memory, simply to be acquainted with Freud's major concepts, albeit with intricacies omitted, is thought to be sufficient. Yet if they looked, nonanalytic critics would find that many of their criticisms and revisions have been anticipated by analytic theorists after Freud. Theoretical changes over the years appear to stem from two main sources: difficulties encountered in following Freud's recommended memory-recovery practices and the introduction of new ideas originating outside psychoanalysis. The present paradoxical situation is that, generally speaking, only those investigators who are skeptical of psychoanalytic theories are interested in preserving Freud's theories in their original, unmodified form.

The first part of Chapter 6 is intended to demonstrate that psychoanalytically derived ideas have been picked up and extended by therapist-theorists who are not themselves psychoanalysts. The ideas of Alfred Adler, who early broke away from Freud, offer considerable contrast. In common with Freud, however, Adler placed strong emphasis on patients' efforts to recall their early memories. And, as elsewhere in Adlerian theory, there is some foreshadowing of theoretical developments in psychoanalysis made by later analysts. Also outlined are the theoretical ideas of two eclectic theorists, D. E. Cameron and William Sargant, who took apparently minor Freudian concepts and expanded them to a surprisingly large number of applications. The second part of Chapter 6 presents my evaluation of the strengths and weaknesses of the theories and ideas related to psychoanalysis that are presented in Chapters 3 through 6. In the book's final chapter, several orthodox and revisionist psychoanalytic concepts that pertain to autobiographical memory are placed in a wider framework that encompasses nonpsychoanalytic ideas as well.

In understanding possible relations between introspection and psychoanalysis, it is useful to note the ambiguous attitude of analysts toward conscious experience. A distinguishing mark of psychoanalysis and other depth psychologies is the unremitting emphasis on the doctrine that we have a near-permanent lack of awareness of many of our memories, especially some of the most important ones. Occasionally a few of these memories surprise us and surface spontaneously. This reservoir of memories can be sampled by using special therapeutic, psychopharmacological, or hypnotic techniques. Thus we are led to wonder how many more memories potentially exist that we will never recall! Nowadays this view is widespread and includes many therapists who have little tolerance for psychoanalysis. But even depth psychologies must inevitably depend on patients' subjective understanding for descriptions of the forms and patterns into which memories are cast. All psychotherapies make use of such reports, though they be but the "tip of the iceberg," and, indeed, parts of psychoanalysis are alleged to give us explanations of Freud's personal memories "writ large." Freud's example notwithstanding, the reigning attitude within psychoanalysis is that the study of memory consciousness is peripheral to the mission of psychoanalysis to investigate the dynamics of the unconscious. More than a few contemporary analysts take the position that autobiographical memories that are too easily recoverable are *ipso facto* irrelevant to therapy.

Although Freud posited a number of seminal ideas that he wove into ingenious and original theories, his views with regard to conceptualizing memory were frequently quite similar to those of the psychologists of his time. Recent historians of psychoanalysis, is searching out the origins of Doctor Freud's theories, have concentrated on medical sources and have ignored Freud's acquaintance and commonality of outlook with turn-of-the-century psychologists. Several theoretical emphases are pointed out that contemporary scholars view as distinctively Freudian which were wholly congruent with an earlier psychological (as distinct from a medical) *Zeitgeist*.[4] Today the related and rival views of these early psychologists are forgotten while Freud's ideas live on.

In Chapter 7 I attempt to trace the early development of the child's memory from the child's standpoint, in contrast to the psychotherapeutic perspective where childhood events are viewed initially from the adult standpoint with subsequent theoretical extrapolations to childhood experiencing. There is a great amount of empirical research on children's memory, but very little of it touches on autobiographical memory. In Chapter 7 I address the views of two developmental theorists, the American psychologist James Mark Baldwin and the Swiss psychologist Jean Piaget. I also describe some ideas of the French psychiatrist and psychologist Pierre Janet that pertain to the development of personal memory. Baldwin was a contemporary of Freud, particularly early Freud, and wrote on children's memory from the perspective of a philosophical psychologist. With regard to children's autobiographical memory, he was a pioneer in spelling out the necessity for social support and validation as children acquire the ability to separate memory content from other thought content. Only one narrow strand of Piaget's voluminous theorizing is discussed. This is Piaget's critique, replete with suggested modifications, of Freud's theory of memory. Some of Piaget's suggestions, partly accepting and partly rejecting Freud's ideas, are fairly novel but have never been followed up by adherents of either Freud or Piaget. Chapter 7 concludes with a short description of Janet's theory of "narrative memory," particularly in its developmental aspects.

Chapters 8 and 9 consider the third approach to autobiographical memory—that given by social, historical, and folkloric perspectives. Developmental viewpoints figure only incidently in these perspectives. In terms of possible candidates I have selected only a very small number of theorists for inclusion in these chapters. Nevertheless, my intent remains firm to make a forceful argument for the necessity of considering societal aspects of autobiographical memory. Chapter 8 presents sociological and historical perspectives on memory, specifically the views of French sociologist Maurice Halbwachs and very briefly those of the American sociologist Edward Shils. Halbwachs was particularly concerned with the effects of group membership and group identification on individual memory. For Halbwachs the framework of society was so important for retention that he scarcely admitted that memories could be formed solely at the behest of an individual. Shils has discussed the role of personal memories in maintaining societal traditions. According to Shils, to constitute itself at all, society must perpetually reenact itself, and in this endeavor we must be guided by our memories, many of which are outside our awareness while others are simply in error.

The professional historian and the psychologist of personal memory are both faced with the serious problem of verification. Historians have uncovered fallacies in relation to determining "what actually happened" that have their counterparts in long-term memory research. For some types of historical information, human memory itself is the court of ultimate resort. The focus is on a number of methodological difficulties found in pursuing historical research that shed light on parallel difficulties in studying human memory. The major source that I cite to draw comparisons between verification problems in history and personal memory is the French historian Marc Bloch. A few ideas dealing with the same problems are also presented from an essay by the American historian William H. McNeill.

It should be noted in considering memory in a social context in Chapters 8 and 9 that psychology, in the interest of scientific understanding, has usually concentrated on the simplified memory-study paradigms of the laboratory. Very little has been done in studying the retention of events where strict control over events is sacrificed for "realism." (The works of psychologist Ulric Neisser and his advocacy of an ecological approach to memory constitute the major exception.) This contrast between manipulative control and realism is a frequent point of tension in social psychology where, for example in the study of attitudes, both laboratory and field studies are performed, often without much theoretical interchange. However, to study long-term retention of events as they occur naturally in society exceeds the ordinary range of psychology; other social sciences and humanistic disciplines must be consulted. In these disciplines time-spans across generations are often studied and conceptualized, and social forces that cannot be simulated in the laboratory are scrutinized. Furthermore, otherwise unnoticed factors that both assist memory and distort retention can be uncovered. What is the possible gain in paying attention to such broad-gauged variables? Most simply put, such attention offers the promise of a better understanding of the nature and function of human memory.

Within academic psychology, autobiographical memory has not only been studied but also frequently conceptualized by assuming that the experimental variables and findings pertinent to laboratory or school studies of memorization must be central to personal retention. In most instances this extension appears to be an unwarranted over-generalization. As evidence, predictions of dominant types of memory errors often fail to transfer from memorization tasks to personal remembering. Throughout this book it will be suggested more than once that data gathered by "learning by heart" followed by retention testing often has very little bearing on the usual *modus operandi* of autobiographical memory.

Chapter 9 touches on a diversity of academic disciplines in describing the cultivation and transmission of memoric information. Topical areas include oral tradition and oral culture as found in both nonliterate and largely literate cultures and "nostalgia" as a category of remembering that represents an inseparable bonding of cognitive and emotional content. It is argued that even the most communicatively advanced societies have many spheres in which interactive patterns are primarily oral, and all children begin life in an oral culture. Dependency on oral memory transmissions, particularly with adults, means that retention considerations must be built into a culture as a social-design feature. Emphasis is put on describing the ways in which retention is brought about by *means other than memorization*. In particular, by extemporizing and combining themes within a formulaic framework and by limiting possible choices, it has been shown that illiterate performers of oral epic poems have achieved the results and appearance of memorization by other means. At least one classical scholar has claimed that operant conditioning furnishes the paradigm for this state of affairs. In many ways, to be sure, this flexible performance model parallels ordinary retention of life events better than a theoretical model that assumes that exact retention is either intended or desired.

A frequently reiterated theoretical point is the ubiquity of the social dimension. Psychoanalysis, like other psychotherapies, considers personal memories from two points of view, the (subjective) rememberer and the (objective) therapist. But this is not a unique observer duality, for in this regard, though more informally, everyone is a frequent listener who on many occasions can infer unexpressed memory content, often by nonverbal indicators. For most of us, this is particularly easy with family and friends. Both psychoanalysts and classical scholars can be found who claim on somewhat different grounds that monologues (even silent ones) do not exist; the apparent monologue is always an implicit dialogue with oneself. Going a step further, it is at least a feasible proposition that we ourselves often act as audience to our own memory evocations so that reminiscent soliloquies to some extent tailor accurately retained memories to self-as-audience expectations.

Chapter 10, the concluding chapter, presents brief assessments of several of the ideas and theories discussed in earlier chapters. Topics that have frequently recurred receive commentary, but no systematic effort is made to assess or collate points of view on all major topics. Chapter 10 also introduces a few new ideas intended to sharpen theoretical perspectives and to arrive at a number of clearly stated, though doubtless debatable, conclusions. The chapter ends with what I believe are neglected areas in research and theory that potentially may lead to profitable investigations.

Separate academic disciplines, with their special vantage points, often produce unique and valuable insights pertaining to autobiographical memories. However, each discipline has been willing to go only as far as satisfying some of its subject-matter interests before stating that a boundary has been reached where expertise is the province of some other discipline. Continuing compartmentalization will achieve only foreordained, limited results until it is recognized that the study of autobiographical memory is necessarily an interdisciplinary endeavor. A major aim of this presentation is to illustrate what a preliminary mapping of a widened theoretical landscape can produce in terms of unified results.

2

Memory Observed
by Introspection

All in all, the dominant trend of the twentieth century has been to emphasize the necessary limitations of personal knowledge and retention. The tradition from Plato and Augustine to Bacon and Hobbes of marveling at the "power of memory" has long been in abatement, perhaps only recently reviving with a renewed sense of wonder fueled by the inadequacies of recent attempts at memory simulation.

The goal of this chapter is to survey a variety of topics, primarily from a subjective perspective, that bear on autobiographical memory. Results and problems pertaining to memory are excerpted from the older introspective psychology and from selected philosophies of memory. The findings of the introspective psychologists were often obtained in laboratory situations where perceptual memories of limited durations were studied. Nevertheless, some of those results can be applied to autobiographical memories.

Unlike psychologists, philosophers of memory have always been concerned mainly with personal memories and have ignored memorization by rote repetitions. I would mention two points about my use of the term *subjective*. First, it encompasses the much-derided "armchair philosophy," which includes logical and other considerations in addition to observational descriptions. Second, I equate *subjective* with *experiential* (except in those meanings that imply a cumulative effect, as in "learning from experience," an emphasis that is often inappropriate when discussing unique autobiographical occurrences).

Topics considered may in some cases seem arbitrary, but most have in common that they give an early perspective on questions that will be raised again in later chapters, which are devoted to better known and more comprehensive theories. It is fair to say, however, that such topics as recognition, memory for emotions, and memory intentionality must figure in any descriptive inventory of autobiographical memory functions. In a few instances I cite current research approaches that formulate old problems in new ways.

The theoretical ideas in this chapter are historical, but because of the strict ukase in later academic psychology against subjectivism, surprisingly few of these older observations have been definitively refuted or supplanted. This does not argue for the invariable correctness of older views, but rather for a lack of interest in subjective descriptions, even when the claims they make are testable.

William James on the "Big" Questions

There are three perennial questions in regard to personal memory that periodically appear in different guises. A century ago William James rhetorically asked and answered all three of these well-worn queries. The questions are of such a general nature that if we are to make any progress toward answers, they must be broken down and researched piecemeal. The first question, to be considered in some detail later in this chapter, is: Do emotional memories result from the retention of emotions as such? James answered no; it was the retained "cause" in the cognitive sphere that produced predictable emotional "effects." The emotions themselves were novel constructions since "new griefs and raptures" result. For James, who claimed to be image-weak, the answer could scarcely have been yes, since according to the psychology of the time, *retained* emotions would have had to be carried by mental imagery or at least by some emotional surrogate that is available to introspection.

The second question is: Can memory be improved? This question refers specifically to memory as a function in itself, not memory for systematic and specialized content. James's answer was again no, and he gathered some data on memorizing poems (enlisting himself as an experimental subject) that he thought supported this conclusion. James's argument against the possibility of memory improvement combined his emphasis on physiologically based habit with his assumption that association is the sole basis for memory. Thus whether memory improvement is brought about by heightened interest, attention, repetition, mnemonic devices, and other reinforcements, only the single mechanism of "elaboration of associates" is involved, while underlying "brute retentative [sic] power" remains unchanged. James poked fun at some excessive memory-improvement claims, but his own view was quite congruent with that of the majority of nineteenth-century mnemonicists who distinguished between "natural" memory, our physiological memoric capacity laid down by heredity, and "artificial" memory, the ability to compensate for a faulty natural memory by artfully practicing the stratagems that the mnemonicists preached. However, the claim has also been made that James became less certain of this position than he had been when he wrote the *Principles*. William McDougall in one of his last books, one dedicated to the "honored memory of William James," asserted that James in his later writings treated the problems of "general retentiveness or tenacity of memory" as a still open question (McDougall, 1926, pp. 296–297).

The third question, nowadays often linked to psychonalysis, is: Is everything personally experienced capable of being remembered? Here James was quite emphatic that although the field of memory might be much broader than ordinarily supposed, especially as shown in pathological cases, most of what happens is actually forgotten; there is no physiological basis for believing otherwise. As a contrary opinion, he cited the hypothesis of Sir William Hamilton, who in 1858 had put forward the argument that since mental activity was a form of energy, "a part of the ego must be detached and annihilated if a recognition once existent be again extinguished." Since this does not occur, memories are necessarily permanent. This reasoning is based on what then was the newly formulated principle of conservation of energy, from which it also followed, according to Hamilton, that it would be more difficult to explain forgetting than remembering (James commented, "Those whom such an argument persuades may be left happy with their belief" vol. I, p. 683.) This peculiar argument is cited here not only to point out that promulgating a theory of universal retention long antedates psychoanalysis but also that there is a mid-nineteenth-century parallel to early psychoanalysis in that memory has to do with mental energy, and what has to be explained theoretically concerns forgetting rather than remembering.

James's negative answers agree with majority opinion today. But dichotomous yes–no answers only tap the surface, and the reasons James gave for his answers were merely sketchy beginnings. Still and all, a hundred years later these questions remain among those for which we would most like to have adequate answers.

Introspective Psychology

Apart from narrowness of content and general artificiality in the analysis of associations and sensations, it is often alleged that the demise of the old introspective psychology was hastened by the lack of agreement obtained between different, somewhat authoritarian laboratories. Lack of agreement there certainly was, but this hardly sets introspective psychology apart from the psychology trumpeting objective methodology that followed. The customary explanation misses an important point of commonality—without exception, controversialists on all sides claimed a sensitivity to shading and nuance of imagery, sensation, and feeling that no longer exists. What were the "feelings of reality" mentioned by pioneer American psychologist Mary Calkins? What about the "feeling of relation" claimed by some of the Würzburg psychologists to be a thought element, but by E.B. Titchener to be a complex? And who now would search for the "feelings of nervous innervation" claimed by Wilhelm Wundt, and the physicists who contributed so much to early psychology, Ernst Mach and Hermann von Helmholtz, but denied at great length by William James and fellow Harvard psychologist Hugo Münsterberg? These latter feelings involved an introspective sensibility to the nerve impulses going out from the brain or spinal cord to the appropriate muscles during motor performance.

No one today would know how to go about the bold reductionism given by James's interpretive self-analysis in his chapter on "The Consciousness of Self":

> When I try to remember or reflect, the movements in question, instead of being directed towards the periphery, seem to come from the periphery inwards and feel like a sort of *withdrawal* from the outer world. As far as I can detect, these feelings are due to an actual rolling outwards and upwards of the eyeballs, such as I believe occurs in me in sleep, and is the exact opposite of their action in fixating a physical thing. (1950, vol. I, p. 300)

A few sentences farther on James admits that it is harder to describe what is involved in the mental activity of consenting and negating, but this does not keep him from attempting a detailed description.

> The opening and closing of the glottis plays a great part in these operations; and, less distinctly, the movements of the soft palate etc., shutting off the posterior nares from the mouth. My glottis is like a sensitive valve, intercepting my breath instantaneously at every mental hesitation or felt aversion to the objects of my thought, and as quickly opening, to let the air pass through my throat and nose, the moment the repugnance is overcome. The feeling of the movement of this air is, in me, one strong ingredient of the feeling of assent. The movements of the muscles of the brow and eyelids also respond to every fluctuation in the agreeableness of what comes before my mind (vol. I, p. 301).

James did not downplay these findings, though giving the customary disclaimers that more was surely involved and that some of this report might be idiosyncratic. Rather, strong summarizing conclusions were given in two italicized statements:

> In a sense, then, it may be truly said that, in one person at least, *the "Self of selves," when carefully examined, is found to consist mainly of the collection of these peculiar motions in the head or between the head and throat.* (p. 301)

And later:

> If the dim portions which I cannot yet define should prove to be like unto these distinct portions in me, and I like other men, *it would follow that our entire feeling of spiritual activity, or what commonly passes by that name, is really a feeling of bodily activities whose exact nature is by most men overlooked.* (vol. I, pp. 301–302)

This confident outlook that important questions could be meaningfully approached and partially answered by paying attention to one's exact sensory feelings was soon to pass away completely, almost without heirs. The psychological historian can attribute it to the onset of the behaviorist revolution, while the social historian can point to introspectionist self-assurance as yet another example of the pre-World War I confidence that has never returned to later generations. The concern here is more limited; surely if such a broad array of questions received introspective answers, the memory experience would be one of them. Although James's musings may appear to the modern investigator as futile exercises, the last few paragraphs have been meant to make the positive point that the psychologists of the turn of the century were experts in introspections and such experts do not exist today, not even among the philosophers of mind. Thus though we may only expect a few crumbs of knowledge from such subjective reports, they may be more nutritious than if obtained from less practiced sources. (A similar argument has been made with regard to the nineteenth-century application of hypnosis. The earlier practitioners, who performed hundreds and even thousands of hypnotic inductions, very likely knew more about technique than the later, objective scientists, who performed a far smaller number of hypnotic inductions [Jenness, 1944].)

I would particularly like to emphasize the views of James and Titchener as representative introspectionists, not just because they were best known but also because they were opposites in regard to the use they made of imagery. Titchener, as is often stated, could be characterized as hyper-imagic. He had visual images of abstract nouns like "meaning"; he could image the conjunction "but"; and he claimed exceptional kinesthetic imagery: "I was not at all astonished to observe that the recognition of a gray might consist of a quiver of the stomach" (1909, p. 179). But this last was not invariable as, "There was plenty of consciousness when gray was *not* recognized, but sometimes none at all when there *was* recognization" (p. 180).[1] Antedating Muzak by several decades, Titchener wrote in 1909 that, "I never sit down to read a book without a musical accompaniment" (p. 9). The accompaniment was not a phonograph record but auditory imagery, and he intimates that this sound imagery was frequently that of the oboe, for which he confesses a special affection. In contrast, James self-confessedly had quite poor imagery, which was on occasion pointed out by Titchener as leading to James's "verbal rushes" rather than systematic descriptions (1909, p. 258).

Introspective Memory Phenomena

Among these introspectionists of note one could surely anticipate some cogent insights with regard to memory phenomena. James, with his admittedly poor visual imagery, espoused a sensationist approach to memory. Considering that James is best known for the James–Lange theory of emotions, by which emotions are defined in terms of one's self-perception of the sensations attributable to physiological changes, it is not out of character that he wrote: "Of our past states of mind we take cognizance in a peculiar way. They are 'objects of memory' and appear to us endowed with a sort of warmth and intimacy that makes the perception of them seem more like a process of sensation than like a thought" (1950, vol. I, p. 223). This kind of sensation is not limited to memories since other experiences also "have that 'warmth and intimacy' which were so often spoken of in the chapter on the Self, as characterizing all experiences 'appropriated' by the speaker as his own" (vol. I, p. 650). But memory occurrences are "*dated* in my past," and consist of "a very complex representation, that of the fact to be recalled *plus* its associates, the whole forming one 'object' " (p. 651). Thus, James, who held the view that memories play an important role in constituting the self and that memory alterations are one of the two principal ways in which mutations of the self occur, linked memories to the self both through a type of generic sensation and through specific associations.

Apparently for the sake of completeness, James does cite the image theory of memory, although in a footnote (vol. I, p. 645); the exposition is that earlier given by Gustav Theodor Fechner and Helmholtz. Fechner was at pains to distinguish between what he called "memory afterimages" and ordinary visual afterimages in which complementary colors appear, as do parts of the perceived visual field that were not initially fixated. Also, the "strain of attention" was inward and not outward as with ordinary afterimages. A short fixation time (estimated by Helmholtz at one-third of a second) was better for producing the memory afterimage; a long fixation time, for the ordinary afterimage. Although the memory afterimage was the earliest occasion on which a true visual memory could be isolated, it was still an afterimage and thus had to be distinguished from the usual memory image that could be reinstated after an indefinite lapse of time.

A few pages later James points out that any image theory of memory is insufficient. He takes the argument from Herbert Spencer that images could never account satisfactorily for remembering that something did *not* happen. With a memory of omission, say for *not* locking the door, imagery pertaining to the door is just as available whatever was done, so explanation cannot rest on the presence or absence of imagery. James does himself attempt a rather lame explanation that there must be a difference in the "mode of feeling the image" which can lead to opposite conclusions. With James's sensationist view the positive recollection of events runs into a traditional problem of the philosophy of memory, difficulty in accounting for the difference between imagination and memory. For something to be a memory, James emphasizes, it is not enough to know it as an event dated accurately in the past; it must be from one's personal past. As James admits, however, the recollected past and the imagined past may frequently be much alike, so that ultimately the distinction between memory and imagination must be based on something else: "*the object of memory is only an object imagined in the past* (usually very completely imagined there) *to which the emotion of belief adheres*" (vol. I, p. 652). It is only the added "emotion of belief" that turns a neutral image into a "memory." This stress solely on feelings as constitutive of memory strikes an unusual chord in modern students of memory, who are accustomed to conceptualizing memory in more cognitive terms.

Titchener was even more detailed than James about the distinctions between memory and imagination. Not unexpectedly, through introspection Titchener was able to find clear-cut differences between memory images and images of imagination, but he claimed that the differences are just the reverse of what popular psychology predicts. "Popular psychology regards the memory-image as a stable copy of past perception, and the image of imagination as subject to kaleidoscopic change. In fact, it is the memory-image that varies, and the image of imagination that is stable" (1910, p. 417). But like James, Titchener claimed that an image is primarily a memory image because of the feeling of familiarity attached to it. The variable memory image is advantageous: "It is, in reality, because the image breaks up, because nervous impressions are telescoped, short-circuited, interchanged, suppressed, that memory, as we have memory, is at all possible" (1910, p. 419). Titchener adds, "if the mental image could not decay, it could not be the conscious vehicle of memory." (At this time Titchener's contemporary, Freud, was writing extensively about the importance of the mechanism of condensation and displacement for both dreams and memories, as described in Chapters 3 and 4.) Thus Titchener finds no merit in the old argument of the British empiricist philosophers that memory images were just weaker copies of earlier perceptions, for in that case "our mental life would, so far as we can imagine it, be an inextricable confusion of photographically accurate records" (p. 419). We thus are given the surprising conclusion by Titchener, representing a psychology dependent on imagery, that image accuracy that is too precise is deleterious to the formation of organized memories.

An image of imagination has attached to it a feeling of strangeness or at least a sense of "something new." Titchener suggests that functionally it is a good thing for the artist and the poet that the image of imagination is relatively persistent and substantial. The reason for this fortunate occurrence is that an image that is conceived for the first time has no associations. Thus associations, contrary to the usual emphasis, detract from stability rather than add to it. In some cases an image of imagination can stir up a few associates that are themselves memory images. But once the imagination image has gone, it might either be rebuilt as an image of imagination or it might itself be recalled later as an image of memory.

In the 1960s Jean Piaget and Bärbel Inhelder performed an extensive study of the development of children's imagery and, somewhat incidentally, obtained indirect empirical evidence concerning Titchener's problem of discerning differences between memory images and those of imagination. Among their imagery tasks were those of *memory* (reproduction) and *imagination* (represented by anticipatory tasks, e.g., tracing the complete path of a rotating stick). Instead of performing introspections, they had children give gestures, make drawings, or offer some other indication of what was being imaged. Among their more important, and to them surprising, conclusions were their findings on the relationship between reproductive images and imaginative anticipatory images.

> If one were to start from the commonly held conception of the mental image as conservation or retention of past-perceived configurations and events, one would reckon on finding a relatively higher occurrence of reproductive images and a lower proportion of anticipatory images limited to extending to unfamiliar situations anything that can be supplied from the stock of familiar reproductions. As for the copy images [drawings obtained with the figure to-be-copied in view], one would have to consider them as scarcely belonging to the domain of images at all, insofar as they are exactly and automatically cast in the form of their perceptual models. *Now we find that the contrary is the case.* The role of reconstitution, reanticipation and anticipation is far more considerable than foreseen: almost without exception, reproductive images [of a moving, rotating object] up to the age of 7 to 8 years are no

more than static images; and direct copy images themselves entail some degree of anticipation and active structuration (Piaget and Inhelder, 1971, pp. 354–55; italics added).

Although the thrust of Piaget and Inhelder's experiments is developmental, results are partially parallel and complementary to Titchener's introspectionist conclusions. By both accounts it is the *imaginative components* that increase the utility of the memory image. In Titchener's theory it makes the image more stable and inspectable; for Piaget and Inhelder it brings a closer match to memory-constructed reality. Fortunately for memory accuracy, the imaginative components increase as subjects' ages increase, for it is just the imaginative aspects of "reconstitution, reanticipation and anticipation" in constituting a memory image that are lacking in young children's retentions. Moreover, Piaget and Inhelder found only hybrid images composed of both memoric and imaginative elements, and this was true even of "memory images" bordering on the perceptual, the copy images. Images that are either purely imaginative or purely memoric probably do not exist except, of course, in the imagination of the introspectionist.[2]

If not the definition at least the scope of what is covered by the term *imagery* has altered in the Piaget and Inhelder description. This is in line with contemporary usage that counts as imagery the functional ability to perform visually mediated tasks requiring internal, nonverbal representations, regardless of whether such representations are themselves readily inspectable. Stephen Kosslyn has stated this viewpoint: "Even if images are not the 'mother of all representations' they may be important as an 'engineering' feature of the mind which is not necessary or fundamental so much as convenient. In particular, recent attention has focused on the role of imagery as a memory aid and as a computational tool" (1980, p. 455). Of course it can be objected that the use of gestures and drawings in charting visual movements are only indirect indices of imagery and are prone to their own kinds of distortion. But in spite of methodological difficulties, rather consistent results have been obtained, certainly more so than when clarity of imagery content is correlated with performance.

The modern "performance approach" to imagery, including memory imagery, where measurement is in terms of task success rather than image characteristics (e.g., the popular psychology classroom demonstration task in which students can usually accurately remember the exact number of windows in their homes regardless of image clarity) greatly lessens the immense variability among individuals always found with the inspectionist approach. Contrary to what is often implied in textbooks, Titchener was quite aware that imagery in general is highly variable and that his own imaging was far from typical. Sensation, he stated, was capable of demonstrating general laws because sense organs were fairly uniform, but imagery was the realm of individual differences because it depended more on the brain, and brains were quite variable. And there were what might be called cross-category difficulties; it was, for example, sometimes hard to tell kinesthetic sensations from kinesthetic images.

Are Titchener's introspectively derived conclusions completely beside the point? I believe to the contrary that they possess a positive originality. It is apparent that Titchener's theory of memory is a constructivist rather than a copy theory. But nowadays this claim is made for almost all memory theories—developmental, information processing, or contemporary psycho-analytic. Where Titchener is unique is in stressing that this characteristic arises not from memoric deficiencies but from memoric necessity. Incomplete and transformed memories are for that very reason often more usable, while imaginings to be usable must tend toward precision and stability. Otherwise, the products of imagination could be neither serviceably manipulated nor communicated.

Recognition Memory in Psychology

A good deal of confusion exists with regard to the meaning of *recognition* and therefore its study as a type of remembering. Although H.K. Wolfe had performed a recognition memory experiment for tone identification as early as 1886, in much of psychology prior to the twentieth century, recognition was something other than the simple determination of yes, an item has been seen before, or no, it has not. Recognition was the final step—a literal re-cognition—in subjectively identifying and perhaps categorizing an object. In this broader interpretation the emphasis was on fitting the cognition of an object or an idea into previously obtained knowledge. Thus in this sense, the one emphasized by Aristotle, recognition was the terminal and uniquely human step in the memory cognition process—not just the kind of memory necessary for appropriate motoric action shared by all animals. The four consecutive processes of memory were learning, retention, recall, and recognition.

> In the sphere of conscious memory, it is common to distinguish two component parts of the event, as the *recall* and the *recognition*—the recovery of something from past experience, and the conscious reference of it to past experience. These two are often indistinguishably blended in the remembering consciousness, but the distinction between them is justified by the frequent instances in which either may occur without the other. (Ladd & Woodworth, 1911)

A related point made by Oswald Külpe was that when recognition is doubtful, recall of the original setting of the object to be recognized aids recognition. This assisting of recognition by recall he called *mediate* recognition in contrast to *direct* or *immediate* recognition (1911, pp. 591–592). But at that time functional psychologists were also considering the developmental point of view, which gave priority to the simpler sense of recognition. James Rowland Angell (1908, pp. 225–226) considered memory "an outgrowth of recognition," emphasizing the vague recognition by the infant of such surroundings as the mother's face, and recognition plays a "fundamentally important part in every one of the cognitive operations."

Titchener's student Walter Pillsbury did not stop at stating that the feeling of familiarity entailed a recognition memory but listed competing options for what he and quite a number of other psychologists were sure subjectively existed, the *mark of recognition*. But Pillsbury acknowledged, "what the mark of recognition is has not altogether been agreed upon" (1908, p. 146). There were four options: (1) it was an old or habitual mode of reaction to the entering mental process, (2) it was a mood or feeling of pleasure that comes with old experiences just because it is old, but it is not further analyzable, (3) it might be produced by the addition of some distinctive and familiar idea to the impression of a re-experienced object, or (4) it might be the reception of the new into a familiar general class by the addition of a word or other generalizing symbol. Pillsbury thought it likely that each of these possibilities could occur but that no single description was true for all forms of recognition, especially as objects or ideas were themselves capable of being recognized in several different ways. Emphasis on the pleasure inherent in acts of recognition, mentioned in option (2), was a widespread idea at that time, even when it was not used to account for recognition itself. Angell's textbook, published the same year as Pillsbury's, states: "Probably the mere act of recognition is, as such, always agreeable, although the object, or content of the thought recognized, is of course sometimes quite otherwise" (p. 228). Freud also made a point of the pleasure received from recognition, as described in Chapter 4.

When Frederic Bartlett wrote his book *Remembering* in 1932 much of the earlier subjective approach lingered, although this emphasis is tactfully ignored nowadays. Bartlett criticized the theories of the time for concentrating largely on the moment of recognition and leaving out accompanying sensory attitudinal reactions that express implicit personal preferences; by this inclusion, something of the desirable earlier meaning of recognition would have been retained. Putting his own preference aside, Bartlett identified four existing theories centered on the moment of recognition. These theories can be termed (1) comparison with an image; (2) fusion; (3) feeling of familiarity, and (4) intellectual judgment. In the first theory the immediate perception of an object is compared with a revived perception or image and a judgment of "likeness" obtained. (Titchener had called this the traditional association theory, but because of his belief in a non-copy memory image, he found the theory false.) In the second theory the revived perception or image fuses with the perceived perceptual pattern. This theory Bartlett believed useless as insusceptible to evidence. In the third theory the feeling of familiarity that occurs on representation of an object is an affective response that needs neither comparison nor judgment. In contrast, the fourth theory states that recognition is an immediate intellectual appreciation or knowledge of similarity. Bartlett, like Pillsbury before him, took the eclectic view that under appropriate circumstances any of the theories (except the second one) could be demonstrated, but a deeper understanding called for perceptual studies, not just studies of recognition occurrence.[3]

Subsequently, behaviorally minded psychologists not only wanted nothing to do with the "feeling" side of memory but also banned the association principle of *similarity* (and sometimes *contrast*) as allowing too much scope to subjectivity. Whenever possible, a contiguity principle should be made to serve. Advocating the importance of a principle of similarity in memory theory as well as in perception were a small group of Gestalt psychologists. They performed laboratory experiments to demonstrate their views but without, they claimed, the highly artificial conditions found in traditional memory and verbal learning experiments. Thus Wolfgang Köhler, in his posthumously published last lectures (Köhler, 1969), reiterated the importance for memory of isolation contrast (von Restorff effect) and of pair formation brought about by similarity, concluding that principles of perceptual organization appear to be equally valid for memory.

Solomon Asch (1969) carried out a more comprehensive attack on association through contiguity by advocating that recognition by similarity must precede recall in most real-life situations. He gives the example of looking at a photograph and recognizing that it is the picture of a friend, even though one has not been thinking of the friend. How do we pull out the particular memory traces pertaining to the friend? Asch believes the most plausible answer to be that "since the photograph is a likeness of the friend, the contact between the perceptual process and the corresponding memory traces occurs on the basis of their *similarity*" (1969, p. 98). Similarity recognition is, however, not often required in the usual highly restricted laboratory experiments which have, according to Asch, been "unwittingly designed" to exclude recognition by never leaving a learner in doubt about the identity of a recurrent situation. Asch concludes, on the basis of some laboratory research, that recognition has a crucial place in a theory of recall and that even "[paired] associate recall is at minimum a two-step process"—that is, recognition is followed by recall.

Philosophical and Phenomenological Viewpoints

Philosophers of memory have, at least until recently, continued to search for the equivalent of a mark of memory ("recognition" now seldom being used in the older sense) by searching for what they termed the "intrinsic memory-event."[4] But as philosopher Norman Malcolm concluded in his 1977 book *Memory and Mind,* the quest has not been fruitful.

> In the case of memory we surveyed the variety of candidates that various authors have proposed: images, feelings of pastness, familiarity, a belief-feeling that belongs uniquely to remembering; and so on. Some of these items are preposterous inventions; other are things that sometimes occur but often do not. And sometimes these latter occur in cases that are not examples of remembering. (p. 51)

Malcolm goes further and closes off future search as hopeless. "When we reflect on the futile endeavors of the memory theorists, perhaps the best reason to sum up the reason for their failure is that the memory event or act they are trying to pinpoint is nothing that does or could exist. People remember things; but nothing that occurs, either inner or outer, *is* the remembering" (p. 53). Malcolm's solution is that we must be completely nominalistic and "identify the remembering, in each context, with the expression of memory that occurs in that context."

Other traditional moves have been made within philosophy in efforts to pin down the elusive nature of memory, particularly personal memory. One approach is engaging in the Cartesian method of all-inclusive doubt in an attempt to establish basic principles of memory justification. The best known doubting hypothesis is Bertrand Russell's (1921) conjecture that there might have been no past at all as the world only came into existence five minutes ago, complete with geological traces, records, memories, and so on. This hypothesis, which is curiously reminiscent of nineteenth-century anti-evolutionary arguments, appears neither susceptible of proof or disproof, although there have been several attempts. Russell (1940) himself later stated the impossibility of memory verifiability more generally: "No memory proposition is, strictly speaking, verifiable; since nothing in the present or future makes any proposition about the past verifiable." A circuitous reply to this skepticism was A. J. Ayer's (1951) argument that it is at least logically possible that we might remember the experience of others. The obvious objection was made against this possibility that such an ability would usually not be termed memory but rather telepathy or clairvoyance. Malcolm shunned counter reasoning intricacies and cut the Gordian knot of memory skepticism by simply asserting that Russell's hypothesis that all memory was false was "not a coherent idea."

Another traditional way of taking the measure of somewhat ill-defined phenomena is to consider the dilemmas given by borderline cases in the hope of delimiting possible boundaries. Here is an example of some complexity with regard to how we might find one sequence of actions more memory-like than another. The example is taken from philosopher Don Locke's (1971) book, *Memory.*

> When my friend tells me that I once saw a partridge in a pear tree, I may be unable to remember it, and have to take his word for it—I learn it again. But on the other hand I might also remember it again, though I had forgotten about it. How are we to distinguish the case in which I now remember that I saw the partridge, because I have been reminded of it, from the case in which I cannot remember it at all, and know that I saw it only because my friend assures me I once told him about it? It seems that the difference must lie in the fact that in one case my present knowledge depends wholly on what is now said, and so does not qualify as memory, whereas in the other it also depends in part on the earlier experience. This has the correct consequence insofar as you are unsure or cannot tell whether my present knowledge does depend on that earlier experience, you will be unsure or unable to tell whether I really do remember it as I claim to. (pp. 59–60)

There would seem to be little cause for disagreement with Locke's conclusion that a memory content reactivated by a reminder is a clearer case of memory recall than taking knowledge on faith, although the two cases are indistinguishable to an observer. But such a conclusion doesn't get us very far. There are innumerable permutations of successive forgettings, rememberings, and re-mindings. Now and again some sequences are sketched out in public juridical and political testimony. (Several interestingly diverse forgetting and reminding sequences were offered by witnesses in the televised proceedings of the Reagan administration "Irangate" hearings.) Nonetheless, the search for some underlying or unifying memory commonality has again dissolved in nominalism.

A potentially more far-reaching approach, one in line with the thrust of this chapter to emphasize the experiential side of memory, is the phenomeno-logical description of memory phenomena given by the French philosopher Maurice Merleau-Ponty. It might seem a plausible assumption that a phenome-nological approach would yield particularly subtle and perhaps poignant mem-ory descriptions. In the case of Merleau-Ponty, however, this assumption would be utterly mistaken. The direction he takes is to argue that too many mental phenomena have been erroneously attributed to memory that are, in fact, more correctly designated as functions of perception. The argument for the pervasiveness of perceptions is pushed as far as possible. Only when the possibilities of perceptual encounters have been exhausted can one ascribe the remainder to memory functioning. (This point of view is succinctly captured in the title of a long essay by Merleau-Ponty, *The Primacy of Perception* (1947), but most of the arguments presented here come from his major work, *Phenomenology of Perception* (1967).

The alleged fallacy of the over-attribution to memory functioning of what is in actuality the outcome of perceptual experience Merleau-Ponty labels the "traditional prejudice of the projection of memories." By *traditional* Merleau-Ponty refers to the fact that such an astute perceptual theorist as Helmholtz believed that gaps in perception were filled by "unconscious inferences" stem-ming from memories. Merleau-Ponty's argument is that the memory claim in such a belief is self-contradictory

> because in order to fill out perception, memories need to have been made possible by the physiognomic character of the data. Before any contribution by memory, what is seen must, at the present moment, organize itself in such a way as to present a picture to me in which I can recognize my former experiences. Thus the appeal to memory presupposes what it is supposed to explain: the patterning of data, the imposition of meaning on a chaos of sense-data. No sooner is the recollection of memories made possible than it becomes superfluous, since the work it is asked to do is done already."
> (1967, p. 19)

To consider a specific example, Merleau-Ponty counters the claim that mis-reading a word results from a projected memory by posing the question: "How could the evocation of memories come about unless guided by the look of the strictly visible data, and if it is thus guided, what use is it then, since the word already has its structure or its features before taking anything from the storehouse of memory?" (p. 20).

Merleau-Ponty makes an additional argument to support his case. If we assume that memories do typically supplement perceptions, how are the exact memories that are a good fit obtained? No mechanism has yet been described capable of "stemming the flood" of memories and yielding "precisely this memory" and not others. And since the purely empirical theory of projection of memories requires a blind, largely automatic process, there is no way of introducing meanings and guarding against the "teeming hordes of memory."

It could be hypothesized that what is being argued for could be accomplished by near-instantaneous memory recognition followed by substantive recall, a double memoric process. The phenomenological claim then would come close to Asch's argument that association by similarity (or resemblance) must in the real world often precede appropriate recall. The phenomenological viewpoint, however, with its strong anti-association presumption, must find such an interpretation unacceptable. Rather, the "recognition" involved is, as Merleau-Ponty makes plain, conceived as a nonmemoric process. Previously cited examples of "recognition" processes, which are partially nonmemoric in that they avoid consideration of cognitive judgments, include Bartlett's "feeling of familiarity" and particularly Pillsbury's "old or habitual mode of reaction to the entering mental process."

Merleau-Ponty makes it clear that there is not just an intellectual judgment involved, but rather an immediate perceptual realization in the initial categorizing recognition. The physiognomic character of the data, mentioned above, produces immediate categorizing. "Physiognomic perception" names a cognitive process first described by psychologist Heinz Werner in 1922, in which perceived objects are immediately sensed and reacted to in terms of motoric and affective dimensions. When they occur these experiential perceptions are instantaneous and inescapable. In Heinz Werner's (1948) major theoretical work he gives the following description.

> All of us, at some time or other, have had this experience. A landscape, for instance, may be seen suddenly in immediacy as expressing a certain mood—it may be gay or melancholy or pensive. This mode of perception differs radically from the more everyday perception in which things are known according to their "geometric-technical," matter-of-fact qualities as it were. (p. 69)

A possibility that Merleau-Ponty does not mention is that physiognomic perception might itself be a source of memory distortion. Erwin Straus, a prominent phenomenological psychologist, postulated that children, in particular, might be susceptible to such errors. For stable memories to be achieved, the child must "allow physiognomic changes no longer to interfere with the constancy of the invariant framework and with the identity of single events" (1966, p. 72).

A perceptually guided account of experience does not by itself constitute an explanation of autobiographical memories. For Merleau-Ponty, perceptions only exist in the present:

> A preserved fragment of the lived through past can be at the most no more than an occasion for thinking of the past, but it is not the past which is compelling recognition; recognition, when we try to derive it from any con-

tent whatever precedes itself. Reproduction presupposes re-cognition, and cannot be understood as such unless I have in the first place a sort of direct contact with the past in its own domain. (p. 413)

Therefore, according to Merleau-Ponty, there must be some temporal concept apart from time as a continuously lived-through experience. Everybody possesses such an autonomous concept of time, but it is more readily acknowledged in regard to our concept of *future* than that of *past,* "since the future has not even been in existence and cannot, like the past, set its mark upon us" (p. 413). In this regard, Merleau-Ponty, like the pre-Socratic philosophers, makes use of the comparison of time to a river to emphasize that a unitary concept can appropriately designate ever-changing appearances.

> Hence the justification for the metaphor of the river, not in so far as the river flows, but in so far as it is one with itself. The intuition of time's permanence, however, is jeopardized by the action of common sense, which thematizes or objectifies it, which is the surest way of losing sight of it. There is more truth in mythical personifications of time than in the notion of time considered, in the scientific manner, as a variable of nature in itself, or, in the Kantian manner, as a form ideally separable from its matter (pp. 421–422).

An autonomous conception of time does not occur by a reasoned intellectual act, nor does it consist of an ordering of recollections.

> If the past were available to us only in the form of express recollections, we should be continually tempted to recall it in order to verify its existence, and thus resemble the patient mentioned by Scheler, who was constantly turning round in order to reassure himself that things were really there—whereas in fact we feel it behind us as an incontestable acquisition." (pp.418–419)

Even for Merleau-Ponty, possessing an autonomous conception of time does not much aid one in temporally localizing past events. The intellect must conduct a search of the personal past and somewhat laboriously construct an appropriate time-frame. In the involved cognitive problem solving that such an effort can entail, key components are often memories of past affective states, as in the following subjective monologue by Merleau-Ponty:

> There are certain identifying systheses, but only in the express memory and voluntary recollection of the remote past, that is, in those modes derived from consciousness of the past. For example, I may be uncertain about the date of a memory: I have before me a certain scene, let us suppose, and I do not know to what point of time to assign it, the memory has lost its anchorage, and I may then arrive at an intellectual identification based on the causal order of events, for example, I had this suit made before the armistice, since no more English cloth has been available since then. But in this case it is not the past itself that I reach. On the contrary, for when I rediscover the concrete origins of my memory, it is because it falls naturally into a certain current of fear and hope running from Munich to the outbreak of war; it is, therefore, because I recapture time that is lost; because, from the moment in question to my present, the chain of retentions and the overlapping horizons coming one after the other ensure an unbroken continuity. The objective

landmarks in relation to which I assign a place to my recollection in the
mediatory identification, and the intellectual synthesis generally, have themselves a temporal significance only because gradually, step by step, the synthesis of apprehension links me to my whole actual past. (p. 418)

In spite of Merleau-Ponty's abhorrence of associationism, "the chain of
retentions and the overlapping horizons coming one after the other" that he
ascribes to his dating determination would pass as serial associations in the
view of many theorists. Much as one might dislike resorting to associations for
explanations (because of their lack of a selection principle and logical rather
than psychological after-the-fact determination), some sort of matching of
events appears to be part of the usual dating procedure. Some linking with a
known dated event or train of events, whether personal or historical, is established; Merleau-Ponty with his acute phenomenological insights finds no other
way. Obviously, however, the chain of retentions is seldom as long as that
given in Merleau-Ponty's protocol.

In researching autobiographical memory, the favorite and often exclusive
empirical question has been, What is your earliest memory? But researchers
have done nothing to elucidate the tricky question of how one would know the
date of such a memory to establish that it is, in fact, the earliest. Certainly as
we grow older we do not keep adding associations to work back to our *Ur-*
memories. There must be other pathways. The process remains mysterious,
particularly with children who do not perform too badly at memory dating in
general. Piaget (1973) is surely wrong when he implies that a serviceable
autobiographical memory must wait until the child is about 7 or 8 years old, at
which point the child has achieved a perfected concept of simple serial order
(as described in Inhelder and Piaget, 1964). But, as some of Piaget and
Inhelder's experiments have shown, correct *recognition* of serial order can be
performed at younger ages, and in many cases of autobiographical ordering
this is probably sufficient.

The problem of reducing the domain of possible memories to just a few or
that single one most relevant is a persistent one. As described above, Asch as
well as Merleau-Ponty, though they hold different theoretical assumptions,
considered orienting (preceding or simultaneous) recognitions a necessity. For
philosophers of memory, some of the energy that in the past went into the
search for the intrinsic memory-event might be more usefully expended in
exploring the topography of memory domains or contexts. There are, after
all, "good" or at least reasonable memory errors as opposed to wild guesses.
The problem is a venerable one in philosophy. It was foreshadowed in the
early seventeenth century by Francis Bacon's concept of "pre-notion" in his
unfulfilled quest for a more intellectual mnemonics.

Order, artificial places, and verse aid memory by giving a pre-notion of what
the thing is we would recall. If we try to recollect a thing and have no pre-
notion of what the thing is we would recall, "we seek and toil and wander
here and there, as if in infinite space." But a pre-notion cuts off infinity and
limits the range of memory. (Bacon, quoted in Burnham, 1889, p. 69)

Déjà Vu and Related Phenomena

All forms of memory are prone to systematic errors. Older classification of more common error types were sometimes called *memory illusions,* apparently after analogy with perceptual illusions. Frequently occuring types of errors were also called *paramnesias*—literally mixing memories with fantasy—with one type of error always cited as predominate, viz., pseudo-reminiscence or *déjà vu.* Quite a wide variety of memory phenomena have been included under these headings, from mere misidentification and mislocating of memories, through feelings of unreality and depersonalization, to an overwhelming conviction that previous experiences are repeating themselves in exact detail. Great strength of feeling has even led some people to claim an experience of metempsychosis, in which memories were alleged to represent actual events from a previous existence. Experiences of *déjà vu* are scarcely a modern discovery, but at the beginning of academic psychology they attracted little notice. Ribot in the 1880s thought them a rather rare occurrence, with only three or four recorded examples. James (vol. I, pp. 675–676) thought that they were a quite common occurrence but found the alleged mystery supposed to be attached to the phenomena unwarranted. James cited several examples in his own experience that were simply cases of partial and indistinct reminiscence where, at least at first, there was just a general suggestion of pastness, as no date could be attached to the reminiscence. Any suggestion of "weirdness" disappeared when the past context grew more distinct and complete.

The golden age of interest in *déjà vu* phenomena was approximately from 1890 to World War I, and it was French investigators who took particular notice. That was, after all, the era of Henri Bergson and Marcel Proust. Pierre Janet (1905) emphasized the diminished sense of reality inherent in the experience, claiming that *déjà vu* was usually more a negation of the present than an affirmation of the past. This lack of reality conviction was but one manifestation of Janet's preferred diagnosis of inadequate coordination of psychological functioning, viz., psychasthenia. Bergson (1908) stressed that we both perceive and remember ongoing events simultaneously. But a memory of a present unfolding event is quite inferior to perception as a guide to action; therefore we ordinarily ignore the rather useless "recollection of the present." Under stress or disturbance of attention, however, recollection of the present breaks through, giving us a paramnesic false recognition, which Bergson characterizes as the "most inoffensive form of inattention to life." In the true Bergsonian manner the question that defines the basic problem is the reverse of what one would expect: Why does one *not* have a recollection of the present all the time rather than on just those few occasions of so-called pseudo-reminiscence? The answer is that future orientation plays a crucial role, holding off memory which is only virtual from actual goal-directed activity.

Titchener (1910) emphasized emotional stress or extreme mental fatigue in bringing about a state where there is abnormal weakness of the associative tendencies serving two phases of a single consciousness. Havelock Ellis

(1922), summarizing his own earlier writings, also emphasized fatigue or other conditions of mental enfeeblement and the possibility of conditions akin to hypnagogic states playing an important role. Under these conditions one accepts the actual fact as merely a representation. Paramnesia thus results as part of a reversed hallucination since there is a diminishment of actual external sensations to mere representations. Ellis also advocated a temporal confusion explanation of paramnesia by claiming that it is often due to the *anteriorisation* of perception. An example open to anyone is establishing the moment at which one has awakened in the morning: ". . . we can never fix the exact moment when we awake. When we become conscious that we are awake it always seems to us that we are already awake, awake for an indefinite time, and not that we have just awakened. If I had to register the exact moment I awake I should usually feel that I was considerably late in making the observation. It seems that the imperfect hypnagogic consciousness projects itself behind" (Ellis, 1922, p. 251). It is such a paramnesic illusion, Ellis contends, rather than an attempt at deception that causes people who have nodded off, and perhaps who have even been snoring, to claim that they have never been asleep at all.

There have been many other theories of false recognition, some of them emphasizing that somewhere there must be a lack of synchrony. Thus quite early in the nineteenth century Wigan (cited favorably nowadays for his pioneer theorizing about differences between the right and left hemispheres of the brain) claimed that in paramnesia the two hemispheres are not acting quite simultaneously. Other researchers thought paramnesia was owing to an asynchrony brought about by hyperesthesia—a perception occurs so rapidly that one concludes it is from past experience. For present purposes, what is of concern is less the possible mechanisms that produce paramnesia and more the subjective range of recognition phenomena.

A number of turn-of-the-century theories emphasized what already has been mentioned, that an initially unnoticed activity could assume the guise of a pseudo-reminiscence when later recognized, and that dreams were often fertile sources for these later recognitions. Freud in a footnote to the *Psychopathology of Everyday Life* (1901), went still further in claiming that a false recognition could often be the reminiscence of unconscious daydreams. More widely quoted is Freud's short paper of 1914 in which he describes two kinds of "false recognition" or "already told" (*déjà raconte*) in psychoanalytic treatment. A patient will frequently state a remembered fact in a therapy session, qualifying it by adding, "But I told you that before," even though the analyst knows that this is not the case. Freud accounts for this mistake by theorizing that such patients once had the intention of giving this information, but resistance (in the psychoanalytic sense) had prevented them from doing so, and that they later confused recollection of their intention with recollection of their performance. The second kind of false recognition sometimes occurs near the close of treatment when, despite all resistances, a patient not only accepts a repressed event but now states that he feels he had known it all the time. This is a favorable sign and indicates that the work of the analysis has been completed.

The study of memory has usually been carried out in terms of correct versus incorrect items, especially in behavioral studies of recognition where there is little else to go on. By definition, a *déjà vu* occurrence is always an error, whereas an error of the opposite sort—failure to recognize the familiar—is sometimes designated as *jamais vu* (never seen). Although this kind of error is common enough and is frequent in senile conditions, it has not attracted theoretical interest. (Titchener at least allowed for a related feeling of "strangeness" that might be complementary to the feeling of recognition.) On those occasions when lapses of interest, distracted attention, perceptual wandering, etc. occur, the causes are probably too various and frequently nonmemoric to suggest a specific theory of memory for *jamais vu;* in contrast, *déjà vu* is always a positive achievement necessitating a feeling of familiarity, however arrived at.

The encoding–retention–decoding model of the psychology laboratory is all too often taken as an acceptable model for personal memory. But it cannot easily apply to personal memory where there is no overt intent to memorize and much recall is fortuitous. I find two of the *déjà vu* theories of particular interest, those of Bergson and Ellis, although neither theory has any connection with the traditional coding model. Bergson's idea of continuous memory registration conducted simultaneously with perception (a view also held by James Mark Baldwin; see Chapter 7) should not be dismissed out of hand. At the same time one need not agree with Bergson's rather fanciful speculation that memory evocation of the present is always imminent, lurking behind a thin covering screen of ongoing perception. The second suggestive idea, Ellis's claim that there is a kind of constant error owing to the "anteriorisation of perception," has as a probable practical effect that recognition of an occurence is typically dated earlier than it happened. This effect, even if substantiated, might only apply to the short-term sleep–waking relation. Conceivably, however, the anteriorzation effect might also apply to other longer-term memories where there is a sudden change of state in consciousness. In any event, so little is known about systematic distortions in relation to memory consciousness that such a specific hypothesis is worth considering.

Memory for Emotions

Do we remember emotions directly as emotions or only indirectly, with feelings being generated and attached to a revived cognition? The latter view has generally been accepted but a vocal minority of investigators has put forth ingenious arguments as to why direct retention of emotions is a possibility. James (vol. II, pp. 474–475), as was stated earlier, took the cognitive approach, claiming that *"The revivability of the memory in emotions,* like that of all the feelings of the lower senses, is very small." We produce "new griefs and raptures by summoning up a lively thought of their exciting cause." Shame, love, and anger are especially liable to be revived by ideas of their object. From this argument, that a lively imagination for objects and circumstances is necessary for an abundant emotional life, James arrived at the conclusion that "it may be better that a man of thought should not have too strong a visualizing power. He is less likely to have his trains of meditation disturbed by emotional interruptions" (vol. II, p. 475). James then mentions, as he has before, that he has poor visualizing ability, even less than when he was younger! Titchener (1910, pp. 494–495) also is generally negative toward direct emotional revival in memory. There may be an occasional exception if one allows that the James–Lange theory is sometimes correct, i.e., that on occasion the perception of organic sensations produces an emotion, and that sometimes these organic sensations produce organic images. But the ability to have such images is rare. Since all intellectual processes, not just memory consciousness, are reflected in the "presence or absence of organic commotion" (the "commotion" is the stimulus for emotion in the James–Lange theory), Titchener concluded there must be innate differences in mental constitution of those capable of such imagery.

French psychologists and writers were again, as with *déjà vu* phenomena, in the forefront among those who opposed the cognitive-intellectualist view of emotion around the turn of the century. Led by the later writings of the psychologist Théodule Ribot, the argument went well beyond the claim that emotions and feelings had their own independent revival (*mémoire affective*), since it was conceivable that emotions and feelings themselves—not just ideas about feelings—had their own associative and generalization rules (*logique affective*). Like Titchener and James, however, Ribot accepted wide individual differences. There were many people with small or no aptitude for pure affective recall, but direct emotional revivability did occur for a gifted minority. (For present purposes I am using the the English word "affect" as a synonym of emotion. In psychological usage it has a claim to be more generic than "emotion" in that it includes feeling as well as emotion, but in the older introspective psychology it could be narrower in that an affect was claimed to be an element of an emotion in the same way that sensation was an element of a perception.) Affective logic remained largely schematic, with stress placed on possible analogies between the logic of emotion and the logic of concepts. In this vein "generalization" was a key concept, as it appeared to mediate qualitatively what otherwise might be considered merely a quantitative variable; thus emotions might be generalized in the form of moods or sentiments (Baldwin, 1913, pp. 143–145).

The evocation of the *mémoire affective* has continued more recently in French philosophy and literary criticism. Jean-Paul Sartre (1940) stated that he was long opposed to the concept of an affective memory but had come to admit its importance through reflecting on the role of imagination and finding in consciousness more than a present cognition of an "abstract emotional present." However, yesterday's feeling is not so much produced for itself but rather as a stimulus, since the "abstract emotion serves as material for a special intentionality that aims through it at the feeling I had yesterday." Moreover, the affective memory, together with the affective imagination, is of considerable importance in engendering feelings of empathy by means of direct, though guided, emotional revival. "For it is by a similar process that we attempt to realize the feelings of a stranger, or of a madman, or a criminal, etc. It is not exact that we limit ourselves to producing in ourselves a real emotional abstraction. Our desire is to evoke the feelings of the madman, the criminal, etc, in an unreal state insofar as these belong to him" (1961, p. 203). Sartre forces us to ask: How would it be possible to empathize or in other ways communicate emotions if we did not at least remember our own vocabulary of affects? Such being the case, it is difficult to believe cognitions are *retained,* while affects are merely *engendered.*

In analyzing memory through the interpretation of literature, the French critic Georges Poulet quotes from Nathaniel Hawthorne's description of odor-arousing memories in the *House of the Seven Gables* and concludes: "In this manner 'the spell peculiar to remembered odors,' occasionally also to sounds, to tastes, less often to sight, produce with Hawthorne, as with Charles-Pierre Baudelaire, Gustave Flaubert, or Marcel Proust, the phenomenon of the affective memory. By association there is unloosed a recollecting motion which gradually brings closer and closer to consciousness the emotions or sensations experienced over a long period of the past" (1950, p. 327). Under this broadened concept of affective memory, the earlier distinction between separate affective and cognitive retention has lost some of its sharpness. Associations, which can scarcely all contain affects alone and must often be cognitively inspired, frequently provoke memories saturated with sensational and affective content. This is much vaguer and more indirect than Sartre's theory where the emotion as directly experienced acts as a stimulus to recover and amplify yesterday's feeling in full. Nonetheless, Poulet must be right in claiming that affective memories are involved; it is not a case of affects being created anew without specific reference to our past experiencing of emotions. Some cognitive participation does not disqualify memories as "affective." Odors, after all, can by most people be seldom if ever literally recalled, and so if not present must always depend on cognitive activity for imaginal reinstatement. (The Freudian interpretation of odor memories is considered in Chapter 3.)

In Piaget's developmental theory the topic of affective memory was discussed in some lectures delivered in the early 1950s. For Piaget, unlike some older affective memory theorists, there is no purely affective or purely cognitive behavior, but separate analysis of each factor can be undertaken.

> [Affective] decentration brings one's past to life again not just by connecting current situations with past ones or linking present perceptions with images from the past. It also recreates feelings and values momentarily forgotten. [Decentration or decentering, a Piagetian theoretical term, refers to a shift away from a concentration or overfocusing on present perceptual aspects that results in distorted or biased understanding.] Since the expression affective memory has been contested, let us say that when a person recalls situations, he relives values as well as memory images. . . . Decentration of values, while presupposing it, is parallel to and cannot be reduced to cognitive decentration. (1981, p. 64).

What produces this decentration of values—the "affective analogue of intellectual decentration"? Piaget was sufficiently independent and disrespectful of fashion to apply the name of a psychologically discarded category to this activity—the *will*. The function of the will is to go beyond given affective configurations by "changing perspectives." At the same time the act of will "consists of subordinating a given situation to a permanent scale of values." To achieve maturity, the retention of affects, like any other function, needs the regulation of permanent values.

Piaget's formulation is different from the tradition that conceptualizes the will and related constructs (e.g., morality) as a combat between two independent forces. Although Piaget kept affect and cognition apart theoretically, he did not believe affects are "copies" derived from earlier experiences any more than cognitions are. Within Piaget's functional framework, no real distinction is made between emotions and motivations. Differences are only a matter of degree; it is the conative or action-producing aspect of affects that matters most. For Piaget, the problem of memory for emotions is, in principle, generally treated as parallel in form to other kinds of retention, even though it must be admitted that his theorizing in regard to affects and emotions is severely limited.

Can an affective memory in the direct sense be attributed to psychoanalytic theory? The answer is both yes and no. Yes, because many psychoanalysts assume that emotions, like perceptions, are individually repressible, but no, because Freud himself did not allow that a true affective memory was possible. In Freud's theory the question of the existence of an affective-memory category hinges primarily on the question of whether emotions can qualify as memories by undergoing repressions related to previous experiences. But Freud finds this to be a contradiction in terms: "It is surely of the essence of an emotion that we should feel it, i.e., that it should enter consciousness. So for emotions, feelings and affects to be unconscious would be quite out of the question" (Freud, 1915b). Yet Freud admits that even at that early date in the development of psychoanalysis, it was common to speak of unconscious love, hate, and anger, but this he avers is only a shorthand approximation since "the affect was never unconscious but its indicational presentation had undergone repression." Thus, as is frequently affirmed with surprise, Freud was in this case, as in a number of other respects, a cognitive theorist.

It would appear probable that frequent misrecognition and displacement errors might be found for affective memories, regardless of whether recall was direct or mediated through cognitive representations. But since no clear method of detecting affective memory errors exists, affective peculiarities are never assigned to a memory category. Inappropriate or bizarre affects are considered to be the outcome of emotional conflicts or inhibitions. This is to affirm that affects must be considered only unidimensionally—affective activity explains manifested affects. The usual implicit premise in psychological theorizing is that if an accurate cognitive representation can be reinstated, then the appropriate emotion will be attached to it in errorless fashion; distortions only occur if *cognitive* memories are faulty. By way of contrast, suppose we were to accept that in some cases affective memories can be directly recalled. Then slippages between accurate emotional recalls and appropriate cognitive designations would be readily acknowledged. For example, recalled emotions of lust interpreted as love and envy designated as sorrow would not surprise anyone. The point is that if emotions are difficult to classify, the linkage between cognitions and emotions must be reckoned as a potential error source, regardless of which element assumes priority in recall.

This discussion of memory for emotions and the previous section on *déjà vu* have some common ground. There is a kinship between the two categories in that it is common for odor, taste, the kinesthetic, and other lesser senses to be cited as stimuli for both *déjà vu* occurrences and specific affective memories. Also, by some accounts, a reinstated affect can be among the recognitions outside of awareness triggering a *déjà vu* experience, whether or not a lesser sense or a cognitive memory content is involved.

In summary, majority opinion from James and Freud to current cognitive psychology is on the side of retention carried by cognitive representations. Notwithstanding, there are those who continue to argue for the "primacy of affect," not limiting their argument to considerations of remembering (e.g., Zajonc, 1984). Most theorists who have concerned themselves with the retention of emotions would be in agreement with Titchener's 1910 summing up (though they would not find the image comparison relevant): "Affection as the technical term goes is always 'actual'; it appears always in the same form; it has no substitute or surrogate, as sensation has in the image" (p. 494). Thus Titchener, as Freud shortly after, concluded that since affection is always "actual," it is contradictory to conceive of emotion as embodied in a memory trace.

But important questions are left unanswered; if cognitions are the exclusive affective carrier, why then do painful emotional memories seem more than others to recur against our inclinations when the cognitive disposition or memory trace itself contains no affect? Can a distinct separation between cognition and affect be maintained when mental functioning is at the level of the primitive, psychoanalytic primary process? One begins to see why even orthodox psychoanalysts often did not follow Freud and instead assumed that emotions could be repressed directly. Must one hold to the extreme cognitive position? Perhaps, after all, there can be some direct linkage of the recalled emotion with the original experienced emotion; Sartre's hypothesis of the retained emotion serving a partial stimulus function would be one intermediate possibility, and in several ways Piaget presents another option. At the other extreme, no one today appears to claim there is a *pure* affective memory, and the development of an affective logic has not yet begun.

The question of the relative contribution of cognition and emotion to the experiential aspect of an affective experience is not often touched upon by current psychological research. The closest active research area pertaining to the retention of emotions and moods is an interest in state-dependent memories. For example, it has often been hypothesized that similarity in emotional milieus between the learning state and the recall state will favorably influence amount retained, while unlike or dissonant states will curtail retention. Concern here is not with retention of emotions as such but rather with emotions serving a stimulus or "cue" function, or the bringing about of a more complete memory, since the replicated emotion is a reinstatement of one aspect of the original occurrence. In academic psychology consonance for hypnotic states versus normal waking states has been a frequent comparison. This consonance principle is being contested, but under some circumstances even rather mild affective states of pleasantness and unpleasantness have been shown to influence retention when emotional moods were similar (e.g., Gage & Safer, 1985). Drug states and, especially, alcoholic intoxication have been popular candidates in folk tradition for states in which it is claimed that a consonance principle holds for memory reinstatements. A related retention idea, also with long folkloric origins, is that knowledge obtained through dreams is best and frequently open to recall only in the sleep state. Obviously, in the study of state-dependent memories the scrutinized situations are invariably complex, and more than an affective memory background is involved.

Intentionality and Memory Automaticity

A rather weak degree of purposefulness is usually attributed to autobiographical memory as compared with the memorization of schoolwork or other didactic material. Traditionally there have been several dichotomies applied to span the volition dimension, e.g., voluntary vs. involuntary, active vs. passive, intentional vs. incidental. These categories are partially overlapping, but in each pair the first term indicates strong volition or the expenditure of effort, while the second term indicates its lack. The intentional–incidental dichotomy is usually applied somewhat arbitrarily to the material to be retained; for example, the subject in an experiment might be requested to remember the form of an object with the retention of the object's color designated as "incidental." In such an experiment it is of interest whether the incidental is retained along with the intentional. In general, for memory registration, the second, or weak, volition term fits autobiographical memory registration, but because both intentional and nonvolitional recalls occur with high frequency, there is no uniformity in the recall of autobiographical memories. There is little attempt made in contemporary psychology to account for volition or even obedience to task requirements. Volitional compliance is a presupposition incorporated into task instructions. But with personal memory, where not even tacit instructions are in effect, volition is totally unassessed.

Here a slight digression is in order to describe a dramatic historical change that occurred in psychological theorizing within a brief twenty-year period at the turn of the century. The change involved the disappearance of the construct of "will" as a psychological category. (A single exception has been noted earlier: Piaget's anachronistic reinstatement of the term "will" in a somewhat idiosyncratic and circumscribed form.) In 1890, "Will" was a chapter of over ninety pages in James's *Principles*. By 1910 discussion of the will had shrunk to just over three pages in Titchener's *Text-book,* and the shorter length of Titchener's book cannot account for the disparity. In the eighteenth century, as Titchener himself pointed out, *will* had been one of the three great divisions of mental phenomena, along with intellect and feeling. Some of the topics formerly treated in the "will" category Titchener redistributed under such headings as "imagination" and "secondary attention." (Secondary attention occurs within Titchener's system when a specific perception or idea is held at the center of attention in the face of opposition.) Furthermore, he states that he would have found it unnecessary to devote any space at all to the "will" category except for the fact that a specific will consciousness exists whose essential factor is the "conscious 'acceptance' of the instruction" in introspective experiments. Thus the "will" construct in late introspective psychology was not only a faded flower but a decidedly artificial one.

The Würzburg school of psychologists, best known for their discovery of an "imageless thought" element, attacked the same volition problem more "task dynamically," as they said. They claimed that the laboratory task or *Aufgabe,* which included instructions, was itself a cause of arousal through "determining tendencies" and "set." More pertinent to present concerns, they also claimed that the "reproductive tendencies" initiated by the task were themselves energizing (see Humphrey, 1951). This treatment of memory reinstatement as itself somehow energizing was more in line with the *Zeitgeist* (including psychoanalytic theorizing) than Titchener's attachment of volition to attention; for the subjective study of attention, too, was becoming passé as the era of introspective psychology drew to a close. Although the Würzburg school ended with the onset of World War I, the theoretically unattached concept of "set" lived on in spite of its well-known ambiguities (Gibson, 1941), leading a shadowy half-life in such venues as introductory psychology textbooks. It should be noted by way of summary that the construct of *will,* in contrast to other taboo topics such as *instinct,* had largely disappeared before the behavorial revolution had begun and that no uniform treatment of volition has taken its place.

Recently some theoretical models put forward by information-processing psychologists to explain performance in simple detection, search, and memory tasks take a descriptive approach to volition in describing "control processes" as a component of the task model. The other distinctive component process in these models tends, not surprisingly, toward the nonvolitional and involuntary and is labeled "automatic processes." The discovery of mechanical or automatic components in human actions has occurred frequently in psychology. With James, the automatic emphasis was placed on *habit,* which in the neutral course of events went from being voluntary to involuntary. "We must make *automatic and habitual, as early as possible, as many useful actions as we can. . . .*" (vol. I, p. 122) Along with this moral injunction, mention was made of the hallmark of habit, that it *"diminishes the conscious attention with which our acts are performed"* (vol. I, p. 114). The diminishment or lapsing of consciousness was the key index to satisfactory habit attainment. Titchener had little to say about habit or learning and therefore found little that was automatic in applying the necessarily "hard introspective labor" that his tasks required. An exception was in the acquisition of the "introspective habit" itself that might be required of the practiced observer, who can eventually not only make mental notes but even jot down written notes "while the observation is in progress, without interfering with consciousness" (1910, p. 23).

Apart from highly practiced habits, application of the "automatic" metaphor to memory phenomena was limited by the introspectionists to the traditional warnings against the mechanical, meaningless associations of mnemonic devices. Possibly, as already sketched, their concern with recognition feeling states and the mark of recognition rather than the narrower yes–no type of recognition worked against finding any component process automatic. As their numerous recognition theories showed, they found variability, not process uniformity.

A highly specific *automatic* memory-encoding hypothesis, based on behavioral data rather than introspective reports, has recently been proposed by Lynn Hasher and Rose Zacks in a number of journal articles. They assert that "several fundamental aspects of experience are stored in memory by an implicit or automatic encoding process." Further, these authors suggest that "frequency of occurrence, spatial location, and temporal location are among those aspects of experience that are continually registered in memory, whatever the age, the ability, the education or the motivation of an individual" (Hasher & Zacks, 1979, 1984). Their criteria for automaticity include the negative ones that neither direction of intention nor explicit training nor information feedback makes a difference. Nor does it make a difference in accurate performance whether automatically obtained knowledge is tested by recall or recognition. The only variable extensively investigated to date is the encoding of frequencies (frequencies beyond ten do not seem to have been tested). Experimental results indicate an ability to accurately encode and retain frequency information from age 4 or 5 to age 70 or more. Not all potential candidates for automatic encoding have passed the empirical test; e.g., temporal order results were negative since both practice effects and large individual differences were found (Zacks et al., 1984). (Other investigators have found limitations in the adequacy of the automatic frequency-encoding hypothesis, but this literature is not of concern here.)

As Hasher and Zacks point out, the idea of *automaticity* is common to a number of investigators of recent years, but their own research focus is more specifically related to personal memory than is that of other theorists, because they stress that their automaticity principle applies to memory for naturally occurring events. With their criterion of age invariance, Hasher and Zacks also differ markedly from other theorists in that automatic memory processing is acquired at a very young age. For most investigators, automaticity occurs only with highly practiced (habitual) activities that require considerable practice.

Walter Schneider and Richard Shiffrin (Schneider & Shiffrin, 1977; Schiffrin & Schneider, 1977) have developed a theory of automatic and controlled processing and applied it to detection tasks and search tasks that require long-term memory. Automaticity is obtained by practice in administered tasks that vary the mix of control and automaticity required. One index of automaticity in detection tasks is that performance is invariant with word lists of different lengths. With this criterion, it is possible to determine which individuals are performing "automatically" and which are not, in contrast to the Hasher and Zacks frequency-retention tasks, wherein automatic performance is universal so that individual differences are unimportant. For both Hasher and Zacks and Schneider and Schiffrin, conscious experience is irrelevant. A contrasting position is taken by Michael Posner and C.R.R. Snyder (1975) in their analyses of several laboratory cognitive tasks: "Automatic activation processes are those which may occur without intention, without conscious awareness and without interference with other mental activity. They are distinguished from operations performed by the conscious processing system since the latter system is of limited capacity and thus its commitment to any operation reduces its availability to perform any other operation" (1975, pp. 81–82). Thus, even within a strict information-processing context, opinion can be divided concerning whether consciousness is irrelevant or a limitation on *automatic* performance.

The Effort Paradox

This brief survey of automatic processing is intended in part as an introduction to a surprising commonality among several memory theorists regarding what can be called the "effort paradox." A number of psychologists of quite differing theoretical persuasions, working in different eras, have independently arrived at the conclusion that the effort to remember inhibits good performance. This generalization goes well beyond the commonplace idea that *anxiety* about remembering leads to poor performance; rather, it is asserted that almost any prolonged *intentional concentration* to remember tends to inhibit good retention both in registration and in recall. This claim admittedly seems quite opposed to the usual recommendations for efficient study habits and the like. But even if only sometimes valid, it might have particularly strong implications for personal memory registration, since autobiographical memory registration is usually quite passive and involuntary, even when not fully qualified as "automatic." Perhaps, after all, seemingly inattentive event encoding might be more efficient than one might suppose on the basis of traditional wisdom.

It was, as described earlier, explicit in the theory of memory afterimages that attention for too long a duration led not to a memory afterimage but to a perceptual afterimage whose distinctive indicator was that it appeared in complementary colors. Such an example might be thought a highly specific case of too much effort in memory-encoding preventing effective registration for what is, at best, only a short-term perceptual memory. The earliest pronouncement that I have found of an inverse relationship between concentrated attention and memory more directly applicable to personal memories is in an 1894 medical congress paper by Dr. Marie de Manaceine cited by Havelock Ellis and titled, "Concerning the antagonism that exists between each effort of attention and motor innervations." Ellis summarizes: "Concentrated attention, she argues, paralyses memory, and there is an absolute antagonism between motor innervation, or real movement, which favors memory, and the concentrated effort which favors attention" (Ellis, 1922, p. 229*n*). A corollary was that although there may be no actual movement in sleep, memory in sleep can still occur because "there is relaxation of motor tension and freedom of motor ideas." Ellis noted, however, that there are other investigations that do not find this antagonism between attention and memory. Certainly the supposition of a tie between motoric components and nonmotoric retention has seldom been supported since. Therefore these claims might be dismissed as an isolated introspective observation based on a speculative neurology but for the fact that two of the most prominent psychologists of the 1930s advanced conclusions disavowing effort efficacy that were directly based on typical laboratory visual and verbal retention tasks.

Psychologist Frederic Bartlett carried out several laboratory experiments in which the subjects learned the meaning of arbitrarily selected or constructed signs for words; subsequently he devoted a section of his 1932 book to the topic "the influence of determination to remember." He gave a fairly detailed analysis of the typical introspections obtained, and he concluded: "Determination to remember was constantly correlated with actual forgetting. It cannot be asserted that this forgetting was directly due to any unpleasing feeling-tone which accompanied the reaction to difficult signs" [the material to be memorized] (p. 117). This assertion is given as one of the main experimental conclusions.

Bartlett's contemporary, the American experimental psychologist Knight Dunlap, went much further in placing an important theortical value on the inadequacies of effort in bringing about good retention. Dunlap is scarcely known today except for his concept of *negative practice,* invariably illustrated by the single trivial example of eliminating the typing error "hte" (instead of "the") by deliberately and repeatedly practicing the incorrect "hte." (A mild effort at reputational resuscitation was undertaken a few years ago by pointing out the numerous ways in which Dunlap's theoretical ideas anticipated those of recent behavioral modification therapists.) Negative practice, or the systematic repetition of undesirable responses, is characterized as an *unlearning* procedure that is useful in many practical psychotherapeutic situations, but Dunlap claimed that it was first demonstrated in dealing with problems of memory, not just motor errors in typing. He adhered to the older meaning of recognition as the identification of past experience, adding that such full-scale remembering usually was unnecessary for practical purposes. "By *remembering* we mean *recalling* with *recognition.* If there is no recognition of what is recalled, the recalling is not remembering. . . . Recognition involves a time factor, or reference to past experiences. The knowledge that is remembered is not merely revived; it is consciously post-dated . . . it may be that remembering is restricted to human beings, and that the only sort of recognition of which the animals are capable is perceptual recognition" (1972, pp. 147–148). What makes these classificatory strictures particularly remarkable is that Dunlap was a pioneer behaviorist and learning laboratory "ratrunner" who had written a *Psychological Review* article at the very beginning of behaviorism (1912) on "The case against introspection.")

Here is Dunlap's forthright commitment to the "effort paradox."

> It is evident, however, that positive effort is in general detrimental to learning. In other words, the effort to learn interferes with learning. The effort to forget on the other hand, is equally detrimental to forgetting, that is, it assists learning. From this another practical role, of especial importance, is deduced. In case of failure to remember, never make an effort to remember, unless the remembering of the particular item is of more importance than the damage the effort can produce. In the vast majority of cases, the adequate procedure when some item cannot be easily remembered, is to dismiss at once the attempt to remember. In this way, remembering at a later time will not be prejudiced, whereas the effort to remember not only reduces the probability of remembering but also may make it impossible even after further learning. In a great many cases, the persistently non-retainable items are non-retainable because at some time, when the learning had been insufficient to produce adequate retention, a prolonged (and perhaps successful) effort to remember the item has been made. . . . The evidence of effort to remember is an important matter in every province in which memory and remembering occur. (1972, p. 165)

This is plain speaking but does not explain either the perversity of the ineffectiveness of effort or, even more paradoxically, why when one succeeds in memory retrieval after considerable effort, subsequent retrieval becomes more difficult. According to Dunlap the ideational and affective factors are of great importance, and volitional exclusion must be very strong to be effective. "In applying the negative method, it should be kept in mind that the involuntary lapsing of the item from attention is not efficacious. The item must not be *allowed* to lapse; it must be voluntarily put out. Probably in this volitional process is the real secret of the effect" (p. 164). Carried to an extreme, Dunlap's retention procedure would not seem unlike the litany of childhood: The more you learn the more you forget; the less you learn the less you forget. Why learn?

Just as the theory of memory afterimages claimed that too long a duration of attention in the original perceptual registration was not optimal, so too Dunlap found for long-term item retention. But during the appropriate *limited* period of study a to-be-retained item should claim full attention. Curiously for a supposed arch-behaviorist, Dunlap uses James's introspective description of consciousness.

> This difference between full and partial attention has been picturesquely described as the difference between the item occupying the "focus of attention" and its occupying the "fringe of attention." This is an important matter. An equally important matter, not sufficiently recognized until recently, is that there is a time-limit of effective attention." (p. 163).

Thus, according to Dunlap, in attempting to retain the name of a place or person, full attention should briefly be given to the name and then it should be ignored as quickly as possible.

It is difficult to conceive of statements stronger than Dunlap's in regard to the "lack of effort" doctrine, nor, as I have tried to indicate, did he stand alone. Nevertheless, despite Dunlap's prominence in academic psychology, his strong claims seem to have had little subsequent impact. There were some experiments in the early 1970s on "directed forgetting," where subjects were given instructions to forget. Efficiency in carrying out those instructions would be a strong counterargument to Dunlap's claims. However, only weak forgetting effects were shown, without convincing evidence that subsequent recognition tests would not show considerable remembering, even when immediate recall was stymied. Nor were Dunlap's rather strict procedures adhered to closely enough to afford a test of his claim that improved retention should ultimately result.

The main conclusion for autobiographical memory (assuming the effort paradox is generally valid) is that many of the situations occurring in ordinary life may often be better for long-term memory retention than are the conditions that prevail in overly motivated laboratory experiments. From this effort-level perspective the results reached in the psychological laboratory are too much like the doctor's office where blood pressure measurements are taken after we are told, "Relax, it will lower your blood pressure." But accepting the *effort paradox* as having some efficacy does not always bode well for one's personal equanimity. What things would we most commonly try to tell ourselves to forget and so inadvertently assist in their retention? Unfortunately, our most unhappy and unpleasant experiences.

Conceptual Summary

Introspective psychologists were a confident and skilled generation of theorists in regard to claiming linkages between mental activities and bodily responding. Such claims were not restricted to psychologists but included scientists of the stature of Ernst Mach and Hermann von Helmholtz. William James linked memory to the "self" and found similar introspective sensations in examining the ideas of memory and selfhood. Visual memory afterimages are a minor memory category, but they are interesting because they are achieved with a shorter visual fixation time than are perceptual afterimages. James, however, believed with Herbert Spencer that any imagery theory would necessarily be incomplete because imagery cannot represent negation or absence. The hyperimagic psychologist E. B. Titchener found images of imagination to be relatively stable and memory images labile, a result he claimed to be the reverse of that held by popular opinion. He said that too much exact imagery is inimical to the creation of organized memory imagery, whereas transformed memory images often are transformed in helpful ways. Images of imagination are relatively stable because they have few or no associates. In some developmental investigations (Piaget and Inhelder) experimental results obtained with young children partially restricted yet basically supported and extended Titchener's conclusions. All obtained images were found to be amalgams of both reproductive and imaginative components, even when direct copy drawings were performed, and imagination in the form of "reconstitution, reanticipation, and anticipation" played an unexpectedly large role. The *memory* images of children below ages 7 or 8 were inferior to those of older children because they made less use of *imaginative* processes.

An older meaning of "recognition" in psychology was that of re-cognition, the conscious referring of an object or event to personal past experience. As such, recognition was the final self-conscious step in memory processing that could occur after recall of memory content. In the early years of the century there was a widespread search for a distinctive "mark of recognition"— multiple means of ascertaining this "mark" were acknowledged. In more recent decades "recognition" has acquired a narrower meaning, referring only to the dichotomous judgment of past presence rather than absence. Gestalt psychologists have suggested that remembering can often be a two-step process, with recognition memory the precursor of recall memory. Two steps are needed where context is not narrowly stipulated (as it invariably is in laboratory experiments); a recognition step invoking a principle of similarity or resemblance is necessary to give topical locus to items before item recall can be accurately performed.

Philosphers continued the "mark of recognition" quest by looking for the "intrinsic memory-event." No such event has been found, and philosophers' efforts often appear less sophisticated than those employed by the older psychologists, because the philosophers have continued to seek universal criteria. Other interests of English-speaking philosophers have been the validity of memory claims, the classification of varieties of memory, and the related problem of determining what can appropriately be labeled "memory" in borderline cases. Generalizable results have been lacking. French philosopher Maurice Merleau-Ponty's phenomenological analysis of memory is more provocative. He asserted that a very common fallacy is the "projection of memories," the mistaken attribution to memory functioning of what in reality is mediated by perception. Of particular importance in this regard is "physiognomic perception" through which perceived objects are immediately sensed and reacted to by the perceiver in terms of affective and motoric responsiveness. Merleau-Ponty has further argued that, to place present perceptually based knowledge appropriately in the past we must possess an autonomous concept of time (a more readily admitted supposition in formulating the concept of "future" than that of "past"), an intuition jeopardized on the one side by common sense and on the other by scientific conceptions of time. To illustrate the process of dating events from one's past accurately, Merleau-Ponty presented a personal protocol of reminiscences that matched experienced affective memories with a chronology of historical events. Other theorists might well find an association process at work in such an event-dating process, but Merleau-Ponty preferred to conceive of it as consecutive "over-lapping horizons."

A great variety of pseudo-reminiscences have been labeled *déjà vu* or paramnesic experiences over the course of the last century and a quarter. Explanations have spanned a range from indistinct reminiscence to metempsy-chosis, and from cerebral asynchrony to over-rapid acts of perception. Two theoretical hypotheses (both lacking empirical substantiation) were particu-larly noted: (1) Bergson's notion that continuous memory registration occurs as a process paralleling ongoing perception, and (2) Havelock Ellis's idea that there is frequent "anteriorisation of perception," so that recognition of an event is believed to have occurred before it actually took place.

A majority view—that of James, Titchener, and Freud, among others—has been that emotions as such are not retained in memory; rather, cognitions are retained which when recalled evoke congruent but newly minted emo-tions. Many psychoanalysts other than Freud have assumed, however, that unconscious emotions could be retained during repression as individuated contents. A few theorists have argued not only for an affective memory but also for an affective logic based on different principles than ordinary logic. Philosopher Jean-Paul Sartre proposed that retained affective memories to-gether with affective imagination are important in producing appropriate em-pathic feelings. Literary critic Georges Poulet claimed that great writers often have invoked descriptions of mixed cognitive and affective associations that bring about the recovery of affective memories in their fictional characters.

In his developmental treatment of affects in children, Piaget advocated a theory somewhat akin to the concept of an affective memory in that "decentra-tion" of affects is postulated as a separate process from cognitive decentration (decentration represents a shift in mental processes toward greater objectiv-ity). The change in affective perspective through decentrations Piaget de-scribed as a "regulation of regulations"; for the affective control function itself, he resurrected the term "will." Piaget noted three assumptions that differenti-ated his theory from others: (1) there is no direct conflict or consequent compro-mise between competing affects (as in psychoanalysis), (2) reinstated emotions are not copies deriving from earlier experiences, and (3) there is no purely affec-tive nor purely cognitive behavior; rather, the cognitive and affective retention strands are on parallel tracks. Piaget's theoretical description of affects is lim-ited in that he concerned himself almost exclusively with subject areas that he personally had investigated, namely, value frameworks and judgments.

If we assume the dominant theory is correct, that cognitive retentions encode situations that engender emotions, the possibility of slippage between these retained cognitions and the expression of appropriate emotions re-mains. Identical cognitions might well produce different emotions. Research on retention of affects or emotions is not a popular area of investigation today. There is, however, some interest in the area of state-dependent memories, where the emotional state of the individual is thought to influence recall—favorably when there is a match between emotion at the time of occurrence and recall. But in these investigations the nature of emotional retention is of less interest than emotions as a recall cue. With his usual gift for grappling with questions to which the popular mind can be attuned , James considered two other "big" questions beyond the form in which emotions are retained. He gave negative answers both to the idea that, by practice or otherwise, one can "improve" one's fundamental memory ability and that, in some way (perhaps not fully accessible to consciousness), we remember everything.

Some older theoretical treatments of intentionality and volition in psychology were summarized. The concept of "automatic" memory, formerly identified with good performance that continued to occur after the withdrawal of conscious attention, has recently been reinstated in terms of automatic memory-encoding processes. The most studied task has been that of memory for frequency encoding, which is presumed to be remarkably accurate over an extremely wide age range regardless of training and information feedback. In studying automatic performances of this sort, the role of consciousness is ambiguous since it has sometimes been presumed to be irrelevant and sometimes a limitation.

The hypothesis of an "effort paradox" rests on the claim by several investigators that too long and too intense concentration on the effort-to-remember is counterproductive, as, for example, Bartlett's finding that "determination to remember was constantly correlated with actual forgetting" and Dunlap's statement that "positive effort is in general detrimental to learning." Dunlap went further with what he termed the "negative method" and claimed that the effort to forget, if intentional and strong enough, assists learning and is detrimental to forgetting. Efficiency in retention, according to Dunlap, also depends on studying an item with full but definitely time-limited attention. To the extent that the effort paradox is valid, study beyond a brief period handicaps remembering, hence it follows that autobiographical memory performance is probably better under the conditions of ordinary life than either laboratory results or common sense would predict. Another inference from the effort paradox is that items learned in the laboratory will subsequently be quite poorly retained because the conditions obtaining for memorization tasks would tend to handicap subsequent retention.

3

Freud's Theory of Memory

From his working out of psychoanalytic theory beginning in the mid-1890s until his death in 1939, Freud presented a range of concepts concerning the functions of retention and forgetting. Screen memories, repression, and childhood amnesia are key concepts of Freudian theory. In addition, Freud examined the role played in memory by different sensory modalities and reality testing.

This chapter is devoted to the key concepts of Freud's memory theory, with emphasis on his early work. It concludes with an analysis of his ideas about the much discussed question of whether there is a distinction between retention of actual early childhood events and the memory of infantile fantasies, and by consideration of the hypothesis that there can be multiple memoric encodings of a single object or event. Although this is chiefly a discussion of Freudian theory, in line with the assumptions expressed by many contemporary psychoanalysts (e.g., Gill, 1976; Rubenstein, 1967; Schafer, 1976) most mental energy explanations have been dispensed with, in particular, libido theory with its concepts of cathexes and anticathexes, bound and mobile energies, and so on. The omission of these descriptions doubtless results in some minor falsification of psychoanalytic points of view as originally expressed, but I am not alone in believing that such descriptions are more tautological than explanatory.

At the beginning of his 1914 article "Remembering, Repeating and Working-Through" Freud briefly recites that changes in analytic techniques up to that time. All of the enumerated techniques had a common goal in that they dealt directly or indirectly with the recovery of personal memories. Three chronological phases were outlined. First was Josef Breuer's catharsis technique, in which there was direct concentration on the events producing symptom formation and an attempt to gain conscious control of one's mental processes. Breuer believed that such control would enable recall of crucial events and expression of strong feelings. "The aims pursued at that time by the help of the hypnotic condition, were 'recollection' and 'abreaction' " [i.e., tension release]

In the second phase, when hypnosis had been abandoned as a psycho-therapeutic technique, the therapeutic task was

> divining from the patient's free association what he failed to remember. Resistances were to be circumvented by the work of interpretation and by

making its results known to the patient; concentration on the situations giving rise to symptom-formation and on those which lay behind the outbreak of illness was retained, while abreaction receded and seemed to be replaced by the work the patient had to do in overcoming his critical objections to his associations. . . .

The third phase, which in 1914 was current practice, gave up concentration on presumed critical situations so that the analyst "contents himself with studying whatever is occupying the patient's mind at the moment" and uses interpretations chiefly to reorganize and make the patient aware of his resistance. When patients do become aware, they can often relate the forgotten situations and connections without difficulty. "The aim of these different procedures has of course remained the same throughout; descriptively, to recover the lost memories; dynamically, to conquer the resistance caused by repression."

For purposes of exposition I take this 1914 article as a mark of the halfway point in Freud's development of psychoanalysis. The first era, as described, was particularly rich in techniques to recover and interpret autobiographical experiences. From this point on there was a greater development in abstract theory as the metapsychological theorizing of the 1910s was already well under way. In the early 1920s came the shift to the tripartite structural theory of id, ego, and superego, in the middle and late 1920s the statements on social psychology and speculative sociology, followed by the partial summarizing statements of the 1930s. During this second half of Freud's theory making, the analysis of resistances and of the transference became dominant as analytic techniques. In fact, some analysts downplayed the recovery of early memories altogether, although considerable theoretical importance was still given to the concepts surrounding infantile memories. Freud, even in his last papers, maintained the recovery of early memories as a theoretical objective. From the more applied standpoint of therapeutic feasibility, however, dependence on obtaining early memories, let alone whether they pertain to actual happenings, has always been problematical. For the majority of later analysts (see Chapter 5) the overriding fact is that early personal memories, whether significant or not, can at best only be inferred.

For a time Freud attempted a frontal attack on memory recovery. During the formative period of psychoanalysis in the 1890s he used the so-called pressure method, in which he pressed his hand on the forehead of the patient whose eyes were closed and urged her to speak freely her thoughts and memories. According to Ernest Jones (vol. I, pp. 243–244), "Freud was still given to urging, pressing, and questioning, which he felt to be hard but necessary work." But this approach was soon given up, "the more confidence he acquired in the belief that relaxing conscious censoring would inevitably lead to the important memories, the less need had he to urge, press, or direct the patient's thoughts." (These somewhat abortive efforts lend further credence to the "effort paradox" described in the previous chapter—direct concentration on memory recovery is counterproductive.) The editorial comment can be added that the majority of Freud's patients in the early period of psychoanalysis, some the protagonists of the classic case studies, were quite youthful, so that recovery of early memories might well have been facilitated when compared with recall attempts of older patients, who were distanced by many years from the incidents they were trying to recall. Perhaps the increased ages of many of Freud's later patients, as well as advances in theory, played a role in encouraging the development of therapeutic techniques that aimed to capture childhood experiences, but indirectly by chains of inferential reasoning.

Screen Memories

In the 1890s Freud had already availed himself of two theoretical mechanisms, repression and screen memories, purporting to explain why memories pertaining to neurosis-producing events required special recovery techniques. These two memory mechanisms could, if necessary, be stretched to cover any memory error, since *screen memories* dealt with the commission of errors and *repression* with memory omissions. Alternatively, as Fenichel has stated, repression deals with words while screen memories deal with compensating ideas, feelings, and attitudes. One would expect these mechanisms to be invoked unequally. In the experimental laboratory, where lists of single words or nonsense syllables are the material of memorization and it is theorized that errors are made because there is "interference" between lists (e.g., the retroactive inhibition paradigm), omission errors are far more common than substitution errors. But where life experiences are involved, it is quite likely that the proportion of distortion errors is much higher. The inertial logic inherent in our autobiographical narratives commonly encourages continuity, even permitting "embroidering the truth" as against discontinuous saltations and outright gaps.

Since screen memories are thought to convey important information, however indirectly, they have always been considered valuable in the psychotherapeutic situation. In the 1914 article already cited, "Remembering, Repeating and Working-Through," Freud stated: "In many cases I have had the impression that the familiar childhood amnesia, which is theoretically so important to us, is entirely outweighed by the screen-memories. Not merely is much that is essential in childhood preserved in them but actually all that is essential. Only one must understand how to extract it from them by analysis. They represent the forgotten years of childhood."

The earliest paper by Freud on screen memories was published in 1899. This concept was enlarged upon through several editions of the *Psychopathology of Everyday Life* (1901). Although it would be possible, as with repression, to draw a theoretical distinction between memories located in childhood and subsequent screen memories, this was not done; Freud's concern was with the distortion of childhood memories, though he did not rule out the possibility that adult happenings could also be *screened* when recalled. Freud starts from the common observation that memories of childhood are often not only sparse and isolated one from another but of very ordinary and indifferent content, so that even to the rememberer they appear to have no special significance. It is puzzling to consider why one would recall them at all. Freud's explanation is that frequently ordinary memories cover up or "screen" a memory of greater import. In the last analysis, however, screen memories are themselves products of repression, since a particular screen memory occurs because of an associative relationship between its content and that of a repressed memory. The juxtaposition of the repressed memory against the screening memory can occur in any temporal order. The most common chronological sequence involves a repressed memory that occurred in early childhood and a screening memory that occurred later in life. But that sequence can be reversed, with the screening memory temporally preceding a later repressed memory, or the two memories may be nearly contemporaneous.

Freud draws a comparison between screen memories and the forgetting of proper names. The two phenomena differ in that screen memories tend to be permanent, whereas forgetting a name is usually temporary. From the standpoint of conscious experience one is aware that substitute names are false, while one is surprised that the screen memory is remembered at all. But the two phenomena are alike in that not only is there a conflict between two possible memory candidates, but more importantly there is a tendentious factor or motive involved.

Screen memories may also sometimes be identified by their experiential content. In considering the often bruited question of how early can one obtain valid childhood memories, Freud concluded that most memories people put forward as fitting this description are probably screen memories. His argument first makes the generalization that there are imagery types (auditory, kinesthetic, etc. as well as visual), but regardless of the imagery dominance one has in later life one is always predominantly visual in dreaming and in infantile memory. (Freud cites himself as an example of one who has good *visual* memory only for his earliest childhood memories.)[1] It is customary in screen memories that apparently insignificant events appear with unexpectedly clear imagery. Regardless of the truth or falsity of early childhood memories, "what one sees invariably includes oneself as a child, with a child's shape and clothes." Freud finds that this literal self-perception contradicts both the self-absorption that one would expect of an infant (i.e., infants would not perform transformations to view themselves externally) and the memories that those who are visual types have as adults, in that these "visuals" do not see themselves in their memories. (This latter assertion—which is at least open to doubt—is supported in a footnote as "based on a number of inquiries I have made.") From this reasoning, almost all early childhood memories are inferred to be screen memories and, in their process of formation, to be analogous to mythical formations. "Thus the 'childhood memories' of individuals come in general to acquire the significance of 'screen memories' and in doing so offer a remarkable analogy with the childhood memories that a nation preserves in its store of legends and myth" (1901). Screen memories may contain inaccuracies, akin to legends and myth, for two reasons; they can include unconscious fantasies, and they are produced by compromise formations between repressed contents and defense mechanisms.

In his first theorizing about screen memories Freud (1899) carried a bit further his interpretation of the observation that seeing oneself in memory is a hallmark of many screen memories. He suggested that such an image means that a childhood memory has been translated into visual imagery only at the time of its revival, and that no reproduction of the original memory ever previously entered consciousness. The reasoning seems to be that since self-perception is impossible, a memory content in which it occurs must be a later representation. In rebuttal one could argue that if all memories result from constructive processes, then seeing the self can, like other constructions, sometimes be an *initial schematic representation* in the service of memory. (See Hebb, 1969, for descriptions of memories whose initial formats depict never-perceived perspectives as well as examples of imaging the self.)

The line is somewhat blurred between screen memories and the direct repression of memories. Anything that distorts the memory of significant childhood experiences can, after all, be considered as acting to facilitate repression, particularly since displacements, mergers, and substitutions occur that will render a memory innocuous. Indeed, screen memories, particularly of early childhood experiences, are said to be analogous to remembering through dreams. Most of the falsification, Freud argues, occurs not while registering the original experience but at a later date, when retrieval is attempted. Freud also assures us that we cannot tell subjectively the difference between true and false memories since the false ones are not tentative but just as sensorially distinct as the true ones. Since memories are not simply revived but are formed at retrieval, we can never know the exact nature of the original experience. This constructivist formation of memories holds for many early childhood memories, so that it may be that all early memories undergo some distortion. Freud concludes that perhaps we have no memories at all from early childhood but only memories *relating* to our childhood. It is pertinent to keep this assertion in mind when it is glibly asserted that Freud believed dogmatically that no experience is ever forgotten.

Repression

The multiple meanings of *repression* have been discussed many times in the literature, probably at greatest length in Peter Madison's (1961) treatment. This is not another such analysis but, rather, a presentation of some of the main ways in which repression touches on memory phenomena. It is clear that the initial use of repression by Freud referred principally to unconsciously motivated forgetting (1893, 1894, 1895). That repression should subsequently refer to many other mental mechanisms involving distortions of cognition is hardly surprising when we realize that for a twenty-year period, from about 1906 to 1926, "repression" and "defense" were synonomous; "its [repression's] meaning grew more complex with every development in psychoanalytic theory. The only uncontroversial point is that the meaning of 'repression' as hysterical amnesia came first and was never abandoned" (Madison, p. 17). Further, Madison points out that in his well-known and much-quoted 1915 paper "Repression" Freud "defined 'repression' in terms of keeping material at a distance from consciousness, a function that is performed quite as well by reaction-formation or projection as by amnesia." After 1926 when Freud had instituted a clear distinction between defense as a general term and repression as a particular mechanism, he was still often inconsistent. Madison makes the even more inclusive argument that defense and repression can *never* be completely separated because repression in the broad sense of keeping material away from consciousness is an aspect of most defensive mechanisms, not just repression as one among many defenses protecting the ego from anxiety. Madison also suggests that this overlap resulted from the fact that Freud's fundamental ideas in this domain were mostly worked out when the conscious–unconscious distinction was foremost in Freud's thinking, before the adoption of the structural theory of id, ego, and superego in 1923. In any event, it is obvious that many of the resistances met with in psychotherapy have little to do with the specific amnesic form of repression that was central to "defense" in Freud's first psychoanalytic theory.

In what follows, much has been condensed in presenting a somewhat simplified description of the way in which repression comes about. To do otherwise would involve considerable repetition of what is readily available from many sources. Any adult repression is dependent on a prior primal repression, brought about by a fixation of an instinct at the infantile period. These primal repressions are fairly automatic, instinctive responses resulting from "over-tension" produced by overstimulation, which can be induced by such occurrences as separation from the mother and, a little later, castration threats. Repressions after the age of 5 or 6, when the superego is formed, are technically called *repression proper* or *after-expulsion,* although when the term "repression" is used alone this secondary repression is usually what is meant. Superego anxiety most frequently supplies the motive for adult repressions, but these repressions presuppose the primal repressions that are needed to exert an attraction on the more recent occurrences. With secondary repression, the pull of the repressed material has often been emphasized as well as the push of the repressing forces and the cost in effort required to maintain repression.

In the description given by Otto Fenichel the manner in which this critical mass of repressed content acts is somewhat indirect:

> The impression arises that the repressed is like a magnetic force attracting everything that has any connection with it, so that it, too, becomes repressed; actually it does not attract associatively connected material into the repressed, but tries to transform it into a derivative, whereupon the same forces that had originally repressed it repress the new material as well. (1945, p. 149).

Chronologically, what has been repressed during primal repression manifests itself in consciousness but is again subjected to a second or "deferred" repression. It should be noted that in this description an associative process still plays a key role, since *derivatives* are defined somewhat vaguely as "associatively connected ideas that are less objectionable to the conscious ego." (Fenichel, 1945, p. 17). In sum, as Freud said in one of his last papers, "all repressions take place in early childhood; they are primitive defensive measures adopted by the immature, feeble ego. In later years there are not fresh repressions, but the old ones persist and are used by the ego for purposes of further mastering instinct. New conflicts are resolved by what we call 'after-repression' " (Freud, 1937a). After Freud's theory revision of 1926, these after-repressions were said to be triggered by a signal anxiety mechanism that developed once the superego was formed.

As Fenichel further points out, the commonest examples of amnesic after-repression occur in the type of phenomena described in the *Psychopathology of Everyday Life.*

> The pattern of repression is exemplified best in the case of the simple forgetting of a name or an intention. Analysis reveals that a name or an intention is forgotten if a suppressed motive resisted it, usually because it was associated with some objectionable instinctual demand. In the case of tendential forgetting, the fact that the repressed still persists in the unconscious is sensed directly in the subjective feeling that one ought to know what has been forgotten, or even that one does know it "somehow," "it is on the tip of the tongue," although actually one does not know it. (1945, p. 148)

What is striking about Freud's exceedingly numerous examples of tendentious forgetting is that no attempt is made to trace causation back to primal repressions. This omission holds throughout Freud's theorizing, both in his early formulations where primal repressions were either exclusively sexual in origin or based on nongratification of other physiological needs, and also after the importance of aggression as a separate instinct was noted in 1920. Surprisingly, recognition of aggression resulted in less theoretical revision than might have been expected. Although Freud gave the aggressive instinct separate status, aggression was not considered by Freud to be an independently repressible motive since it was invariably associated with sexual motives.

In spelling out repression more definitively in his 1915 article Freud made a distinction between two components of the same idea or group of ideas that underwent repression, viz., the charge of affect and the cognitive representation of the idea—that is, the idea itself. Freud regarded the affective charge as both more important and more complex, for though it may appear to be repressed, as was discussed in the last chapter, repression does not in fact occur. Possible outcomes include the affective charge being transformed into anxiety or producing an affect of a particular qualitative tone, although the notion of transformation into anxiety was later discarded. (It can be noted that Freud's [1915b] theoretical description of the fate of affects coincides with the widespread interest shown in affective memory at that time by philosophers and psychologists.)

Informed commentators on Freud are nowadays quick to state that it is a

vulgar error to equate repression simply with a form of forgetting. Nevertheless, the forced-forgetting component of repression remains, even when
unemphasized. Recent Freudian theorists like to point out the paradoxical in
the repression–memory relation. For example, the chronological sequence
may be reversed and the lifting or undoing of a repression be followed by
heightened recall, rather than recall dissipating repression. George Klein
notes, "Recalling an event does not necessarily undo repression; indeed recall
may be *facilitated* by the removal of a repression, as memories are seen in a
new light and are *therefore* remembered. It is not a memory, but the *meaning*
of a memory that was condemned" (Klein, 1976, p. 248). Franz Alexander, a
pioneer in shortening the duration of psychoanalytic therapy, had put forward
a similar view in the 1930s. Indeed, most of those who advocate brief psychotherapies believe that increased recall of troublesome memories simply vali-
dates the success of the treatment.

A further turnabout from the usual emphasis is to point out that repressed
memories are, after all, preserved so that repression is not just forgetting but
also a special form of retention. "It is obvious that the process by which a
repressed memory remains unconscious is quite different from the quiet and
passive fading undergone by impressions of insignificant events. When, for
instance, a repressed wish produces a powerful compulsion, a blatant error or a
slip of the tongue, we cannot believe that it has lost its basic organization"
(Klein, p. 249). In terms of memory organizational factors, construing memory
in a broad sense, many of the theoretical constructs of psychoanalysis added
after the early period of concentration of amnesic repression can be classed as
partially repressed organized patterns of retention, e.g., transference, repeating (acting out), and repetition compulsion. The transference mechanism occurs when the patient transfers to the analyst "mental attitudes that were lying
ready in him and were intimately connected with his memories".

For Freud the transference is a memoric *faute de mieux,* the communication of memory content through action, though in somewhat stereotypical
form. Freud asserts that the patient "would like best to repeat in his relation
to the analyst *all* the history of the forgotten period of his life. So what he is
showing us is the kernel of his intimate life history: *he is reproducing it
tangibly, as though it were actually happening, instead of remembering it"*
(1926b, p. 226). But as Jean Laplanche and J.-B. Pontalis (1973) emphasize,
transference is more a process of actualization of unconscious wishes than a
repetition of literal events. Therefore: "what is transferred, essentially, is
psychical reality—that is to say, at the deepest level, unconscious wishes and
the fantasies associated with them. And further, manifestations of transference are not verbatim repetitions but rather symbolic equivalents of what is
being transferred" (1973, p. 460). The same authors note that Freud, unlike
most contemporary analysts, never considered the analysis of transference an
adequate substitute in any respect for memory recall. "Freud never abandons
the view that the ideal of the treatment is complete *recollection* and in cases
where this turns out to be unattainable he falls back on constructions to fill in
the gaps in infantile history. Furthermore, he never esteems the transference

relationship for its own sake, either from the point of view of the abreaction of childhood experiences or from that of the rectification of unrealistic modes of object-relationship" (p. 459).

It can be concluded that, over the years, emphasis in psychoanalytic theory shifted from the study of specific memories to broader action patterns that were also in great part the product of repressions. Memoric manifestations were still the point of focus, but to trace these partially disguised action patterns to their origins was so indirect and tortuous as to be dauntingly difficult. Instead, therapy concentrated on contemporary actions that could, to some degree, yield reconstructions of critical events in the patient's autobiography.

Childhood Amnesia

One of the most discussed psychoanalytic memory phenomena in the nonanalytic psychological literature is what Freud called *childhood amnesia* (also known as *infantile amnesia*), the inability to recall autobiographical events from the early years of life. The time at which the veil lifts and more or less continuous life memories begin is placed at age 6 to 8 in the first description given of this phenomenon (1905a), but age 5 is also suggested in a later description (1916–17). This repression is not worldwide. It is thought not to apply to primitive races where sexual repression is not a necessary concomitant of civilization, and it is not universal in the West since it applies in "the case of most people, though by no means all" (1905a). One reason Freud advances as to why we should be surprised at this lack of remembrance of early childhood is the somewhat dubious assertion that "the memory is more efficient at an early age, since it is less overburdened than it is later" (1916–17). Nevertheless, from the perspective of the adult there are some important early memories that are acknowledged to be retained after all. These memories, seemingly neutral in emotional value and unimportant in content, are the "screen memories" discussed at the beginning of this chapter. Freud makes an even more sweeping statement about the ability of screen memories to penetrate childhood amnesia than he had in 1914: "with a thorough analysis everything that has been forgotten can be extracted from them" (1916–17). Also, impressions from the earliest years often are retained in dreams and so are susceptible to analysis. Thus the childhood memories do exist but are considered to be blocked and inaccessible because of a widespread and ordinarily never-to-be-undone repression, which Freud compared directly to hysterical amnesia. Theoretically, Freud first attributed widespread childhood amnesia mainly to the decay of the Oedipus complex, with the resultant formation of the superego at around age 5 or 6. Later, Freud (1924, 1930) acknowledged that there was something developmentally organic or phylogenetic about the dissolution of the Oedipus complex and that one should *not* overestimate superego conflict in the obtained infantile amnesia (see later under "The Sense of Smell and Organic Repression").

What are the more important events for which the child is amnesic? Near the top of the list would have to be the critical, wounding events that lead to neurosis, the well-known concept of infantile "traumatic incidents." That one cannot practice psychoanalysis without examing the difficulties of infancy is made clear by Freud in one of his last works, *Moses and Monotheism* (1939), where he finds it "nonsensical to say that one is practicing psycho-analysis if one excludes from examination and consideration precisely these earliest periods—as happens in some quarters" (1939). In this same work Freud gives us two slightly different age ranges during which crucial traumas might occur, "All these traumas occur in early childhood up to about the fifth year. Impressions from the time at which a child is beginning to talk stand out as being of particular interest; the periods between the ages of two and four seem to be the most important . . ." (1939, p. 74). Several pages later Freud writes: "What children have experienced at the age of two and have not understood, need never be remembered by them except in dreams; they may only come to know of it through psycho-analytic treatment. But at some later time it will break into their life with obsessional impulses, it will govern their actions, it will decide their sympathies and antipathies and will quite often determine their choice of a love-object, for which it is so frequently impossible to find a rational basis" (1939, p. 126). Thus the age-period birth to 2 years and that of 2 years to 4 years each appear to lay claim to a special determinative importance for later memories of possibly traumatic significance.

Is there always a single crucial traumatic incident, or is there cumulative early learning that tends to set the infant into a pathological pattern of responding? Freud in his later writing is rather open-minded on this point. It is largely a matter of individual differences dependent on whether certain experiences made "too many demands on the personality" so that "with one constitution something produces a trauma whereas with another it does not." But in principle Freud concluded that it was unimportant whether single or multiple experiences were involved; in either case, such experiences occurred before the age of five. In Freud's later theorizing the exclusively sexual emphasis of crucial early experiences had somewhat broadened to include interlinked aggressive and narcissistic experiences.

> The experiences in question are as a rule totally forgotten, they are not accessible to memory and fall within the period of infantile amnesia, which is usually broken into a few separate mnemic residues, what are known as "screen memories." They relate to impressions of a sexual and aggressive nature, and no doubt also to early injuries to the ego (narcissistic mortifications). In this connection it should be remarked that such young children make no sharp distinction between sexual and aggressive acts, as they do later (cf. The misunderstanding of the sexual act in a sadistic sense). The predominance of the sexual factor is, of course, most striking and calls for theoretical consideration. (1939, p. 74)

In spite of the somewhat flawed claim to universality for childhood amnesia, many theorists have sought to enlarge, amend, or give altogether different explanations than Freud did. The most popular explanations within academic psychology have been those of Ernest Schactel (1947) and Ulric Neisser (1967). Neisser pointed out the importance of Schactel's work and presented his own information-processing view. These theorists believe that the categories the infant possesses for registering and organizing perceptions and wishes that subsequently become memories are inaccessible as the child becomes older. Their views make use of a constructivist schema theory in which forgetting becomes an inability to reconstruct earlier events from the categories and information available to the child at an older age. Neisser stressed the discontinuities in cognitive development of which the transformation from the preverbal condition to language use and school entry are among the more important. He claimed that these acquired ways of categorizing are not reversible, thereby offering little possibility of recovering the now mismatched few fragments of infantile constructions that might be retained.

As a psychoanalyst, Schactel had to allow for the possibility of memory recovery by interpreting screen memories, free associations, and dreams. Unlike Neisser, he claimed that all experience leaves something like a memory trace behind, so that the developmental memory discontinuities characteristic of childhood are rather like those found between waking and dreaming states. Schactel also emphasized the shift from dealing with nebulous odors to easily retained visual perceptions, a shift that he believed occurred in early life: "it is significant that the olfactory sense, so important in infancy, throughout life is least, practically not at all, capable of objectifying stimuli, whereas the more spiritual and later developed sense of vision cannot but objectify the stimuli by which it is affected" (Schactel, 1959, p. 302). According to Schactel, recovery of early screen memories and other involuntary recalls of a Proustian variety are therefore sensationist in nature since they are

> not in the conscious, purposefully remembering mind and its memory schemata, but in a sphere which is more adequately if vaguely described as memory of the body or, rather, of the psychosomatic entity (what Piaget has referred to as sensorimotor memory). The forgotten experience is revived by the recurrence of a sensation which has left a record, a trace behind; or it is revived by the understanding and reliving of the bodily attitudes, muscular and vegetive, which the forgotten experience produced. (1959, p. 315)[2]

The Sense of Smell and Organic Repression

There is a common set of assumptions for both Freud and Titchener that lends special interest to the sense of smell or olfaction. (Olfaction had almost no interest for William James, despite his sensationist inclinations in theorizing.) Titchener makes the point that the sense of smell is of "peculiar interest," partly on account of the role it has played in evolution. It is, he says, mainly a land sense in that both mammals that have a water habitat and birds have a weak sense of smell; "and our own disregard of smell sensations is largely due to our assumption of the upright position" (1910, p. 116). Nevertheless, "both in range of quality and in discrimination of intensity it holds its own as against the other senses", and "there is no evidence for the statement, often as it is made, that in man the sense of smell is degenerating." More provocatively, Titchener states that whether "the sense of smell has any large share, primary or derivative, in the sexual life of man is a disputed point," but "on the whole, the evidence is decidedly in the affirmative."

Almost twenty years after Titchener wrote, a similar evolutionary theme is taken up by Freud in order to speculate on why the sexual function so often fails to yield satisfaction and is deflected from its aim. He states that his "deepest conjecture" in the regard is to the effect that

> with the assumption of an erect posture by man and with the depreciation of his sense of smell, it was not only his anal erotism which threatened to fall a victim to organic repression, but the whole of his sexuality; so that since this, the sexual function has been accompanied by repugnance which cannot further be accounted for, and which prevents its complete satisfaction and forces it away from the sexual aim into sublimations and libidinal displacements. (Freud, 1930, p. 106*n*)

Why the sense of smell is of particular interest in a discussion of autobiographical memory is owing to Freud's concept of *organic repression*. Freud, as mentioned, had earlier written about the need to consider organic repression (i.e., repression as an inevitable structural containment of experience independent of particular life events), but now somewhat later he commits himself to the assertion that "the deepest root of the sexual repression which advances along with civilization is the organic defense of the new form of life achieved with man's erect gait against his earlier animal existence." Deterioration of the human olfactory sense, mediated by a shift from olfactory to visual dominance (an assumption not accepted by Titchener), is for Freud an index of the historical shift in sexual mode, which tended toward universal and not just individual sexual repression: "The diminution of the olfactory stimuli seems itself to be a consequence of man's raising himself from the ground, of his assumption of an upright gait; this made his genitals, which were previously concealed, visible and in need of protection, and so provoked feelings of shame in him" (1930, pp. 99–100*n*).[3]

This postulation of an organic basis for repression has consequences that clearly are different from those repressions brought about by the punitive morality of the superego or the external pressures of the environment. In both of these cases an actual event has occurred that is subsequently acted on by the forces of repression, even if it is only a thought that has not come fully into conscious awareness. But Freud's description of an organic repression resulting from an evolutionary sequence could conceivably lend itself to warding off potential threats and avoiding perceptual encounters so that repression can act to prevent behavior. Thus the extended meaning of repression that is so widespread among contemporary analysts and often far from possessing any memory connotation—e.g., repressed impulses, fantasies, perceptions, and affects (see Klein, 1970, Ch. 11)—receives blanket justification when repression is construed as *organic*. In this context repression can occur *before* rather than *after* the fact.

A consequence of the "diminished" sense of smell brought about by organic repression is that it possesses a now unobtrusive place in the mental economy in that smell perceptions are among the least likely to become conscious. "Of the phenomenon of consciousness we can at least say that it was originally attached to perception. All sensations which originate from the perception of painful, tactile, auditory, or visual stimuli are what are most readily conscious" (Freud, 1939, p. 97). Olfactory perceptions are conspicuously absent from this list.

To account for the devaluation of odor experiencing in our culture, Anna Freud had no need to resort to an explanation in terms of "organic" repression. Instead, she gave a developmental explanation and described how the infant must learn to reverse his natural preferences as part of the socialization process, particularly in regard to the pleasure he takes in the smell of feces. She argued that immaturity and lack of discriminatory ability cannot account for such perverse preferences. "Whoever has carefully observed a small child of about two years of age must have noticed that he distinguishes with extraordinary exactitiude between the different smells. His difference from the adult lies in his different appraisal of the various smells. . . . But what smells horrid to us smells good to the child. Of course, we can if we like, consider the child naughty because nasty smells give him pleasure!" (A. Freud, 1979, pp. 54–55).[4]

Still another approach to odor deprecation is put forward by Schactel, who takes a social psychoanalytic position that the sense of smell possesses animalistic connotations and has therefore undergone a cultural taboo that results in poor representational schemata for retention, including the lack of an adequate vocabulary.

> especially smell and taste are neglected and to a considerable extent even tabooed by Western civilization. They are the animalistic senses *par excellence*. Engaged for thousands of years in a battle for control and mastery of nature outside and inside himself, man, and especially Western man, does not want to be reminded that he is not only man but also nature, also animal. Because of the cultural taboo on smell and taste—smell even more than taste, but the two are inseparable—it is even possible for the adult to realize clearly the effect which the discrepancy between experience on the one hand and language and memory schemata on the other hand has on the capacity for recall, especially voluntary recall. English, like the other Western languages, is conspicuously poor in words for the description of smells and tastes. (Schactel, 1959, p. 298)

It can be concluded that our civilization's systematic deemphasizing of odor sensations and their retention is, in the psychoanalytic sense, *overdetermined,* since three somewhat different arguments have been made. Indeed, the arguments agree that odor sensations are more focused on by infants than by older children and adults, and that odor sensations become fully conscious less frequently than other sensations. Of greatest importance, however, smells appear to be an important vehicle for infantile affects, about which Freud tells us that "infantile feelings are more intense and inexhaustibly deep than those of adults." Titchener is, perhaps, also partially correct in that the sense of smell (on occasion attenuated through food and drink) is more nearly holding its own in the culture of today, even for adults.

Experimental research on odors supports the idea that young preschool children can well tolerate odors found extremely unpleasant by adults (Engen, 1982). A similar conclusion was also reached in an earlier study by E. Peto (1936), who tested a sample of nearly 300 children below age 5. While such findings do not speak to the evolutionary basis of "organic repressions," they do emphasize that odors disagreeable to adults, as argued by both Anna Freud and Schactel, very early come under a social taboo that, in most cases, leads to rapid sensory learning of the socially correct preference. Insofar as few older children and adults can ever recall finding "nasty" smells tolerable, the question can be raised as to whether this preference reversal results from repression or forgetting by relearning, a frequent dilemma in categorizing the fate of young children's memories.

Auditory and Visual Imagery and Reality Testing

It has often been remarked that Freud, and through him psychoanalysis, insists that the patient should aim for full understanding expressed in language, whereas most other therapies from hypnosis to behavioral modification do not. For Freud, perception and consciousness (in early Freudian theory the system Pcpt.-Cs.) are adjacent to but apart from the memory system (true hallucinations constituting an exception). Lacking a general theory of language, Freud stressed the memorization factor in language usage and viewed retained "verbal residues" as primarily derived from auditory perceptions (*Ego and the Id,* 1923), with secondary contributions made by visual and motor images. In some ways this verbal and auditory emphasis might be thought unexpected because of the importance Freud attributed to dreams and his own much greater interest in the visual arts of painting and sculpture than in music.

When it becomes desirable to think of concrete things, "optical mnemic residues" come into their own. Although the optical mode is favored by some people, its main limitation is "that what becomes conscious in it is as a rule only the concrete subject-matter of the thought, and that the relations between the various elements of this subject-matter, which is what specially characterizes thought, cannot be given visual expression" (1923, p. 21). Freud concludes that, owing to this deficiency, thinking in pictures "stands nearer to unconscious processes than does thinking in words" and in fact is "only a very incomplete form of becoming conscious." In his first schematic diagram of the tripartite structural theory, the ego was given special representation, which was illustrated in a diagrammatic sketch of what Freud called a "cap of hearing," while no locus was given for the visual sense. Visual images, while not so liable to be unconscious as sensations of odor, nevertheless, like dreams and childhood memories (recall that Freud found these almost entirely visual), are not free of distortions from unconscious influences. (Examples of memory-derived, symptomatic visual imagery described in the *Psychopathology of Everyday Life* are discussed in Chapter 4.)

One of the definitive characteristics of dreams is that they cannot ordinarily be differentiated from reality while they are occurring. But in the waking state it is important that one distinguish clearly between thoughts and ideas generated internally and perceptions occasioned by the external world. Thoughts and ideas are largely made up of memories, and "since memory-traces can become conscious just as perceptions do, especially through their association with residues of speech, the possibility arises of a confusion which would lead to the mistaking of reality" (*An Outline of Psychoanalysis,* 1940, p. 199). It would seem, then, from Freud's reasoning that auditory memories, particularly those with verbal content, would much more likely be confused with reality than visual memories,and the majority of dreams, being dominantly visual, would be less likely candidates for confusion. But this modality distinction was not remarked on by Freud in regard to the "institution of reality testing," the function that distinguishes internal from external perception and makes it possible for the ego to operate in accord with the "reality principle." Nowhere, in fact, does Freud follow up on his imagery assumptions and clearly spell out the mechanisms that make reality testing a generally valid enterprise.

Infantile Memories (or Fantasies?) and Deferred Action

A crucial point in Freudian theory that seemed firmly established until recently was an important change that came about in 1897, when Freud recognized that women reporting experiences of sexual seduction by their fathers were in reality remembering infantile fantasies. Jeffrey Masson (1985) and others have challenged this important doctrinal change and argued that Freud's switch to an emphasis on infantile fantasy was not motivated by evidence but by nonscientific considerations, such as a desire for professional acceptance and ingratiation with his peers. At issue in the present discussion are not the facts about the history of Freud and psychoanalysis but whether infantile fantasies are remembered as actual events, with the possible outcome that neurotic illness can be caused by remembered fantasies as well as veridical memories. In the 1930s Sandor Ferenczi had argued that real seductions rather than sexual fantasies were the operative factors, and in 1973 "Dr. Robert Fliess, a psychoanalyst and son of Freud's onetime close confidant Wilhelm Fliess, quoted Ferenczi approvingly and added: 'I would now contradict him [Freud] head on: no one is ever made sick by his fantasies' " (*New York Times,* Aug 25, 1981). (It is Masson's further startling contention that Robert Fliess himself suffered sexual abuse at a young age from his father Wilhelm [Masson, 1985, pp. 141–143].)

Freud's most detailed analysis of a probable fantasy taken for a memory did not concern explicit sexual fantasizing but occurred in his monograph *Leonardo da Vinci and a Memory of his Childhood* (1910b). The memory in question, as recalled by Leonardo himself, was exceedingly brief: "It seems that I was always destined to be so deeply concerned with vultures; for I recall as one of my very earliest memories that while I was in my cradle a vulture came down to me, and opened my mouth with its tail, and struck me many times with its tail against my lips" (1910b, p. 82). We are concerned here only with interpretation of the memory–fantasy relation and not with Freud's lengthy commentary on the content of this memory, the unconscious fixation on the mnemic image of the mother, the foreshadowing of Leonardo's homosexual orientation, or even that, as later research has shown, Freud was factually mistaken in that the bird in question was a kite rather than a vulture.

On the basis that there are two improbabilities involved: (1) that the memory occurred as early as the suckling period (violating the premise of general infantile amnesia) and (2) that the bird actually opened the infant's mouth with its tail, Freud concludes that Leonardo's alleged memory was not an event memory at all but a fantasy that he formed at a later date and transposed to his childhood.

> This is often the way in which childhood memories originate. Quite unlike conscious memories from the time of maturity, they are not fixed at the moment of being experienced and afterwards repeated, but are only elicited at a later age when childhood is already past; in the process they are altered and falsified, and are put into the service of later trends, so that generally speaking they cannot be distinguished from phantasies. (1910b, p. 83).

Here Freud makes explicit what he has put forward implicitly elsewhere: infantile memories are especially prone to distortion because there is no short-term representational revival, because personal memory dating is mobile and unreliable, and because recalled events are intertwined with fantasies. Memory identification can be complicated in yet another way, since in response to a review by Havelock Ellis, Freud conceded in a footnote added in 1919 that there is an alternative way in which positive childhood memories originate, namely, inculcation by the mother. Freud states that, indeed, it is quite plausible that the mother observed a large bird visiting her infant son and repeatedly told him about it afterwards.

Whatever the channel by which early distorted childhood memories originate, it is evident that for Freud they are a variant of his screen memory classification. The significance of what is screened, however, remains problematic and is perhaps not so much an event memory as a motivational desire.

> It happens, indeed, as a general rule that the phantasies about their childhood which people contruct at a late date are attached to trivial but real events of this early, and normally forgotten, period. There must have been some secret reason for bringing into prominence a real event of no importance and for elaborating it in the sort of way Leonardo did in his story of the bird, which he dubbed a vulture, and of its remarkable behavior (Freud, 1910b, 1919, pp. 82–83*n*).

One of Freud's favorite analogies is here invoked, the chronological development of personal memory is compared with the history of nations.

> A man's conscious memory of the events of his maturity is in every way
> comparable to the first kind of historical writing [which was a chronicle of
> current events]; while the memories that he has of his childhood correspond,
> as far as their origins and reliability are concerned, to the history of a
> nation's earliest days, which was compiled later and for tendentious reasons.
> (1910b, p. 84)

Hence it will be hard grubbing to obtain accurate childhood memories, even
for Freud, if one can reasonably equate them with national origin myths.

A naturally occurring question concerning early sexual memories (be
they actual or fantasy) is whether they are subsequently remembered at an
older age as they were originally encoded, or whether they are recalled and
better understood in terms of the greater maturity that obtains at the time of
recall. Freud is quite clear that the mature level of understanding prevails:
"In every analysis of a case of hysteria based on sexual traumas we find that
impressions from the pre-sexual period which produced no effect on the
child attain traumatic power at a later date as memories, when the girl or
married woman has acquired an understanding of sexual life" (case of
Katherina in *Studies on Hysteria,* 1895). This later realization and comprehension of the meaning of earlier events falls under the psychoanalytic heading of "deferred action."

In the more detailed and extended case history of the "Wolf Man" (1918),
at least a partial "deferred action" is alleged to take place at a much earlier
age, well before puberty. An infant boy at age one-and-a-half had a primal
scene observation of the copulation of his parents that was recalled in disguised symbolic form through a dream at age four, an experience Freud
attributed to the boy's increase in intellectual development. Understanding at
this age is presumed to be at least sufficient to consider the primal scene
memory as threatening. Full conscious understanding, however, only came
about twenty years later during the course of analysis. Freud attempted to
meet the suggestion that there might have been no originating event as such
and that content might have all been a fantasy, particularly since at no time
did the patient spontaneously give a clear recollection of his primal scene
observation.

> It seems to me absolutely equivalent to a recollection if the memories are
> replaced (as in the present case) by dreams, the analysis of which invariably
> leads back to the same scene, and which reproduce every portion of its
> content in an indefatigable variety of new shapes. Indeed, dreaming is an-
> other kind of remembering, though one that is subject to the conditions that
> rule at night and to the laws of dream formation. It is this recurrence in
> dreams that I regard as the explanation of the fact that patients themselves
> gradually acquire a profound conviction of the reality of these primal scenes,
> a conviction which is in no respect inferior to one based upon recollection.
> (1918, p. 51)

Thus dreams with similar recurrent content can sometimes be a criterion indicating that event memories are being invoked rather than extraneous fantasies. The Wolf Man memory of a presumed actual observation and the Leonardo memory of a part fantasy both appear to be of equal importance for analysis. Nor does it seem to make any difference that the Wolf Man memory was of an unshared, singular event while Leonardo evocation was very likely fantasized repeatedly or perhaps inculcated by the mother on several occasions. Thus, for Freud, the distinction drawn between a presumed actual event (Wolf Man) and a probably fantasized event (Leonardo) results in remarkably little theoretical or treatment difference. In spite of the great biographical importance imputed to Freud in his giving up the "seduction theory" as fact, there appears to be no reason to expect a theoretical distinction between early fact and fantasy, when both are strongly remembered. This was also Freud's conclusion in his 1914 *History of the Psychoanalytic Movement* when he stated: "If hysterical subjects trace back their symptoms to traumas that are fictitious, then the new fact which emerges is precisely that they can create such scenes in *phantasy,* and this psychical reality requires to be taken into account alongside practical reality" (pp. 17–18). Other analysts have disagreed; Robert Fliess, for one, as cited earlier in this chapter. (See also Chapter 5.)

Edward S. Casey (1980) attempted a synthesis of the ideas of Piaget and Freud to explain "deferred action" by equating this concept with Piaget's demonstration that some memories increase in accuracy over a period of months or years in accord with the child's changing levels of schemes of intelligence. Assuming that dependence on schemes of intelligence can account for deferred understanding, it is also probable that changing cognitive schemes can at times account for some of the distortions and omissions found in autobiographical memory. Such a consideration is related to the explanations of childhood amnesia given earlier in this chapter, particularly those by Schactel and Neisser on the mismatch between cognitive levels at the time of event occurrence and the time of recall.

Multiple Registration of Childhood Events

At this point it is appropriate to consider one of the several statements Freud made that, in spite of the distortion of screen memories and difficulties in separating actual memories of events from fantasies, perhaps nothing is really forgotten.

> Since we overcame the error of supposing that the forgetting we are familiar with signified destruction of the memory-trace—that is annihilation—we have been inclined to take the opposite view, that in mental life nothing which has once been formed can perish—that everything is somehow preserved and that in suitable circumstances (when, for instance, regression goes back far enough) it can once more be brought to light. (1930, p. 69)

Freud then goes on to imagine the City of Rome as analogous to the mind. To make the comparison accurate, all buildings, past and present, would have to be simultaneously present. "In the place occupied by the Palazzo Caffarelli would once more stand—without the Palazzo having to be removed—the temple of Jupiter Capitolinus; and this not only in its latest shape as the Romans of the Empire saw it, but also in its earliest one, when it still showed Etruscan forms and was ornamented with terra-cotta antefixes. Where the Coliseum now stands we could at the same time admire Nero's vanished Golden House" (p. 70). But Freud breaks off the description since he concludes that in this case a pictorial analogy of the mind is impossible, as the same space cannot have two different contents. Freud considers whether a biological analogy would be more appropriate, but "the embryo cannot be discovered in the adult. The thymus gland of childhood is replaced after puberty by connective tissue, but is no longer present itself." Thus this analogy is also inadequate. "The fact remains that only in the mind is such a preservation of all the earlier stages alongside of the final form possible, and that we are not in a position to represent this phenomenon in pictorial terms" (p. 71). Freud then puts in the qualification that even in the mind some things may be effaced or absorbed to such an extent that they cannot be restored, but nevertheless, "It is rather the rule than the exception for the past to be preserved in mental life."

This explanation of "never forgetting" has ramifications that tie in with the previous discussion. At least in infancy and the preschool period, Freud suggests, there are *multiple registrations* at different times of the same objects or activities. And at this early period many of these registrations are mutually isolated from one another and unrecognized as having a common referent. To bring about this result one does not have to go so far as to suppose either that regression is necessarily invoked or that changes in the cognitive state of the developing infant make inaccessible a previous registration, though each may make a contribution. The inaccuracies inherent in such fragmentary and duplicative registrations must be kept in mind when Freud states that there is "good reason to believe that there is no period at which the capacity for receiving and reproducing impressions is greater than precisely during the years of childhood" (1905a, p. 175). This is not quite the same as Bergson's claim (Chapter 2) that there is reason to believe adults can register memories continuously. In adults, even granting the possibility of continuous registration, awareness of duplication and redundancy must discourage much perceptual registration from consideration as memory content.

An explanation for multiple registrations put forward in developmental psychology is that, for the infant, consistent "object constancy" takes time to achieve. During this period multiple registrations that from an adult standpoint are nonindependent and overlapping are particularly likely. Even in later childhood at levels of more global identification there is the possibility that a lack of knowledge coordination encourages further multiple registrations. A well-known example of such a lack is illustrated by children's frequent failure to acknowledge that disparate social roles can be played by the same person. Thus a daddy and a policeman cannot be embodied by the same man. For the growing child the categories that give the world sense also progressively reduce its novelty, as well as the memory burden that excessive unrelated registrations can entail.

This idea of multiple registrations had been put forward much earlier in a 1907 footnote added to the *Psychopathology of Everyday Life* (1901), but without any illustrative visual analogy.

> The most important as well as the strangest characteristic of psychical fixa-
> tion is that all impressions are preserved, not only in the same form in which
> they were first received, but also in all the forms which they have adopted in
> their further developments. This is a state of affairs which cannot be illus-
> trated by comparison with another sphere. Theoretically every early state of
> the mnemic content could thus be restored to memory again, even if its
> elements have long ago exchanged all their original connections for more
> recent ones. (1901, p. 275*n*)

Personally I find the multiple registration concept more provocative than that of mass childhood amnesia. While the multiple registration tendency feeds into Freudian assumptions about the prevalence of early childhood memories in neurotic conflicts and dreams, it does not depend on any alleged universal cultural taboo or special biological mechanism in addition to immaturity. Freud also must have regarded this concept as among his most fruitful, for prominent in his last theoretical musings, written when he was in exile in London in 1938, is the following entry:

> June 16.—It is interesting that in connection with early experiences, as
> contrasted with later experiences, all the various reactions to them survive,
> of course including contradictory ones. Instead of a decision, which would
> have been the outcome later. Explanation: weakness of the power of synthe-
> sis, retention of the characteristic of the primary process. (*Standard Edition*,
> 1941, vol. 23, p. 299)

This chapter can be divided into two parts. In the first part, the best known Freudian concepts related to memory—screen memories, repression, childhood amnesia—have been described, including a discussion of some important ambiguities. It is characteristic of Freud's clinical interests that these well-known concepts all deal with forms of forgetting. The second part of the chapter deals not only with forgetting but also with possible ways in which memories are registered and maintained. Discussion focuses on memory imagery and the distinctiveness of childhood memory.

Chapter 4 goes beyond these concerns and illustrates that the range of Freud's ideas that implicate memory is much wider than is usually represented. This chapter also demonstrates the extent to which Freud touched on all manner of questions dealing with memory, not limiting his interest to psychopathology. Some of his descriptions can stimulate us to determine whether they are matched in our own memory experiences.

4

Additional Freudian
Memory Concepts

Freud's concepts of remembering and forgetting in this chapter have been less central to psychoanalytic memory theory than those previously described. Many of the same concepts have also been somewhat tangential to the practice of psychotherapy—repetition compulsion perhaps being an exception—and most analysts would altogether disown the concept of "archaic memories" with its overtones of Jungian theory, particularly since Freud makes a specific avowal that memories can be inherited.

This chapter is devoted to a description of some of these tangential memory concepts and concludes with consideration of Freud's own self-confessedly excellent memory. It is not altogether far-fetched to view Freud's strong emphasis on personal memory probing—emphasis persisting through his last theoretical writings—as stemming from his exceptional memoric abilities which, at the least, motivated and made feasible his own self-analysis.

Subjective Descriptions and a Functional Association Memory Model

In the *Studies on Hysteria* (1895) and in the prior "Preliminary Communication" (1893), which he co-authored with Breuer, Freud consistently mentioned the "astonishing freshness," "affective strength," and "undiminished vividness" of the "pathological memories" causing hysterical phenomena. "*It may therefore be said that the ideas which have become pathological have persisted with such freshness and affective strength because they have been denied the normal wearing-away processes by means of abreaction and reproduction in states of uninhibited association*" (1893, p. 11). This theme was to continue unabated in Freud's writing, even though hypnosis was abandoned and other treatment procedures were introduced. Recovered repressed memories had a hallucinatory quality. The same notion is taken up again in one of Freud's last papers, "Constructions in Analysis." In some analyses, Freud points out, when a construction consisting of a plausible sequence of childhood events is given to patients, they have had "lively recollections called up in them—which they themselves have described as 'unnaturally distinct'—but what they have recollected had not been the event that was the subject of the construction but details relating to that subject. For instance, they have recollected with abnormal sharpness the faces of the people involved in the construction or the rooms in which something of the sort might have happened. . . ." (1937b). These images of abnormal sharpness occurred either in dreams immediately after the construction had been put forward or in daydreams. Freud interprets this displacement onto items of minor significance to be a compromise betwen repressed material striving to get into consciousness activated by the analytical construction and the resistance attempting to keep the recollection out of consciousness.

Freud then goes further and suggests that although the recovered memories are like hallucinations this does not itself mean they lack veridicality. Actual hallucinations tend to have a core of historic truth behind them. This leads to a suggestion for the therapeutic treatment of delusions in which

> the vain effort would be abandoned of convincing the patient of the error of his delusion and of its contradiction of reality; and, to the contrary, the recognition of its kernel of truth would afford common ground upon which the therapeutic process could develop. That process would consist in liberating the fragment of historic truth from distortions and its attachments to the actual present day and in leading it back to the point in the past to which it belongs. (Freud, 1937b)

The contrast with the views of later analysts is striking. Subsequent theories have often argued that early memories are largely fantasies, but Freud himself stressed that even certified hallucinations possess a solid memoric core. Freud's most quoted statement concerning memory and neurosis had been made 44 years earlier in the "Preliminary Communication": "Hysterics suffer mainly from reminiscences." Freud concludes his 1937 paper by enlarging and clarifying the scope of this psychoanalytic shibboleth.

> Just as our construction is only effective because it recovers a fragment of lost experience, so the delusion owes its convincing power to the element of historic truth which it inserts in the place of rejected reality. In this way a proposition which I originally asserted only of hysteria would apply also to delusions—namely, that those who are subject to them are suffering from their own recollections. I never intended by this short formula to dispute the complexity of the illness or to exclude the operation of many other factors. (1937b, p. 285).

There are other phenomena that remained unchanged from the beginning to the end of Freud's theorizing. One constant is faith that the patient knows his own mind and cannot be led astray by the suggestions of the analyst. Thus,

> *we are not in a position to force anything on the patient about the things of which he is ostensibly ignorant or to influence the products of the analysis by arousing an expectation.* I have never once succeeded, by foretelling something, in altering or falsifying the reproductions of memories or the connection of events; for if I had, it would inevitably have been betrayed in the end

by some contradiction in the material. If something turned out as I had foretold, it was invariably proved by a great number of unimpeachable reminiscences that I had done no more than guess right. (1895, p. 295)

In 1937 Freud's view was: "Here, at the very start, the question arises of what guarantee we have while we are working on these constructions that we are not making mistakes and risking the success of the treatment by putting forward some construction that is incorrect." He argues that false construction is mainly a waste of time and furthermore that, "The danger of our leading a patient astray by suggestion, by persuading him to accept things which we ourselves believe, but which he ought not to, has certainly been enormously exaggerated. An analyst would have to behave very incorrectly before such a misfortune could overtake him. . . . I can assert without boasting that such an abuse of 'suggestion' has never occurred in my practice."

Two other points were made in the earlier writing that were never outmoded by later theoretical developments, although they did not receive much specific later affirmation by Freud. They nicely illustrate the specificity of detail Freud was attuned to in considering his patients' memory processing. One assertion is that there is no reminiscence in an analytic session that is without significance. "An intrusion of *irrelevant* mnemic images (which happen in some way or other to be associated with the important ones) in fact never occurs" (1895, p. 295). Some exceptions are more apparent than real, in that while they may be unimportant in themselves, they are needed to form a bridge between two important memories.

The second and much more complex claim begins with the concept that only a single memory is contained in consciousness at any one time and the length of time during which a memory remains in consciousness is in "direct proportion to its importance." Furthermore, one's total memory is organized in separate "files" that pass through the "defile" of consciousness. If the single memory in the "narrow cleft" of consciousness cannot be dealt with, consciousness is blocked. Freud seems to be attempting a kind of precise breakdown of the old simile that thought is like a moving train of memories or ideas.

That Freud was working out details in meticulous fashion and not just giving a graphic analogy is illustrated by his statement about Breuer's case of Anna O., in which he found that the single theme of "becoming deaf, of not learning" was differentiated according to seven headings, and under each of these headings 10 to more than 100 individual memories could be collected in a chronological series. "It was as though we were examining a dossier that had been kept in good order." Part of the *order* is that in reproducing memories they are reversed from the order in which they originated, with the freshest and newest put first, and last of all the experience with which the series began. The file order is but one dimension; there are two others. The second dimension displays each theme "stratified concentrically around the pathogenic nucleus." "The most peripheral strata contains [*sic*] the memories (or files), which belonging to different themes, are easily remembered and have always been clearly conscious. The deeper we go the more difficult it becomes for the emerging memories to be recognized, till near the nucleus we come upon memories which the patient disavows even in reproducing them" (1895, p. 289).

The third and most important dimension is arrangement according to thought content, which though stressing logical connections, is dynamic rather than morphological in character, as the other two dimensions were. Spatially, connections in this dimension would be irregular, but with logical chains that, in general, traverse from the periphery to the central nucleus while touching intermediate points. Freud likens these zig-zag connections to the chessboard knight's move. Further, "The logical chain corresponds not only to a zig-zag, twisted line, but rather to a ramifying system of lines and more particularly to a converging one. It contains nodal points at which two or more threads meet and thereafter proceed as one; and as a rule several threads which run independently, or which are connected at various points by side-paths, debouch into the nucleus" (p. 290). This latter point, Freud emphasizes, is what results in symptom overdetermination.

Anyone at all familiar with the associative memory computer models introduced into academic psychology in the 1960s and continuing with added refinements until the present day cannot fail to be impressed that there is a remarkable similarity between Freud's description (in his own terminology) of files, pushdown memories, nodal points, and the structural framework of contemporary memory models. It is also obvious that without something akin to a computer, few practical results could be realized. Working against further elaboration of this "model" of the 1890s was the subsequent broadening and blurring of the meaning of repression and defense and the greater emphasis put on the dynamic and agentic functions of the unconscious. These theoretical changes could not well be assimilated to a purely associationistic model, even one that advocated multiple association chains. Freud's memory model was, from the psychoanalytic perspective, "old fashioned." The much discussed neurological model contained in Freud's "Project" was being written by him at almost the same time (1895) as the above-quoted final chapter ("Psychotherapy of Hysteria") of Breuer and Freud's *Studies on Hysteria*. Up until the present day, the straightforward functional approach, of which this description is a brief synopsis, has predicted future theoretical developments better than the *memoric model* contained in the "Project," which specified hypothetical neurological parameters.

Normal Forgetting

For Freud some characterization of "normal" forgetting was a desirable foil for highlighting his description of the uniqueness of repressed memories. The previous section quoted Freud's statement that normal forgetting or wearing-away processes occurred for most experiences "by means of abreaction and reproduction in states of uninhibited association." But what is "uninhibited association?" Freud gives two examples of the setting straight of psychical trauma through "rectification by other ideas" that can occur when associations have free play. "After an accident, for instance, the memory of danger and the (mitigated) repetition of the fright become associated with the memory of what happened afterwards—rescue and the consciousness of present safety. Again, a person's memory of humiliation is corrected by his putting the facts right, by considering his own worth, etc. In this way a normal person is able to bring about the disappearance of the accompanying affect through the process of association" (1893, p. 9). (This type of association sequence was common in psychological writings of the time and looked back to the nonempirical English associationists such as Alexander Bain.)

Associations of this sort are obviously, in part, volitionally directed. Can something like repression also be instigated consciously? Some of Freud's earliest psychoanalytic writings suggest that it can. Freud's editor, James Strachey, wrote in a footnote to the "Preliminary Communication" that "On some of its earlier appearances the term 'repressed' is accompanied (as here) by the adverb 'intentionally' (*'absichtlich'*) or by 'deliberately' (*'wilkürlich'*). Nevertheless, Strachey argued that the use of these qualifiers indicates only "the existence of a motive and carries no implication of *conscious* intention." (The possibility of assimilation to later Freudian emphasis of Strachey's part seems likely.) The customary solution within later psychoanalytic theory is to consider success in voluntary forgetting as a separate mechanism, *suppression*—a rather minor one since the psychoanalytic hallmark of unconscious motivation is lacking.

> One is no more aware of "repressing" something than one is of forgetting something. The only thing one can be aware of is the end result. However, there is a conscious activity which is somewhat analogous to repression. This activity is usually referred to as *suppression* in the psychoanlytic literature. It is the familiar decision to forget about something and to think no more about it. It is more than likely that there are intermediates between suppression and repression and it may even be that there is no truly sharp line of demarcation between the two. (Brenner, 1973, p. 83)

"Forgetting in its proper sense" is the forgetting of experiences, which Freud sets apart in the *Psychopathology of Everyday Life* from the forgetting of proper names, foreign words, and the forgetting of sets of words. The mechanisms of forgetting in its proper sense are those that figure largely in the dream work, particularly distortion and condensation. The field of parapraxes or "motivated errors" (i.e., mistakes are made where performance is ordinarily error free) is, of course, considerably wider than forgetting and includes misreadings, slips of the tongue or pen, and bungled actions, among other errors. But the temporary forgetting of proper names is tagged as the most frequent occurring of all parapraxes. Although many anecdotal examples were added to the text after 1901, Freud asserted that because many of the examples in the *Psychopathology of Everyday Life* were taken from his own life, the selection of examples was biased in that to avoid embarrassment he excluded sexual matters. Yet this bias is not seen as a complete nullification of representative content, since there are other than sexual sources of parapraxes derived from suppressed motives such as egoistic, jealous, and hostile impulsions and feelings. And it is even the case that "at other times it appears to be from perfectly innocent objections and considerations that the disturbing thoughts arise" (1901).

My main point is that here Freud is far from the sexual reductionism of motives that one finds elsewhere in his writings at this time. A considerable economy in categorizing could have been brought about if Freud had recognized aggression as a major category, but this was not to occur until some twenty years later. Even accepting this limitation, one can hardly take sexual motivation as either the ultimate primitive, or as invariably linked with aggression when no examples are given. Thus it does not quite ring true when Freud claims that the mechanism of the parapraxes corresponds in its most essential points with the dream-work mechanism in dream formation. However, Freud ignores the common motivation question and stresses the commonality in *form* of dreams and parapraxes. "In both cases *the appearance of an incorrect function is explained by the peculiar mutual interference between two or several correct functions*" (1901, p. 278). Freud then goes on to compare parapraxes with neurotic symptoms and finds that, indeed, "two frequently repeated statements—namely, the borderline between the normal and the abnormal in nervous matters is a fluid one, and that we are all a little neurotic—acquire meaning and support." The common link between neurotic symptoms and parapraxes is in both cases an upsurge of incompletely repressed psychical material.

With two such open-ended mechanisms as distortion and condensation, and the assumption that these are equivalent in their operations to dream-work functioning, Freud's statements on forgetting as parapraxis add little to what he states elsewhere, with one notable exception. He concludes that time, and therefore memory decay, plays no role in forgetting, and this seems to apply both to conscious and to unconscious memories. "As these processes of condensation and distortion continue for long periods, during which every fresh experience acts in the direction of transforming the mnemic content, it is generally thought that it is time which makes memory uncertain and indistinct. It is highly probable that there is no question at all of there being any direct function of time in forgetting" (1901 [1907 note], p. 274). Note that this temporal nullification in the forgetting of memories means that apparent "freshness" or vividness of memories is unrelated to recency of memory registration, as is indeed claimed for screen memories and recovered repressed memories.

In his book on *Jokes and their Relation to the Unconscious* (1905c) (where jokes also are assimilated to dream work) Freud offers a little better explanation of what happens in lieu of decay.

> I have been able to show that condensation is a regular and important process: namely the mechanism of normal (non-tendentious) forgetting. Unique impressions offer difficulty to forgetting; those that are analogous in any way are forgotten by being condensed in regard to their points of resem-

blance. Confusion between analogous impressions is one of the preliminary stages of forgetting. (1905c, p. 168*n*)

This confusion is not because impressions are indistinct and blurred by condensation; rather, the opposite conclusion is reached, that condensation becomes the basis for the formation of concepts since this progress leads to isolation and consequent clearer cognition (1901, p. 134*n*). But the price to be paid is that the full uniqueness of any individual impression is lost. Thus, without using the term, a *schema* is obtained representing analogous impressions. In the same footnote Freud specifically states that "repression makes use of the mechanism of condensation and produces a confusion with other similar cases"; but there is no obvious reason why this would not also be true in "normal forgetting" as well. As Frederic Bartlett emphasized, schema formation must work to the detriment of the memory of specific experiences. (As for American academic psychology, it was not until about 1930 that John McGeoch and other functional psychologists were able to discredit the temporal decay theory of forgetting and overthrow it by making "interference" theory dominant. Confusion between similarities was an important dimension of functional interference theory, but it was based in large part on formal similarities such as sound and spelling.)

Freud has some interesting remarks on *recognition* in the 1905 book on jokes. He regards humor as a problem in psychical economy. That which minimizes expenditure of psychical energy tends to figure in the making of jokes.

> In a second group of technical methods used in jokes—unification, similarity of sound, multiple use, modification of familiar phrases, allusions to quotations—we can single out as their common characteristics the fact that in each of them something familiar is rediscovered, where we might instead have expected something new. This discovery of what is familiar is pleasurable, and once more it is not difficult for us to recognize this pleasure as a pleasure in economy and to relate it to economy in psychical expenditure. (1905c, p. 120)

Further,

> In view of the close connection between recognizing and remembering, it is not rash to suppose that there may also be a pleasure in remembering—that the act of remembering is in itself accompanied by a feeling of pleasure of similar origin. (p. 122)

The Forgetting of Intentions

The forgetting of intentions is pointed out by Freud as the parapraxis in which it is most transparent to the general public that a counter-force opposes the supposed desire to carry out an action. In particular, forgetting to do one's duty is invariably interpreted not as accidental but as akin to conscious evasion in the two cases of a love relationship and acting under military discipline.

> Both the service of women and military service demand that everything
> connected with them should be immune to forgetting. . . . No one forgets to
> carry out actions that seem to himself important, without incurring suspicion
> of being mentally disordered. Our investigation can therefore only extend to
> the forgetting of intentions of a more or less minor character; we cannot
> consider any intention as being *wholly* indifferent, for otherwise it would
> certainly never have been formed. (1901, p. 154)

Thus an intention must not be too strong or the counter-force can have no
effect. The reverse limitation also applies: If the counter-force comes to be
recognized as sufficiently strong so that one knows the original intention will
not be carried out, then the forgetting of an intention cannot be considered a
parapraxis. The requirement that countervailing forces be somewhat equally
matched is actually a more important criterion for classifying a phenomenon
as a prapraxis that whether or not an individual has some awareness of a
counter-force. For in analyzing "slips of the tongue" Freud acknowledges as
parapraxes instances in which individuals were aware of a hostile attitude but
had intended to inhibit its expression, as well as cases where there was a
vigorous denial of the presumably unconscious counter-force.

Freud's first example of a parapraxis in the *Psychopathology of Everyday
Life* concerned his mental search for the name of the painter of the famous
frescoes preserved in the Orvieto cathedral in Italy. In describing his attempt
at directed remembering he gives an account of his subjective hunches and
wrong guesses. I omit the details of this frequently reproduced example, as I
wish to stress Freud's emphasis on imagery rather than on association. The
name-search procedure is quite similar to the approach taken much later by
Roger Brown and David McNeil (1966) in a well-known experiment in which
they labeled the subjective search for a known but temporarily inaccessible
word the "tip of the tongue" phenomenon.[1]

Freud was particularly concerned with cases in which not only a name was
forgotten but substitute names could also be produced that were properly
identified as incorrect. Thus at least a partial memory for the true name can
be inferred. As with screen memories and neurotic symptoms, the outcome
obtained was described as a compromise between the genuine intention to
remember the name—in this instance *Signorelli*—and the repressed intention
which was not the name of the painter but something which "contrived to
place itself in an associative connection with his name." But is it necessary
that substitute names appear in order that tendentious forgetting caused by
repression can be claimed to occur? Freud thinks not, instead of substitute
names, other elements may be spontaneously emphasized, e.g., image intensity and clarity.

> It would seem that substitutive formation occurs even in cases not marked
> by the appearance of incorrect names as substitutes, and that in these it lies
> in the intensification of an element that is closely related to the forgotten
> name. For example, in the *Signorelli* case, so long as the painter's name
> remained inaccessible, the visual memory that I had of the series of frescoes
> and of the self-portrait which is introduced into the corner of one of the

pictures was *ultra-clear*—at any rate much more intense than visual memory traces normally appear to me. In another case, . . . which concerned a visit which I was very reluctant to pay to an address in a strange town, I had forgotten the name of the street beyond all hope of recovery, but my memory of the house number, as if in derision, was ultra-clear, whereas normally I have the greatest difficulty in remembering numbers. (1901, p. 13*n*)

Elsewhere in the *Psychopathology of Everyday Life* Freud lists two more examples of "ultra-clear" images given independently by other people in analogous cases of repression. These cases are obviously related to the hallucinatory quality of recovered repression images, but in these instances the recovery is not, strictly speaking, even partial but only an associated aspect of the repressed content. By extending the symptomatic products of repression from a substitute name to a more subjective criterion, the ultra-clear quality of an image, Freud is able to broaden the extent of his claim that the repressive theory of forgetting, as indicated by *incomplete* repressions, is extremely widespread.

Ideational Mimetics

Freud may seem to emphasize the sensory side of cognition with his stress on the ideational and imagic aspects of memory, especially as spelled out at length in his description of associative processes. But he was sufficiently a creature of his times to put a strong emphasis on the importance of the introspective analysis of motoric sensations. As pointed out at the beginning of Chapter 2, some of the founders of academic psychology—Helmholtz, Mach, Wundt—specifically argued for the introspective experience of sensing the innervation produced by the efferent flow of nervous energy. Freud's motoric theory of "ideational mimetics" did the same and, in fact, was a representative exemplar of this popular trend. A question Freud raised in *Jokes and their Relation to the Unconscious* was: "But how is it that we laugh when we recognize that some other person's movements are exaggerated and inexpedient?" His answer was: "by making a comparison, I believe, between the movement I observed in the other person and the one I should have carried out myself in his place. The two things compared must of course be judged by the same standard, and this standard is my expenditure of innervation, which is linked to my idea of the movement in both of the two cases" (1905c, pp. 190–191). But in this comparison is memory involved, and if so in what way? Freud elaborates: "I have acquired the idea of a movement of a particular size by carrying out the movement myself or by imitating it, and through this action I have learned a standard for this movement in my innervating sensations." And in the footnote that comments on this last statement, Freud further generalized beyond more immediate motoric comparisons.

The memory of this innervatory expenditure will remain the essential part of my idea of this movement, and there will always be modes of thinking in my mental life in which the idea will be represented by nothing else than this expenditure. In other circumstances, indeed, this element may be replaced by another—for instance, by visual images of the aim of the movement or by a verbal image; and in certain kinds of abstract thinking a token will suffice instead of the full content of the idea. (1905c, p. 191*n*).

To determine whether a movement is of greater or lesser size in someone else, "the surest way to an understanding (an appreciation) of it will be for me to carry it out by imitation." But instead of imitation, "I have an idea of it through the medium of my memory-traces of expenditure on similar movements." Thus ideation replaces performance, a point made in many Freudian texts, particularly in regard to the superiority of secondary process thinking over primary process thinking. But ideation is in this case, as with Wundt and other introspectionists, linked directly with physiological sensation since, "even during the process of ideation innervations run out to the muscles, though these it is true correspond to a very modest expenditure of energy" (1905c, p. 192). The idea of a larger movement would therefore be the one accompanied by the larger expenditure of energy.

It would be misleading to indicate that the memoric component is the only one involved in the understanding and evaluation of humorous situations produced by physical movements, for, indeed, Freud acknowledges that anticipation and expectancy also play an important role. But again abstract thought need not be involved, since "It is quite obviously true of a number of cases that motor preparations are what form the expression of expectation . . ." (p. 197). Freud gives a rather unexpected example of "at least one case in which the expenditure on expectation can be directly demonstrated measurably by physiological experiments on animals" (p. 198). Cited by Freud at this point are Ivan Pavlov's then newly published conditioning experiments, wherein the amount of saliva secreted is proportional to whether dogs' expectations of being fed have been confirmed or denied.

To turn back to the memoric aspect of motoric innervation expenditures, what are its practical consequences? Freud finds that retaining not just sensations but quantity of sensation forms the basis for expressing such attributes as largeness or smallness through expressive movements. The descriptive use of these expressive movements Freud labels *ideational mimetics*. He finds these ideational mimetics in particularly uninhibited form among the naive of the world—children, the common people, "a member of certain races"—where these mimetics supplement verbal language narrations or descriptions. The immediate occasion for the theory of ideational mimetics is Freud's theory of the comic which, briefly put, is that "a person appears comic to us if, in comparison with ourselves [presumably using one's personal ideational-mimetic calibrations], he makes too great an expenditure on his bodily functions and too little on his mental ones," for in this case we feel a sense of superiority. But if the situation is reversed and the other person's physical expenditure is less than ours or his mental expenditure greater, "we are filled with astonishment and admiration" (pp. 195–196).

Freud finds his newly coined concept suggestive: "I believe that if ideational mimetics are followed up, they may be as useful in other branches of aesthetics as they are here for an understanding of the comic" (p. 193). Jack Spector (1972) in his book on *The Aesthetics of Freud* agrees: "Freud's undeveloped suggestion of an 'ideational mimetics' would have crowned his theories of art with a device allowing essential contact between the psychological workings of the individual mind and the external world of other people and of things, including art" (p. 184). I have in my discussion here, however, downplayed Freud's originality and emphasized the point that he was following a strong, and at the time very active, tradition in academic psychology, that could perhaps ultimately be traced back to the French philosopher-psychologist Maine de Biran and the stress he put on the "feeling of effort" early in the nineteenth century.[2]

Mnemic Symbols

The term *mnemic symbols* occurs rather frequently in Breuer and Freud's *Studies on Hysteria*. Mnemic symbols come about when an experience is accompanied by a large amount of affect that cannot be discharged or worn away by associations, so that the affect is said to remain in a "strangulated state" and the memory of the experience is cut off from consciousness. This affectively dominated memory nevertheless manifests itself through hysterical symptoms, which at the same time can be regarded as symbols of the supressed memory; these symptoms in their symbolic aspect are therefore *mnemic* symbols. Thus the pains in the limbs of Frau Emmy von N., "which were associated only accidentally with those experiences [nursing her sick brother], were later repeated in her memory as the somatic symbol of the whole complex of associations" (1895, p. 71*n*). As another example, in the case of Katharina, Freud speaks of the "legacy of the mnemic symbol [of the hallucinated face]" (1895, p. 133). A graphic illustration of mnemic symbols was attempted in the *Five Lectures on Psychoanalysis*. "The monuments and memorials with which large cities are adorned are also mnemic symbols" (1910a, p. 16). Freud cites two London examples, Charing Cross of the thirteenth century and the Monument to the Great Fire of the seventeenth century. He says that it would be quite outlandish to feel the grief of contemporary mourning in front of these memorials today, yet hysterics and neurotics act in an analogous way for "not only do they remember painful experiences of the remote past, but they still cling to them emotionally; they cannot get free of the past and for its sake they neglect what is real and immediate" (p. 17).[3]

The term *mnemic symbols* might seem to be more descriptive than explanatory, but in a later book, *Inhibitions, Symptoms and Anxiety* (1926), mnemic symbols are taken as the appropriate analogy for the large and vexing problem of affective retention and revival. "Affective states have become incorporated in the mind as precipitates of primeval traumatic experiences, and when a similar situation occurs *they are revived like mnemic symbols*. I do not think I have been wrong in likening them to the more recent and individually acquired hysterical attack and in regarding them as its normal prototypes" (1926a, p. 93, emphasis mine). Freud then speculates that the act of birth "the individual's first experience of anxiety, has given the affect of anxiety certain characteristic forms of expression." However, it is going too far to suppose that "something like a reproduction of the situation of birth goes on in the mind" whenever there is an outbreak of anxiety, and hysterical attacks that were "originally traumatic reproductions" can, on occasion, subsequently change their character. In this usage mnemic symbols are not so much remembered incidents as lived-through experiences that have impressed the individual sufficiently to provide a prototypical marker for subsequent life activities.

Moreover, anxiety is far from being the sole affective state to which mnemic symbols are attached. Freud also somewhat enigmatically hints at a collective memory not contingent on individual experiences. "In my opinion the other affects are also reproductions of very early, perhaps even preindividual, experiences of vital importance; and I should be inclined to regard them as universal, typical and innate hysterical attacks, as compared to the recently and individually acquired attacks which occur in hysterical neuroses and whose origin and significance as mnemic symbols have been revealed by analysis" (1926a, p. 133).

This postulation of pre-individual and innate hysterical attacks as the precursors of universally remembered affects is constructed on a speculative basis (see the later discussion of Archaic Memories for a fuller exposition). Nevertheless, as Freud made clear much earlier in his case of Elizabeth von K. (1895), this type of interpretation, in spite of its off-putting language, is conceived of as following the Darwinian evolutionary approach set forth in *The Expression of Emotions* (1888). Charles Darwin, Freud says, taught that emotions are expressed by actions that originally had a meaning and served a purpose. For example, "What could be more probable than that the figure of speech 'swallowing something,' which we use in talking of an insult to which no rejoinder has been made, did in fact originate from the innervatory sensations which arise in the pharynx when we refrain from speaking and preventing ourselves from reacting to the insult?" (1895, p. 181). The description was probably once meant literally, therefore "hysteria is right in restoring the original meaning of the words in depicting its unusually strong innervations. Indeed, it is perhaps wrong to say that hysteria creates these sensations by symbolization. It may be that it does not take linguistic usage as its model at all, but that both hysteria and linguistic usage alike draw their material from a common source." Again, as with ideational mimetics, there is a strong emphasis on the memory of innervatory sensations, a thoroughly introspective analysis in the Wundtian mode.

A point to be made concerning the theory of affective states as analogous to mnemic symbols (1926) is that hysteria is the paradigm of affective expression. It is often asserted that the dream-process paradigm replaced that of hysteria in psychoanalytic theorizing after 1900. Obviously this is not completely the case; considering hysteria the paradigm for repression and symptom formation both in itself and as a model for memory retention, including affective expression, was never completely supplanted.

Repetition Compulsion

It a nice coincidence that Freud and one of the most caustic of his critics, Karl Popper, both made considerable theoretical use of the everyday observation that young children display a frequent and untiring demand for exact repetitions. Oddly enough, Popper (1976), who characterizes Freudian theory as "psuedoscientific," provides only a literary reference. "This infantile dogmatism has been observed by Jane Austen: 'Henry and John were still asking every day for the story of Harriet and the gypsies, and still tenaciously setting [Emma] . . . right if she varied in the slightest from the original recital." In a similar vein Freud states: "And if a child has been told a nice story, he will insist on hearing it over and over again rather than a new one; and he will remorselessly stipulate that the repetition shall be an identical one and will correct any alterations of which the narrator may be guilty—though they may actually have been made in the hope of gaining fresh approval" (1920, p. 35)

Popper continues:

> My main point was that the dogmatic way of thinking was due to an inborn need for regularities, and to inborn mechanisms of discovering; mechanisms which make us search for regularities. And one of my theses was that if we speak glibly of 'heredity and environment' we are liable to underrate the overwhelming role of heredity—which among other things, largely determines what aspects of its objective environment (the ecological niche) do or do not belong to an animal's subjective, or biologically significant, environment. (Popper, 1976)

This appetite for repetition by young children who "urgently need discoverable regularities around them" is considered a key concept by Popper (as it was for Freud) in that it is a requisite biological foundation for the learning process. Furthermore, the "compulsion to repeat" is attributed to biological heredity by Freud as well as by Popper. In the 1914 paper "Remembering, Repeating, and Working-Through," (see Chapter 3) Freud mentioned the "compulsion to repeat" as a clinical phenomenon, but in his 1920 work, *Beyond the Pleasure Principle,* repetition had acquired "the characteristics of an instinct."

For Freud, the repetition compulsion, though inevitable, is frequently an obstacle to full remembering in the therapeutic situation.

> The patient cannot remember the whole of what is repressed in him, and what he cannot remember may be precisely the essential part of it. Thus he acquires no sense of conviction of the correctness of the construction that has been communicated to him. He is obliged to *repeat* the repressed material as a contemporary experience instead of, as the physician would prefer

to see, *remembering* it as something belonging to the past. These reproductions, which emerge with such unwished-for exactitude, always have as their subject some portion of infantile sexual life—of the Oedipus complex, that is—and its derivatives; and they are inevitably acted out in the sphere of the transference, of the patient's relation to the physician." (Freud, 1920, p. 18)

The therapist's goal is "to keep this transference neurosis within the narrowest limits: to force as much as possible into the channel of memory and to allow as little as possible to emerge as repetition," and the patient must be persuaded "to recognize that what appears to be reality is in fact only a reflection of a forgotten past." At the same time it is obvious that what is repeated is not "forgotten" only mislocated in the present. The earlier credo for hysteria that "patients suffer mainly from their reminiscences" could here be attenuated to state that patients suffer because they are unable to identify their repetitious behavior as reminiscences.

The repetition compulsion in the guise of a therapeutic obstacle seems rather far removed both from Popper's Jane Austen citation and Freud's claim of children's demand for exact story repetition. Compatibility between these usages is achieved in Freud's theory by viewing the repetition compulsion as a developmental phenomenon which, in the normal course of events, should disappear with increased maturity.

> In the case of children's play we seemed to see that children repeat unpleasurable experiences for the additional reason that they can master a powerful impression far more thoroughly by being active than they could by merely experiencing it passively. Each fresh repetition seems to strengthen the mastery they are in search of. Nor can children have their *pleasurable* experiences repeated often enough, and they are inexorable in their insistence that the repetition shall be an identical one. This character trait disappears later on. (1920, p. 35)

For children, then, the repetition compulsion is not only benign but a positive good in aiding mastery.

Why are repetition compulsions positive for the child but negative for the adult? Freud is not altogether clear here, partly because he wants to emphasize that, even for small children, repetition compulsion applies to both pleasurable and unpleasurable experiences; repetition of the unpleasurable in an attempt at gaining mastery is one way in which actions commonly go "beyond the pleasure principle." Yet we can understand this apparent reversal in approbation—positive for the child and negative for the adult—a little bit better if we consider that the repetition-compulsion concept is substituting theoretically for what was then (and is sometimes now) often considered a necessary developmental—perhaps biological—principle, namely, imitation. Any giving in to a *strong* imitation principle could play havoc with Freud's insistence on an ultimate motivational linkage to infantile sexuality, which clearly cannot be grounded on imitation. (Limited imitation was not denied and was, for example, a component of ideational mimetics.) But we can note that if a drive to imitate had been put in the place of the autonomous repetition-compulsion process the positive valuation for the child versus the negative valuation for the adult would scarcely have been remarked. That imitation is of common occurrence and highly appropriate for children but mostly undesirable on the part of adults seems a truism.

Ernest Schactel (1959) devotes seven pages to what he calls "focal exploration and repetition compulsion." In opposition to Freud, who in his later writings "characterizes it [repetition compulsion] by its conservative nature and considers it to be the expression of an inertia principle, of a drive to return to an earlier state, and, in the final analysis, of the death instinct" (1959, p. 259), Schactel claims that absolute repetition is a necessity for the child in the interest of obtaining a dependable base from which to make cognitive forays. Before the child can read, insistence on exactitude is the only way that the child can be certain that the story is the same one that was heard before. This need for "object constancy" (mentioned in the last chapter as putting an end to the infantile period of multiple memoric registrations) is given an affective valuation in that "learning about object constancy, thus, is probably closely linked emotionally with the degree to which the infant experiences the constancy—that is, depend-ability—of the most important object, the mother." In this emphasis, Schactel is close to Freud in the first example of repetition compulsion described in *Beyond the Pleasure Principle,* in which a wooden reel with a string attached is made to disappear and reappear by a little boy of age one-and-a-half. This act Freud relates to "the child's great cultural achievement—the instinctual renunciation [that is, the renunciation of instinctual satisfaction] which he had made in allowing his mother to go away without protesting" (1920, p. 15). In speaking of a "great cultural achievement" Freud, as Schactel suggests, seems to be undercutting his claim that there is a return to an earlier state propelled by a death instinct. In this same vein Schactel, like Freud, finds some auxiliary motives involved in children's need for repetition; these include enjoyment of mastery and the overcoming of anxiety by controlling a situation.[4]

Archaic Memories

To determine the possible inventory of what memories an individual can know and potentially express is nearly impossible when one takes into account what Freud himself calls a "fresh complication." For there probably exist in "an individual's psychical life not only what he has experienced himself, but also things that were innately present in him at his birth, elements with a phylogenetic origin—*an archaic heritage*" (1939, p. 98). Foremost is the universality of speech symbolism that continues to manifest itself in dreams in the same way in all peoples. But, more germane to present considerations, Freud asserts that "the archaic heritage of human beings comprises not only dispositions, but also subject-matter—memory traces of the experience of earlier generations" (1939, p. 99). Specifically, Freud gives examples of a neurotic child's reactions to the Oedipus complex and the castration complex that can only be understood phylogenetically in relation to the experiences of earlier generations. Freud states that if this smacks of the presumably discredited biological doctrine of inheritance of acquired characteristics, it is not a misunderstanding for, "I cannot do without this factor in biological evolution"— whatever the strictures of biological science.

At the same time Freud acknowledges that the case for the existence of archaic memories in humans is not quite equivalent, though probably it is a derivative of or closely related to, the more general and more specifically biological doctrine of inheritance of acquired characteristics. Freud here invokes a comparative argument based on the fact that lower animals have instincts that allow them to function without going through a learning process. Thus,

> if any explanation is to be found of what are called the instincts of animals, which allow them to behave from the first in a new situation in life as though it were an old and familiar one . . . it can only be that they bring the experiences of their species with them into their own new existence—that is, that they have preserved memories of what experienced by their ancestors. The position in the human animal would not at bottom be different. His own archaic heritage corresponds to the instinct of animals even though it is different in its compass and contents. (1939, p. 100)

Memories are most likely to be inherited when experiences are important enough or repeated frequently or, better yet, both. But these inherited memories tend to remain in the id in an unconscious state until, in analogy with what occurs in some neuroses, there are multiple causes for memory recovery. A real repetition of a similar event is often the decisive factor in memory recovery.

Why postulate archaic memories when one could for much of human history invoke strong oral traditions as a less scientifically dubious mechanism for transmitting information across generations? Freud explicitly rejects the adequacy of oral transmission. First, there is the obvious point that quite young infants produce some of the best examples of quasi-instinctive, memoric behavior. The second point, which Freud spells out in some detail, is that the inherited memories sheltered in the id demonstrate two features of repressed material—obsessive characteristics and "freedom from the coercion of logical thinking." Freud's example of the recovery of repressed content is his favorite *bête noire,* religious beliefs. "It [religion] must have undergone the fate of being repressed, the condition of lingering in the unconscious, before it is able to display such powerful effects on its return, to bring the masses under its spell, as we have seen with astonishment and hitherto without comprehension in the case of religious tradition" (p. 101). Two brief comments are in order. One, Freud finds in reports of religious experiences the ultra-clarity and freshness characteristic of recovered repressed material; these sensation attributes underline the "obsessional quality" of many religious experiences. Two, archaic memories are for Freud a bridge to social, group memories that manifest themselves in such phenomena as "national character." Here, too, Freud finds explanations in terms of oral traditions totally inadequate. It can be pointed out that Freudian concepts that transcend personal experience such as archaic memory and organic repression put Freud partially in the camp of the older biological theorists of memory (e.g., in the late nineteenth century, Ewald Hering, and in the early twentieth century, Richard Semon and Eugenio Rignano).

Freud's Personal Memory

It would not be surprising to find—as has been suggested with varying degrees of seriousness—that psychological theorists sometimes present in their theories aspects of their own personality. Freud's stress on the importance of autobiographical memories could be taken as a prime example, since there is considerable evidence that his memory was far above average. His biographers have emphasized the labor of memory involved in Freud's original psychoanalysis of himself in the late 1890s, with its concentrated focus on the critical importance of his early infantile memories. But even apart from this most influential memoric achievement, there are several of Freud's own statements concerning more mundane memory accomplishments, written in a seemingly modest, somewhat self-deprecatory style, which indicate that his memory was very exceptional. In the 1933 introduction to his *New Introductory Lectures on Psychoanalysis* Freud remarks in passing that the second half of his original *Introductory Lectures* of 1916–17 "were made during the intervening summer vacation at Salzburg, and delivered word for word the following winter. At that time I still possessed the gift of a phonographic memory." In 1917 Freud was 61 years old.

But years before this, in 1901 at the age of 45, Freud was already complaining that his memory was not what is used to be. In his personal search for reasons for forgetting in the *Psychopathology of Everyday Life* he wrote that he made it a rule to submit to psychological analysis those instances in which he was surprised at his own forgetting.

> I may add I am not in general inclined to forget things (things I have experienced, that is, not things I have learned!), and that for a short period of my youth some unusual feats of memory were not beyond me. When I was a schoolboy I took it as a matter of course that I could repeat by heart the page I had been reading; and shortly before I entered the University I could write down almost verbatim popular lectures on scientific subjects directly after hearing them. In the period of tension before my final medical examination I must have made use of what remained of this faculty, for in some subjects I gave the examiners, as though it were automatically, answers which faithfully followed the words of the textbook that I had skimmed through only once in the greatest haste. (1901, p. 135)

It is noteworthy that Freud lays claim only to a strong autobiographical memory, not to good retention for things learned. One might be inclined to quibble that textbooks are usually thought of as material to be learned, but in this instance, the fact that the book contents were seen once only can put such nonrepeated experiencing on a par with autobiographical events where there is also no event repetition. Freud follows the quoted paragraph by stating, "Since then the command that I have over my store of memories has steadily deteriorated. . . ." But then he gives us two more types of memory feats that he can still (1901) perform with great accuracy. Freud says one example occurs, "when I meet a distant acquaintance and inquire after his small children. If he describes their progress, I try to think at random of the child's present age. I afterwards check my estimate by what the father tells me; and at the most I am wrong by a month, or with older children by three months, although I am unable to say on what my estimate was based" (1901, p. 136). His own explanation as to how he performed this mnemonic feat was characteristically Freudian, as he invoked "my unconscious memory, which is in any case far more extensive."

Perhaps Freud's unusual memoric competence helps account for the abstemiousness he recommended in regard to the use of memory aids on the part of both analyst and patient. Freud considered it undesirable that notetaking occur during psychoanalysis. This would, he claimed, have interfered not only with patient rapport but also with the associative nuances that the therapist might obtain from the patient's dialogue. Outside of the psychoanalytic session the patient was also discouraged from keeping a written record of the dreams which might later be reported. Freud felt that the important themes, conflicts, and overriding concerns would be remembered adequately without resort to artificial aids. Forgetting the unimportant details was, in fact, considered an aid to dream clarification. One can wonder whether these procedural recommendations might have been less stringent if Freud's own memory had been closer to the average.

Although the Freudian concepts that have been discussed in this chapter are not those that are best known, the themes that underlie these concepts are the familiar ones—memory motivations, the role of consciousness, symbol-based associations, and the biological hereditary contribution to memory. A prominent Freudian theme that I claim has been neglected is sensory memory imagery. In Chapter 3, Freud's imagery ideas were discussed in regard to the modalities of odor, vision, and audition. *Ideational mimetics,* discussed in this chapter, can be interpreted as extending Freud's interest in imagery to the kinesthetic dimension. *Mnemic symbols* make use of symbolic images, since they are said to come about through actions that were originally overt and that receive symbolic and metaphorical expression in persistent memories.

Chapter 5 describes psychoanalytic memory emphases and concepts introduced after Freud's death that amplified, modified, and substituted for his original memory concepts. Major interest has centered on the determination of how theoretical concepts can be implemented in psychotherapy. New concepts have been introduced into psychoanalysis, some from neighboring fields such as psychology, but concepts of greater novelty have been introduced from disciplines that focused on literary and linguistic analyses. Revisionism continues apace, abetted by the doctrinal fractionation of psychoanalysis into diverse theoretical groups.

5

Psychoanalytic Continuations

The Freudian tradition has continued in two ways, first through several more or less orthodox successor lines and, more diffusely, as an influence on diverse nonpsychoanalytic groups, including anti-Freudians. A third position is that we live in a post-Freudian age. The meaning of this frequent assertion is debatable, but it is usually taken to indicate that the major Freudian insights have been so thoroughly digested and so general that we must look elsewhere for individualizing causal explanations. Except for an overly simplified concept of repression, however it can be safely concluded that the general public has remained largely unaware of most of Freud's range of ideas about memory functioning, and this is to a considerable extent true of most of academic psychology as well.

Memory Concepts of Ernst Kris

The immediate successors to Freud, beginning at the end of the 1930s, can be taken to be the psychoanalytic ego psychologists, largely an American movement composed of European emigrés. A chief aim of this group of theorists was to make of psychoanalysis a general psychology, which led them to be more open to psychological ideas that had not originated within psychoanalysis than were members of previous psychoanalytic schools. The leading theorist of this movement in regard to memory topics was Ernst Kris, whose views are outlined below as representative of post-Freudian psychoanalytic developments. Though far from being universally accepted, Kris's ideas definitely come closer to much of presentday psychoanalytic theory and practice than Freud's earlier views. But at the same time, later theorists have found fault with some of his conceptions.

Three points that derive in part from Freud's later writings, but that were also considerably influenced by the work of Anna Freud, serve as a theoretical base for Kris's theorizing. The first is that aggression is given equal billing with sexual libido. In fact it is aggressive energies that tend to maintain repressions. Second, repression itself is no longer the exclusive source of motivated forgetting and distortions. Repression acts causally in concert with other ego-defensive mechanisms. Here Kris frequently elaborates on Anna Freud's *The Ego and the Mechanisms of Defense* (1936). He goes so far as to claim that only in cases of pure hysteria is repression the sole mechanism involved. The third emphasis is on the research findings obtained from psychoanalytic child psychology, particularly during the preoedipal period. Kris makes the point in this regard that Freud was unable to study *object relations* (i.e., early social attachments and understanding) and ego functions developmentally and that these are as important as the psychosexual maturation that Freud did depict. Thus Freud's view was only partially developmental, and for this reason even the most developmentally worked-out of Freud's case studies, the Wolf Man case, would "appear in a different light" if Freud had had this later knowledge available. I will elaborate on these three points, but some of Kris's other ideas in relation to memory recovery—some less avowedly in the Freudian mainstream—will also be outlined.

Unlike most other psychoanalysts and psychologists, Kris goes to some pains to point out how autobiographical memory differs from other memory functions, to which other functions he attaches the generic name "general memory ability." Autobiographical memory, he believes, arises near the end of the first year of life in the infant's attempts to find the initially needed and later beloved object, the mother. Out of this "memory matrix" other memory functions soon emerge, including general memory ability. But memory functions that are autobiographical—those that concern the self—are, in a most important sense, different from general memory functioning. The primary distinction is in degree of autonomy. A high degree of autonomy is possible with regard to most informational material that one learns. What will be retained or repeated is often a matter of choice. Where the self is concerned, however, one has very little autonomy. This distinction obtains not just because of a lack of flexibility in registering material given once and fleetingly, but even more because distortion is inevitable in that needs and affects always play a significant role in personal memory. This leads Kris to a somewhat different perspective on childhood amnesia than those previously outlined. He finds that the "amnesia" for early childhood events is almost entirely restricted to autobiographical memories but does not affect the retention of skills, conceptualizations, reality testing, or much of the other information acquired during infancy and early childhood.

In addition to the difficulty caused by the lack of autonomy with regard to personal memories, there is another aspect of the child's early development that works against accurate retention. Young children do not clearly differentiate between motivational investment in the goal of an activity and the activity itself. Thus the child may become more interested in the process of remembering than in memory content. The memory process itself may give a pleasure that can recur throughout life, a tendency whose near-pathological extreme Kris calls a "Proustian pleasure at reminiscing." In early childhood this pleasure in the process of remembering gains in impact up to about the age of four. This state of affairs might seem favorable for accurate memory recovery, but at the same time there is a growing motivational investment in fantasy. The allure of fantasy in distorting memory can hardly be evaded since, as Kris states, "in fantasy the lost is always near and the wish always fulfilled." The intertwining of fantasy and memory leads to a specific memory concept formulated by Kris as the "personal myth."

What then is the "personal myth"? It is an extension of Freud's screen memory concept discussed earlier, it is the "autobiography as screen." Sometimes almost the whole life history is involved with an apparent but spurious clarity since "the firm outline and the richness of detail are meant to cover significant omissions and distortions." But more frequently, Kris claims, it is only isolated stretches or some well-defined periods of the personal history that are involved. Individuals possessing such autobiographical screens are fully confident in their belief that they possess "the certainty that things could not have been different, that their recollection was both complete and reliable." Nonetheless, those possessing such well-developed screening patterns often maintain them rather secretively, and they are infrequently communicated to family and friends. As the previous paragraph suggested, the roots of the personal myth are found in early childhood as they "stem from a time when fantasy and reality were not sharply divided." The function of early fantasy, however, goes beyond its blending with memories, since "the relation of the course of life to an infantile fantasy is a more general phenomenon which plays its part in almost every analytic treatment." One is left with the impression that even the most veridical autobiographical memory has a bit of personal myth in it. For Kris, memories are distorted not just "to make a better story" or for personal aggrandizement but also quite frequently because we are acting a part in our own personal myth.

More than other analysts, Kris, who made popular the concept "regression in the service of the ego" in his studies of artistic creativity in the 1930s, emphasizes that regression often goes hand in hand with evoking personal memories. Characteristically this regression leads to "acting out" without awareness, so that, citing Freud's paper on "Remembering, Repeating, and Working-Through," there is a substitution of repeating for remembering. In Freud's theory, which emphasized the great ability and tenacity of infantile memory, there was somewhat less need for a regression mechanism in order to recover memories. As indicated above, Kris himself was well aware of his differences from Freud's views and considered his theoretical emendations as theoretical advances brought about through empirical study of the developmental process.

Kris paid special attention to the distinction between recognition and recall memory. Recognition potentiality is roughly equated with the preconscious level of retention, so that much material can be known through recognition without being subject to verbalization or recall. This function for recognition is important because Kris views two routes that repressed material can take in becoming conscious. Some memories emerge from repression suddenly in the fashion traditionally described, while other piecemeal derivatives enter the preconscious ego gradually. These preconscious memories slowly become part of an associative trend of thought that is available enough to be recognized but not subject to recall. This slow route to consciousness is claimed to be of common occurrence, since Kris, along with other ego analysts, places strong emphasis on functioning at the *preconscious* level: "Some and perhaps all significant intellectual achievements are products or at least derivatives of preconscious mentation" (Kris, 1950).

The fact that these preconscious memories establish themselves only slowly does not, however, mean that they cannot again be lost to accessibility. It is part of the work of reconstructive psychotherapy to fit seemingly unrelated memories in the "stream of thought" into causal connections in the patient's personal history. The recovery of such an insight protects available preconscious memories from subsequent disappearances resulting from repression and other defense mechanisms. Even at the threshold level, where there is only minimal awareness, a memory occurs as an associatively related entity. The analyst has little interest in isolated memories; a *connected* memory for Kris must relate to the patient's personal history. Memories bereft of personal associations are useless. Indeed, the description of the variety of personal memories in this book—where memory form and structure is emphasized more than content—comes close to what Kris characterized as the "libidinization of memory" where the search leads (in Kris's words) to "intellectualized epiphenomena."

Not surprisingly, Kris is dubious about the possibility of recovering original memories. An essential aim in psychoanalytic reconstructions is to discover the strong, instinctively derived motivations (or affective investments) attached to certain "nodal point" memories. Hence reconstruction is "regularly concerned with some thought processes and feelings that did not necessarily 'exist' at the time the 'event' took place" (Kris, 1956a). Such thoughts and feelings may either never have reached consciousness or may have emerged at a later time during the "chain of events" to which the original experience became attached. Following Anna Freud, Kris asserts that what is reported as a single childhood memory is often a typical experience that may have occurred many times, while a single dramatic and shocking event, e.g., a seduction experience, is usually somewhat blurred in recall. Accurate registration of events is not enough to ensure good recall, since the further course of life helps determine which experiences gain significance as traumatic events.

As mentioned, Kris saw repression as but one mechanism by which memories were made inaccessible. And with the exception of hysterical disorders, repression seldom acts without the participation of other defense mechanisms. In accord with his emphasis on associative chains, Kris particularly emphasized the interaction of repression with the defense mechanism of *isolation,* in which some experiences are excluded from associative chains by the occurrence of suppressions and interruptions. Isolation, Kris claimed, is a general phenomenon of normal mental life and participates in defending against many things, not just memories. Isolation in itself is somewhat less drastic than repression, because memory isolation can take place preconsciously. The interaction between repression and isolation is particularly significant in obsessional neuroses, where isolation tends to be directed against the implicated affect. Kris claimed that he was expanding on Freud, who had not written about an isolation mechanism until 1926, though the 1914 article that has been so frequently cited had put forward an analogous mechanism.

Closely related to isolation is the claimed negation of an actual event, wherein a person remembers the event but doubts whether it occurred. Kris conceives this outcome to result from repression supplemented by a mechanism of *denial* (more commonly referred to as *negation* in the psychoanalytic literature). The acknowledgment that mechanisms other than repression are crucial removes much of the theoretical contradiction from the claim made by some psychoanalysts that lifting repressions enables early memories to surface. With memory inaccessibility only partially accounted for by repression, the lifting of a repression can be either cause or effect in memory recovery.

By way of recapitulation of Kris's ideas about memory development in children, an approximate chronological sequence can be given for the development of autobiographical memory. Near the end of the first year of life, memory functions arise in the refinding of the needed and later the beloved object, in most cases the mother. Out of this matrix all further memory functions develop. High motivation for the experience of the process of remembering for its own sake, apart from specific content, continues up to the age of four, but the contents dealt with frequently contain a rich mixture of internalized fantasy. Just after this time the onset of the Oedipal conflict leads to repression of memory contents of low autonomy—that is, the strictly stipulated memory functions concerning the self—although this repression does not interfere with the freer general memory functions of high autonomy, where the self is uninvolved. A year or two later, after the consolidation of the superego, fully fleshed out autobiographical memory functioning tends to develop with a "continuous and relatively integrated memory identity as part of the self-representation" (Kris, 1956b). But even before this fairly complete consolidation occurs, a considerable integration of the past takes place under the influence of the implicit question the child has already asked: "How did it all come about?"

Nevertheless, at all times autobiographical memory is in constant flux, "constantly being reorganized" and "constantly subject to changes which the tensions of the present tend to impose." Pressure for memory changes is great during the preadolescent latency period, but a heightened "scanning" of memories occurs in adolescence "when the need for a past becomes particularly pressing." What should be most stressed is that Kris is not concerned with everyday event memory or even with the psychoanalytic "traumatic incident," but with autobiographical memory as an integrated life narrative.

Memory in Psychoanalytic Ego Psychology after Kris

After Kris's death in 1957, a shifting group of more than two dozen psychoanalysts continued consideration of the topics he emphasized. They formed the Kris Study Group. (Discussions relevant to present concerns occurred in

1958–1959 and 1960–1961, but nothing was published until 1971 [Fine, Joseph, and Waldhorn, Eds.]. The group chairman both years was the prominent ego analyst Rudolph Lowenstein.) The work of the group dealt with the fundamental psychoanalytic concept and activity of *reconstruction,* and was published under the titles "Recollection and Reconstruction" and "Reconstruction in Psychoanalysis." (The key Freudian reference was the 1937 article "Constructions in Analysis," but Freud's work was not the focus; Kris's precepts were central.) The guiding assumption of the Kris Study Group was that "constructions," or in more frequent use nowadays "reconstructions," arc at the heart of the psychoanalytic process. The Kris Study Group defined reconstructions as a special form of interpretation on the part of the analyst, which has the quality of an analytic intervention in that it supplies information not previously available to the patient. More specifically, a reconstruction "deals with memory traces and affects (usually of the past) that the patient does not as yet consciously recall but which may be brought together through the analyst's synthesis to explain later events or behavior" (1971, p. 63). But a reconstruction can also be based on the interpretation of a fantasy, with the emphasis on childhood situations. The reconstructions are, of course, not neutral or in any sense value-free but are based on the theoretical assumptions of the analyst.

The study group seemed to feel fewer compunctions than Kris himself had about stating differences with Freud's original positions and pointing out areas where Freud's dicta were thought to be inadequate. Thus, "For Freud, the reconstruction of specific childhood data and traumata was always an essential part of clinical psychoanalysis. . . . Others like Kris maintain that the therapeutic efficacy of reconstruction of events and childhood memory recovery are sometimes anachronistically exaggerated, their importance having diminished with the advent of the structural theory and ego psychology" (1971, p. 123). But exaggeration does not mean doing away with early memory recovery, as the somewhat hedging statement that immediately follows the above conclusion indicates: "For Kris a reconstruction is a historical interpretation which aims particularly at producing at least eventual recall of, or conviction about, repressed and defended-against experiences" (p. 123). The group also pointed out that as Kris enlarged the role of defense mechanisms, he also limited the therapeutic role of reconstructions, since "the less important repression was in any constellation of defenses, the less important reconstruction and memory recovery were in any individual's analysis" (p. 123). This conclusion follows from Kris's belief that, in addition to repression, other defense mechanisms prevent memory recovery. "He [Kris] described how the functional distribution of defenses in individuals and in the major psychopathological entities influenced the memory recovery process. For example, intellectualization will often contaminate the process in obsessive-compulsive neurosis because of the prominence of affective isolation as a defense in this condition" (p. 124). Not only the downplaying of early memory recovery but also a widening of the sphere of reconstructive activity was suggested by some of the members of the group, who "maintained that the reconstructed experiences might be psychically significant recent ones, as well as those from early life which are the traditional contents of reconstructions" (p. 123).

As pointed out earlier, the meaning of repression has broadened to include affects and percepts as repressed contents in ways beyond those specified by Freud. But the core meaning of repression seems to have been retained to a much greater extent than has been the case for *screen memories.* "The term 'screen memory' is used in a much wider sense currently than when it was first introduced by Freud in 1899. At that time it referred to a specific type of memory with certain formal characteristics. Under the influence of modern ego psychology the tendency today is to regard almost all memories as screen memories" (p. 60). This seemingly bland generalization "screens" some rather far-reaching and even startling conclusions, as illustrated by the following considerations.

In line with earlier theorists, particularly Otto Fenichel, the Kris Study Group considered as a strong possibility the hypothesis that "screening goes on constantly in a fluid and ever-current resynthesis of memory traces, a process which can be observed in the course of analysis" (p. 61). Memory traces as such may not antedate analysis at all but are evoked and "synthesized only at the moment of their presentation" and they thus do not form part of the personal autobiography. A more unexpected hypothesis still further from Freud's original formulations concerning screen memories was also put forward. The question was broached of "whether all so-called traumatic memories may not themselves be screen memories in which there is the summation and condensation of a number of events significant in respect to the ego developments and conflicts at a particular maturational level" (pp. 61–62). Thus a screen memory need not represent a real event but could be a condensation of several events. This conclusion raised a question about the nature of traumatic memories, in earlier theorizing considered to be difficult of recovery but not necessarily disguised by a neutral screening or covering memory. It was agreed that *trauma* was in the mind of the patient since trauma depends not on the nature of the event but on how it affects the individual; trauma can at times also result from a meaning an event acquires after the fact. But in form the traumatic memory is similar to the screen memory, for it can represent a nodal point of conflict crystallization and "epitomizes best the multiple aspects of the conflict." Therefore the screen memory and the traumatic memory appear to be structurally more alike than unlike, since the traumatic memory has in common with the screen memory "a telescopic quality and the tendency to summation and condensation."

Not only was the expansion of key concepts over time acknowleged explicitly, but also Freud's ultimate lack of resolution regarding the perennial problem of whether the memories of fantasies could be distinguished from the memories of actual events was reexamined (cf. Chapter 3). "Freud struggled inconclusively throughout his career with the question of whether it was ordinarily necessary, or even possible, to distinguish between fantasy and reality in analytic reconstructions. Since then, other analysts have never fully resolved this issue either" (p. 124). (Such a conclusion puts Freud's "heroic renunciation" of his belief in the actuality of childhood seduction into a per-spective that is rather different from that given by Ernest Jones and most of Freud's other biographers.) For Kris this problem was much less central than for Freud, since, to quote the study group, Kris "doubted the necessity for, or the possibility of, ordinarily reconstructing and recovering real, discrete trau-matic experiences from childhood because such events become molded into vastly complex, constantly transferred dynamic patterns. In his opinion, it is with these patterns that the analyst works, rather than with individual events" (pp. 124–125). Nonetheless, the Kris Study Group had considerably more to say on the subject of whether any important distinction was to be made between the memory of a fantasy and the "reality" of events that actually occurred.

Freud had not only equivocated on the fantasy–reality question through-out his career but he even stated contradictory conclusions in the Wolf Man case study. Kris, on the other hand, somewhat finessed the point of whether the distinction is consequential, since he did not believe that unique trau-matic memories could ordinarily be recovered. "He doubted that single, important traumatic experiences, which he called 'shock trauma,' were com-monly recoverable in analysis or distinguishable from long-lasting deleteri-ous situations which he designated 'strain trauma' " (p. 117). The actual traumatic events were but the raw material for the "dynamically meaningful patterns" with which the analyst worked, although these patterns were them-selves "ever-changing."

The Kris Study Group was open-minded enough to consider this problem further and to hear a point of view that asserted that the memory of *actual* traumatic incidents was of special importance for psychoanalysis, even as Freud had originally claimed. Phyllis Greenacre, a prominent analyst who upheld such a theoretical view, was therefore invited to take part in some of the study group's discussions. (Recognition of the importance of the distinc-tion between fantasized and real events does not, of course, necessarily mean a commitment to any common theoretical position. See the remarks of Jeffrey Masson and Robert Fliess in Chapter 3, who also stress the importance of this distinction.) The study group summarized Greenacre's discussion as follows: "Greenacre maintained that . . . whether significant childhood experiences are actual traumatic events or fantasies is often of major significance; this has frequently been overlooked in the reaction against the earlier traumatic theory of neurosis" (p. 114). Furthermore, real preoedipal traumatic experi-ence tended to create greater fixations and to disturb subsequent develop-ment more than those occurring at an older age. Contradicting the views of Kris, she held that ego state distinctions, for example, a regression to the archaic ego state, does not play a significant part in the usually slow process of reconstruction.

Greenacre applied the screen memory concept to two groups of patients who had suffered early traumas. In one group prepubertal traumas were very clearly remembered by patients who attributed subsequent and lasting distur-bances to them. The prepubertal trauma, derived from the acting out of repressed, screened, and severe early Oedipal traumatic experiences, was regressively revived by the emerging pubertal drives. "The later memory of the prepubertal trauma in these cases was then retained because of its intense screening function against earlier trauma . . ." (p. 115). Since this appears to be a case of *the bad screening the worse,* it can be readily understood that this group of patients suffered from severe problems.

As mentioned in Chapter 3, reverse or retrogressive screening is also possible, wherein later childhood memories are "projected" onto earlier ones, the earlier memories acting as a screen. According to Greenacre, such retrospective screening was found for a group of patients in whom the crucial, powerful organizing traumas of later childhood and infancy were stubbornly repressed and screened by earlier infantile *fantasies* on which the later-occurring *events* were projected, thereby enhancing as well as adding elaborations to the early screen memories. Although problems in this group were less severe than those of the other group with earlier traumas, the actual traumas inflicted on both groups of patients made it therapeutically desirable that the analyst's reconstructions recognize this and attempt to recover the "real traumatic, organizing experiences of development."

Greenacre felt that most significant traumatic experiences in early life were sexual and that, when they were not, the retained memories screened sexual experiences. Especially noted were "primal scenes, seductions, violence, and childbirth scenes." She did not deny that fantasies and individual experiences strongly interact in childhood, but she emphasized that fantasies are invariably colored by individual experiences. Greenacre contrasted her emphasis on the genetic basis of neurosis and character disturbances with those analytic approaches that "utilize the repetitive demonstration of conflict and defense in current situations, which may easily deteriorate into indoctrination" (p. 116).

Some suggestions were offered by Greenacre for ways in which an analyst could detect whether actual traumas had occurred. One clue to real trauma was a transference distortion of an almost delusional character in a nonpsychotic patient. Other indications included acting-out tendencies, the frequent appearance of dreams that reproduced reality events exactly but were peculiarly devoid of associations, and insistently recurring discrepancies of age or place that were inappropriate to the events with which they were associated. Related to these are what she called "vacuoles of memory," where there are either conspicuously omitted substantive areas or incongruous repetitions. To no one's surprise, the Kris Study Group seemed to favor Kris's position over Greenacre's, although Lowenstein, the group chairman, agreed that it is often important to distinguish actual traumatic events from unconscious fantasies. At that time it could scarcely have been imagined that thirty years later, owing to publicity given the widespread problem of child abuse, the theoretical question of children distinguishing suggested and fantasized events from actual physical molestations would be a staple of daily newscasts.

Other trends in regard to psychoanalytic reconstruction were more unanimously agreed upon. The uncovering of aggressive impulses, stressed by Kris, played an even more important role for the study group. Sexual motives were much more in the background than they had been for Freud (and for Green-acre). In fact, in the first year during which the Kris Study Group met, all the reported clinical examples dealt with reconstructions of situations in which the main content was aggressive rather than sexual. This concentration on aggression was justified in part by stressing the role of aggression in the most fundamental of all psychoanalytic building blocks, the Oedipal situation. "In the classical form of the Oedipal complex, the little boy's love for his mother is not dangerous *per se*. It is warded off because of the aggressive impulses directed towards the father, which would mean destruction of an object that is also loved" (p. 75). Leaving the father aside, a second source of aggression occurs in this conflict situation in that the intensified libidinal drives toward the mother are inevitably frustrated, and this frustration "stimulates aggressive impulses which threaten the destruction of the loved object and must be defended against." This description is seen as a possible explanation of why "primal scenes are always felt to be aggressive acts."

By way of commentary I would note that the pervasive saturation of infantile actions with aggressive motives has some theoretical advantages over Freud's complex libidinal interpretations. For example, a frequent criticism is that Freud endows infants with abilities that exceed their developmental capacity. Superficially, Freud's description of the Oedipal situation is alleged to posit mental representations and long-matured jealousies of which infants are incapable. In contrast, fear of the loss of the loved ones through an infant's own aggressive actions gives an account of the infant's behavior at a cognitive level that appears to be a better fit with the observed behavior of infants. This considerable shift in relative motivational emphasis must, of course, result in changes in what is looked for in the reconstruction of patients' memories, as well as altering the theoretical explanation for childhood amnesia.

Like aggression, superego functions were expanded by the study group to include two new ideas; neither concept had a place in psychoanalytic theory when Freud made his early formulations concerning memory functions. The group suggested that superego functioning could sometimes lead to resistance on the part of a patient, who is intent on winning superego approval, and who might therefore accept incorrect memory reconstructions in order to shore up defenses against the strictures of the superego. In contrast, superego functioning may be helpful at times in that the analyst's reconstructions can represent superego commands that lead the patient to remember. Also related to the occurrence of the Oedipal conflict is the possibility that some memories may be made permanently inaccessible through identification mechanisms that incorporate attitudes of the Oedipal period into the permanent character structure of the individual. "The Oedipal memory is handled by identification in order to ward off the aggression which can destroy the loved object [one or both parents]. The object is protected by fusing part of it with the self-representation" (p.75). When this perspective is taken and difficulties are diagnosed as "character disorders," the chance for recovery of actual memories appears to be almost negligible. "Analysis of the character of the adult should result in recovery of the 'original' aggressive impulses and/or its associated memory, but perhaps the memory itself is no longer recoverable" (p. 76). An analyst would then be able to observe only "shifts in aggressive energy from the superego back to id and ego, with the resultant character changes supplying the necessary confirmation." (The difficult inferential reasoning required to recover memories in this account of the Oedipal situation would likely be even more complicated for the female than for the male, whose situation is taken as the paradigmatic one in psychoanalysis.)

Great importance in the process of reconstruction was given to a mentalistic conception that exudes an aura of the old introspective psychology, "the sense of conviction" that a patient has about the veracity of the reconstruction. If a reconstruction is factually true but the patient remains unconvinced, it is therapeutically useless; therefore "the sense of conviction" has pride of place over the ability to recall personal memories. The Kris Study Group stated, "unlike recall, it [the sense of conviction] is considered the *sine qua non* of the validity and effectiveness of reconstruction." It is obvious that the sense of conviction can occur over a wide orbit and is not limited to memory reconstructions; examples within psychoanalysis itself include "convictions in the service of narcissism or denial, as well as the truthfulness of a screen memory" (p. 76).

There was also recognition that the sense of conviction may be "false," sometimes "misused" by the patient, and even delusional. The criteria put forward to distinguish between "true" and "false" convictions regarding reconstructions were numerous yet weak in explanatory power. As an example, "A true, objective or scientific sense of conviction can be compared with a genuine feeling which does not have within it any degree of ambivalence or struggle." But by itself this feeling of harmony is not enough. "However, as primary process thinking is superseded by secondary process thinking the subjective sense of conviction may become more objective" (p. 77). It would appear that reconstructive phenomena are too diverse to allow specific generalizations. (There was, however, a stab at classification in terms of orthodox psychoanalytic character types based on "the clinical observation that a strong sense of conviction is often found in intensely oral characters, as contrasted with the doubts so typical of anal characters" [p. 79].)

In a generalized description that the Kris Study Group put forward to show how progress is made toward developing strong convictions about reconstructions, it is evident that the straightforward recovery of memories plays a secondary role; instead, emphasis is placed not only on the gradual diffusion of understanding of cognitive memory contents but also, and just as importantly, on the reinstatement of primitive affects from an earlier period.

> As the reconstructive work proceeds many factors occur which may strengthen the sense of conviction. The analysis of the transference neurosis, with its release of affects in vivid form and the neutralization of cathexes, permits the emergence of additional confirmatory screen memories. There is a gradual elaboration, modification, and building up of the understanding of earlier situations. The sense of conviction does not come only because the

analyst said something and the patient feels that the analyst must be right. It comes from the very reconstruction of the patient's problems, which explains more and more of the phenomena with which the patient is troubled. Often aided by the transference, a reconstruction may bring unquestioned sureness by arousing strong primitive affects appropriate to the time represented (1971, p. 78).

A Sampling of Contemporary Psychoanalytic Theorists

Psychoanalytic ego psychology, which had been the dominant theoretical trend for almost three decades,[1] was challenged by a perhaps inevitable reaction within psychoanalysis that developed in the 1970s. A particular focus was against the use of metapsychological explanations that applied such theoretical hypothetical constructs as mental energy attachments (cathexis and anticathexis) and mental energy displacements (the "economic" point of view) to structures of id, ego, and superego. A theme of many theorists was that the attempt to represent psychoanalysis in a physicalistic manner was not only misguided but also extraneous to what in fact happens in psychoanalytic praxis. New formulations were sought in which psychoanalysis was defined as dialectical and hermeneutical and more closely allied to the humanities than to the natural sciences, or even the social sciences. Psychoanalysis, it was argued, should not aim for an all-encompassing psychological theory but should more modestly attempt a theory that arises out of and could be helpful to clinical practice. I have chosen to present the views of several representatives of this trend—Roy Schafer, Stanley Leavy, Anton Kris, Samuel Novey, Donald Spence, Paul Ricoeur—not because of their part in this fairly widespread psychoanalytic reformation but because of what they say specifically that is pertinent to autobiographical memory, particularly in their writings on psychoanalytic interpretations and reconstructions. It is characteristic of these theorists thay they place great emphasis both on language and on linguistic theory. As two examples, Schafer (1976) has formulated an "action language" for use in theorizing that largely dispenses with the physicalistic terms of energy, force, structure, and mechanism. Leavy (1980) has been strongly influenced by recent French psychoanalysts (particularly Jacques Lacan), whose dominant emphasis has been on language and its nuances as structuring not only conscious thought but unconscious mentation as well.

Schafer considers *Freudian* psychoanalysis as a 'life-historical discipline." He is scrupulous in pointing out that there are other *psychoanalytic*, but what he calls *non-Freudian*, theories such as Harry Stack Sullivan's interpersonalistic theory. Psychoanalytic theory is concerned with narratives—i.e., stories—with the "story line" dictated by the particular school of psychoanalysis to which the analyst belongs. The piecemeal recollections of the patient do not in themselves constitute the narrative; rather it is the retelling of the life story by the analyst. But, in accord with the theoretical persuasion of the analyst, certain forms are used as contents and other forms are excluded.

Thus the similar thematic forms of particular schools help account for "plot" similarities. Although personal historical analysis is necessary, "the point of the historical inquiry is the elucidation of the present world, especially in its disturbed aspects" (1978, p. 15). Using the categories of infancy such as those dealing with bodily organs, bodily excretions, bodily contacts and movements, the therapist establishes for the patient a perspective on psychic reality as "primarily a child's atemporal, wishful, and frightened construction of reality, and as such a construction that is in principle modifiable. To accept this modifiability is itself a new action, and one of the most important a person can ever perform." For Schafer the narrative itself is neutral in regard to its truth value and also its reality value, since multiple versions are possible. To some extent, however, a criterion of consistency can be applied, "*As much as by its basic categories of past and present life-history and experience, Freudian interpretation is distinguished by its conception of personal existence as actions with multiple and transformable meanings*" (p. 27).

Schafer places considerable stress on personal agency and intentionality in interpretations. It is of great importance that patients look at their life history in such a way that they do not *disclaim actions,* including the "so-called mechanisms of defense," by blaming them on others, and do not indulge in *excessive claiming* (for example, responsibility for the death of family members) by assuming responsibility for what they were in no way responsible. In both respects, here as elsewhere in the narrative life history, though no criterion of truth value can be assessed, a criterion of consistency can be applied. Thus the weakness of relying exclusively on a "sense of conviction" is partially got round.

Of special relevance here is Schafer's (1981) argument that verbal interchanges during psychoanalytic therapy sessions do not and should not lead to the construction of a *unitary* life history on the part of the analysand (patient). Schafer claims that remembered events are given different meanings to construct alternative life histories. These multiple "recontextualizations" can possess equal validity. In any event, if good psychoanalytic technique is followed, a chronologically ordered history is unlikely to result from obtained memories since, "Temporally, the psychoanalyst works in a circle. He or she uses the present to raise questions about the as yet unremembered or unorganized past and even to fill in gaps or make other changes in the past" (1981, p. 38).

One reason that there are multiple life-history versions is that as analysis progresses new life histories are concocted, but earlier versions still retain some validity. The earliest telling of the past can be used as a basis to "raise questions about the as yet inadequately defined or unintelligible present. The past is even used to locate and to fill in gaps in this undeveloped present." The nearest that analysands approach to a chronologically ordered account, in Schafer's view, is that "to a limited though significant extent, linear time, especially in the form of distinctions newly drawn between the past and present, does figure more prominently and more reliably in these revised stories than it did before." The optimal outcome of psychoanalysis is that "analysands learn through analysis to become more versatile, sophisticated and relativistic historians of their own lives. Some indeterminacy of temporal location is one of the things they learn to accept and work with." This limited goal for psychoanalysis Schafer contrasts favorably with the many case histories that "present single, life-historical accounts, chronicled in linear time, as though these are unproblematic summaries of purely objective facts that have been encountered or uncovered by analysis and whose latent significance has been revealed by interpretation." Furthermore, even theoretically, a somewhat muddled chronology is not an indication of failure, since the goal of psychoanalysis is only incidentally to obtain a literally true account of the analysand's life history.

Crucial to the interpretive enterprise are the axioms of the psychoanalytic theory of development whose basic outlines were themselves laid down by obtaining retrospective recollections: "This knowledge of development was in the first instance arrived at retrospectively or historically; its basic shape has been not so much altered by the findings of child analysis and psychoanalytic observation of infants as filled in, refined, and confirmed by others" (1978, p. 12). Schafer, it should be emphasized, is here at the opposite pole from Kris, who thought a still-living Freud would have modified his theory in line with the new knowledge gained through later child development research. In Schafer's view, the past of each patient was considered inevitable enough to be sturdily anchored in psychoanalytic theory: "One may say that the analyst uses the general past to constitute the individualized present as a basis for inquiry into the individualized past. Thus, while moving with the analysand back and forth through time, the analyst bases interpretation on both present communication and a general knowledge of possible and probable pasts that have yet to be established and detailed in the specific case" (pp. 13–14). It can be noted that in following this procedure the possibilities for recollective memory have been so strongly scripted by psychoanalytic developmental theory that even *potential* memories can be incorporated into the narrative.

In regard to autobiographical memories, it can be observed that in Schafer's approach the likelihood of finding new or surprising theoretical constructs is much diminished. This is true to an even greater degree in some other contemporary psychoanalytic theories in which, unlike Schafer's "temporal circle" approach, obtained memories of actual events and emotions become beads strung on the life-story string. Perhaps in any field it is inevitable that where the amount of theoretical doctrine increases, room for surprise arising from additional empirical content decreases. But what is special to psychoanalysis, as Shafer suggests, is that by deemphasizing retrospective memories, the original source of theorizing is done away with. This consideration may also help partially answer the lament about why we no longer see psychoanalytic case studies that are akin to detective investigations into life histories, like the ones the early Freud produced in his classic cases—Dora, Little Hans, Rat Man, Dr. Schreber, Wolf Man.

Stanley Leavy's theoretical analysis of the "psychoanalytic dialogue," detailed in his 1980 book by the same name, clashes in no important way but rather extends remarks by Schafer that autobiographical experience is reconstructed through dialogue, not by introspection. Analysis of the psychoanalytic transference, asserted by Leavy to be the principal source of the recovery of the past, is "inseparable from the conditions of dialogue," and (following Lacan) the transference itself is characterized as a kind of memory distortion in that it is a "misrecognition of the other in the dialogue." By Leavy's reckoning, even an apparent monologue is counted as dialogue, and one especially liable to distortion, since "to be at all is to be in dialogue, whether the other participant is actually present, or only a mental representation and hence subjected to even greater stresses from the realm of the imaginary than when actual" (p. 109). Nevertheless, like Schafer, Leavy asserts that "at every stage of the recovery of the past the [personal] *history* is inevitably a *story*" (p. 99).

Leavy also has a fondness for comparing what the analyst does in supplying interpretations with the interpretative process performed by professional historians. Especially noted is that causal explanations in analysis are more like those in history than those in the physical sciences—and in neither personal nor general history can success be equated with predicting the future. But, admittedly, analytic interpretation deviates from ordinary historiography in that cohesiveness is more important than strict veridicality. "It would also be naive to claim that our progress in analyzing is also a progress away from the fictive to the realistic narrative; all we can claim is a more inclusive and coherent story as the basis of our history" (p. 109). Both general history and personal history are subject to subsequent and fairly continuous revision. Personal history is always changing, whether through intellectual knowledge or subjectively lived experiences. "An experience of the past acquires new contextual experience with the advance of personal history," and "a present experience reveals something about the past that was hitherto unknown" (p. 115). Thus Freud's concept of deferred action and understanding is an all-pervading tendency. For Leavy, as for Ernst Kris and other ego analysts, it is only the interpreted pattern that counts; isolated memories, veridical or not, are useless. Even when apparently valid recollections are obtained "on the proper territory of psychoanalysis," namely, the memories of infancy, Leavy finds such memories to be irrelevant. These isolated memories are merely "those precious bits of recollecting from the cradle in which some people take great pride, and some analysts find such impressive demonstrations of the truth of our theories;" but Leavy terms them simply *disjecta membra*.

What, then, can be recovered by means of recollections, particularly of infancy, that helps construct the life-history narrative? In many contemporary views, Leavy's in particular, the ground of the earlier argument has shifted. It is no longer a major concern whether recollections are real or fantasies; instead, the most valuable and sought-after recollections are those that represent *unconscious fantasies*. Although Leavy believes that we can often distinguish true memories from false ones, "it is irrelevant to psychoanalysis whether the recovered past is grounded in an objectively recognizable event or not. Paradoxical as it may seem, the only sure reality of the memory of the past is fantasy—the cluster of imaginings, wishful in nature, in which it exists"

(p. 103). Until they are constructed in psychoanalysis, these fantasies may have always remained unconscious, paralleling Freud's earlier claim that important early event memories may never have been expressed until psychoanalysis recovers them. But the unconscious fantasy is known *only* as a construction produced by dialogue, not as a direct recollection.

Other analysts have emphasized the great importance of understanding patients' unconscious fantasies, but no other theorist has placed them so exclusively at the center of reconstructions as Leavy did. Leavy is careful to spell out what he means by unconscious fantasies. In ordinary usage, he points out, a fantasy may be any imagining, but in psychoanalytic parlance it carries with it a wishful element, so that "to fantasize something is to think about it in its absence with an accompanying desire" (p. 84). Unconscious fantasies may guide and direct conscious fantasies, and, looked at the other way round, he believes that analysis of many conscious fantasies may lead to the one unconscious fantasy inherent in all of them. He concludes that these unconscious fantasies, primarily from the "prehistoric" period of the preverbal individual when the imaginary mode has free reign, may "yet be the most elementary unit and the most inclusive" (p. 85).

It is clear that Leavy, Schafer, and to a considerable extent Ernst Kris and other ego analysts, are representative of the many modern analysts who have little interest in the recovery of early memories *as such*. Leavy and Schafer are more explicit theoretically and less merely programmatic than some others in spelling out what it is they are interested in obtaining and interpreting from early childhood. But they do see a necessary determinism issuing from infancy and Oedipal conflicts as central to difficulties later in life. As they view it, a belief in the crucial role of early life events is an irreplaceable axiom of Freudian psychoanalysis. Therefore the past *must* influence present action, even if it is only indirectly detectable through transference, free associations, acting out, or guiding fantasies.

But what kind of memory is this that concentrates on (to reverse the William Blake phrase) the "lineaments of *un*satisfied desire?" I think one way to view this question is to consider the threefold classification of psychological subject matter into cognition, affection (emotion), and conation (motivation)—a classification espoused by the British functional psychologists at the turn of the twentieth century, and as recently as the 1920s by William McDougall (1926). In this classification what the analyst is obtaining by tapping retention of early experiences comes under the heading of *conation,* including, dictionaries tell us, impulse, desire, volition, and striving. Contemporary psychology ordinarily treats conation under such headings as motivation or drive, but what is to be emphasized is that treatment of the retention dimension of motivation per se is almost wholly lacking. The conative memory emphasis found in psychoanalysis is an original one and seems to fill a previously empty ecological niche in memory investigations. As has been outlined, the conditions under which the track of this kind of memory may be located can be quite peculiar. For example, no cognitive formulation of memory content need have taken place; what is disclosed may be more like an implicit summarizing trend than an actual event;

and the past is reinstated by dialogue not by recall. All in all, Freud's therapeutic prescription has proved overly optimistic; the discovery process is closer to *repeating* than *remembering*.

From another perspective, memories of earlier strivings, impulses, and desires can be considered part of the character structure—or as academic and popular psychology would usually put it, *personality*—rather than being just memories. (One way this outcome can occur was given by the Kris Study Group in suggesting that attitudes of the Oedipal period can be incorporated into the character structure by the mechanism of identification.) When this is the case, however phrased, the little that remains from an early experience as a recoverable memory is scarcely more than psychic scar tissue. What is certain is that there is a tension here in psychoanalytic thought between what is memory and what has passed over into some unmodifiable mental structure of the individual during the malleable period of infancy. If desires are wholly embedded in character and personality, much of the necessity for theorizing about repression and screen memories has vanished. And the fragile thread linking infantile events with specific actions of later life becomes ever more frayed.

Nevertheless, it seems unlikely that putting the major emphasis on a character and/or personality approach is a viable option for psychoanalysis. The anamnestic emphasis on an integrated personal history is too imbedded in psychoanalytic methodology (particularly when compared with other psychotherapies), even when the search for early traumatic memories advocated in Freud's initial theorizing plays scarcely any role. As currently practiced, the detection of past occurrences may appear to concentrate on the incidental and indirect, but, nonetheless, it is the past as known in the present that counts. Revealing the past, even if only by claiming to find guiding unconscious fantasies, implies some optimism for therapeutic change. In contrast, analysis of the allegedly *permanent* traits of personality or character structure implies considerable pessimism regarding therapeutic change. Furthermore, adopting such an approach would not, in itself, eliminate the need for careful scrutiny of the early life history. For when particular traits or predispositions of character or personality have been identified as endowed with a degree of permanency, they can ultimately be adequately explicated only by linking them to a recollected past, however unreliable its recall.

No contemporary psychoanalytic theory fails to stress the importance of transference phenomena. The specific role assigned to memory processes is frequently left unclear, however, beyond stating the obvious fact that memory is centrally implicated in the partial misrecognitions on which the transference is founded. Theorists who do elaborate on modes of memory involvement often stress that the relevant memories operate exclusively at an unconscious level and largely leave it at that. An interesting delineation of how memory is involved in transference was given by Anton Kris, the son of Ernst Kris. In considering transference in relation to free association, he claimed as a necessary element not only the direct operation of an unconscious memory of some past relationship but also "the unconscious re-creation of this old relationship so that thoughts, feelings, wishes, sensations, and images are directed toward the analyst and the analysis in place of the person or, less frequently, the nonhuman partner (e.g., an animal or an institution) involved in the original relationship" (1982, p. 61). This is obviously giving a more inclusive scope to transference than that given by the usual definition. And Freud himself had considerably widened his conception of transference in the two decades from 1905 to 1925.

Anton Kris, with an approach through free associations, found the same core problem that earlier ego psychoanalysts had struggled with: "Is the organizing principle of the patient's associations an unconscious memory of a past relationship, operating directly, or is it an organized part of the adult personality, operating in a similar unconscious fashion?" (pp. 62–63). Only in the former case can the situation be a true instance of transference. Kris distinguished true transference from three different types of nontransference reactions that focus on the analyst: (1) reactions influenced by present-day hopes, wishes, fears, and other expectations; (2) reactions that represent characteristic patterns of behavior; and (3) reactions that derive from externalization of one aspect of inner conflict (p. 63). The inappropriate interpretation of one of these types of reactions as "evidence of childhood experience can only dissuade the patient from attaching any importance to understanding unconscious aspects of his present feelings."

More generally, mulling over present experience in terms of past experience, even when partly performed unconsiously, and *recalling* past experience rather than *reviving* it in the patient's relationship to the analyst are both occasions where analyzable transference has *not* taken place. Thus it is evident that for memories to be analytically valuable and useful in "transference analysis," compulsive recurrence is more important than controlled volition, and repressions take precedence over suppressions. Early memories are of most interest when they persist in remaining for a long time, and perhaps permanently, beyond the reach of the patient. Attempts at memory recovery on the part of the patient are neither practical nor worthwhile. A too accessible memory disqualifies it from possessing major importance; it is suspect as not having been an unconscious memory after all. Kris expressed contemporary dilemmas insightfully in factoring out the influence of the past on the present, and he has the virtue of being unusually precise and unambiguous in his specifications. But we can wonder if it is possible to perform such distinctions in every instance, say, between unconscious transference memories and characteristic behavior patterns. We can also question whether the devaluation of conscious experience, including any accessible personal memories, has not been carried to an extreme.

A different dimension of memory recovery was considered by the psychoanalyst Samuel Novey, whose work was published posthumously in his book, *A Second Look* (1968). It can be acknowledged, he argues, that sometimes in analysis and quite often on other occasions there is an urge to explore old diaries and papers and to return to the physical settings and persons important in an earlier period of life. From the analytic standpoint there is frequently ambivalence and resistance on the part of the patient in undertaking such investigations. Novey claims that an advantage in carrying out such activities is that they can stir up old memories and feelings useful in psychotherapy and psychoanalysis. However widespread such actions may be, memory-seeking activity has sometimes been criticized by analysts as departing too much from the strictly verbal interchanges that take place within therapeutic sessions. For, Novey implies, correct methodology insists that words speak louder than any kind of action. That such procedural rigor has been carried too far is illustrated for Novey by the "gradual extension of the term 'acting-out,' which was originally intended only to describe the 'living-out" in the situation of things which should be talked out in the analytic situation." But, Novey adds, eventually the meaning of this term was "extended to include all sorts of behavior which was felt to be neurotic in nature in the general sense," and even applied as a "kind of epithet" (1968, p. 76).

In many instances, Novey claims, there is a compulsive need to carry out biographical investigations even though they yield pain as well as pleasure and can be labeled as "acting out." A great advantage of such activities is that through coming in contact with the physical setting a gratifying reality is established for situations that previously were felt to be dreamlike and some of which perhaps had a nightmarish quality. Nevertheless, historical emphasis should not be carried too far; some deference must be paid to the psychoanalytic aphorism, "when the patient becomes too preoccupied with the past, it is the analyst's duty to bring up the present—and the reverse" (p. 80). Investigation of one's biography is especially useful with obsessive-compulsive patients and those manifesting other disorders where there is resort to the omnipotence of words and the isolation of feeling.

> If thinking is the preparation for action in the normal, in the obsessional the fear of action and its associated affect prompts him to use thinking regressively, as a defense. It is because of this that doing instead of thinking becomes a way of overcoming the isolation. Doing in this context is not simple impulsivity but also behavior in the interest of interrupting a regressive pattern and of lifting repression. (p. 82)

Novey further claims that it is sometimes necessary to re-experience through the senses in order to lift repressions by visiting settings from the past or looking at certain documents. Re-expressing can be effective in two ways; either the sensory experience may precipitate an affect producing a memory, or the experience may precipitate a memory with subsequent affect. Attention is called to the parallel with *déjà vu* phenomena, at least insofar as a particular *déjà vu* experience rests on memories of prior experience. He stresses that many *déjà vu* experiences are accompanied by a "vague sense of unease and the uncanny." According to Novey, actual revisitations allay this anxiety of the present with the "reassuring experience of dealing with the realities of previously experienced objects" (p. 83). Novey also views biographical investigations as important to the "working through" process, which he characterizes as largely preconscious, nonverbal and highly affective in character. ("Working through" is identified by Laplanche and Pontalis as "the process by which analysis implants an interpretation and overcomes the resistances to which it has given rise . . . a sort of psychical work which allows the subject to accept certain repressed elements and to free himself from the grip of mechanisms of repetition" [1973, p. 488].) In some cases, because of significant resistance on the patient's part, an act such as revisitation to geographical sites that figure in one's life history may come only after a long period of analysis and prior working-through experiences.

The value of giving in to the autobiographical impulses described by Novey is something of a side issue, although it can be seen as encouraging the current movement to combine some behavioral modification techniques with psychoanalytic approaches. But like Freud's consideration of sensory imagery as an aspect of memory recovery, Novey's "acting out" prescription has had little follow-up in the psychoanalytic literature.

A book by Donald R. Spence, *Narrative Truth and Historical Truth* (1982), returns us to the overriding theme of this chapter, the extent to which autobiographical memories can be recovered, reconstructed, and described by psychoanalytic procedures available in therapy sessions. Spence, a psychoanalytic practitioner, not only pulls together many of the objections raised by earlier analysts in finding only "narrative truth" possible but also cites some objections that are so inclusive that any recovery of even quite recent memories would seem to be impossible. "Memory is more fallible than we realize, and it is vulnerable to a wide range of interfering stimuli. Substitute memories are perhaps much more frequent than Freud had assumed, and in fact, one might ask whether any kind of veridical memory exists" (1982, p. 91).

To some extent, then, Spence's argument would seem to constitute overkill, since the scope of his doubts about obtaining veridical memories extends well beyond psychoanalysis. He makes general claims against the possibility of verifying memories similar to those made by philosophers in their role as memory skeptics. A lengthy argument is put forward that we must always distort and falsify recall when we try to recapture lived experiences by means of words. Remaining within a strictly verbal dimension scarcely brings improvement; any tape-recorded interview is necessarily incomplete since we cannot adequately know the historical contexts of the speech acts. Also, analysts cannot remain neutral in listening to patients but produce unwitting interpretations since everyone has different associative contexts. Therefore, Freud's (1912) specification that the analyst should maintain "evenly hovering attention" while listening to patients is not usually possible and is often not desirable.

Spence is greatly impressed by Elizabeth Loftus's (1979) experiments on eyewitness testimony, which show that, apart from dynamic factors, accidents of similarity and contiguity have an important role in memory distortion. Emphasis is also placed by Spence on the undoubted fact that the visual and pictorial can never be accurately reproduced verbally. "The assertion that the form of the dream or memory *corresponds* in some significant way with some other data requires us either to produce the original visual stimulus or to demonstrate that our mode of translation is exhaustive and systematic and captures *all* essential features of the image. We never have the former—and can only rarely claim the latter" (p. 75). Obviously, for Spence, historical truth is impossible to attain and is not what historians (or anyone else) can hope to find. Thus, Spence strongly disagrees with the contemporary philosopher Adolf Grünbaum, who states that reconstructions in psychoanalysis attempt to obtain veridical reconstruction of the events that are causally relevant in the patient's current and early life. For Spence, neither long past memories nor recent ones can ever be verified by "pieces of the past."

In a number of ways, previous lines of reasoning within psychoanalysis are carried further by Spence, and conclusions are reached that in earlier years would have been thought anti-psychoanalytic. As previously discussed, it was formerly taken as axiomatic that adult conflicts were historically linked to Oedipal and pre-Oedipal conflicts. Even if direct recalls could not be obtained, the origin of the conflict or mode of defending would be represented by some memory remnant in the transference, resistance, free association, or acting-out behavior. Obviously, for Spence, links to infancy can only be established by applying the tenets of developmental psychoanalytic theory through inferential reasoning. No usable memories from infancy are recoverable.

A peculiarity of Spence's exposition is that in his book-length treatment touching centrally on the claims of psychoanalytic memories, *repression* is referred to only once. The mention of repression occurs in one of several attacks Spence makes on Freud's oft-repeated comparison of psychoanalysis with archeology.

> Although Freud was fond of describing the process of uncovering the past as a kind of archeology, we have little reason to believe that the memories that emerge can be trusted very far. More than we realized, the past is continuously being reconstructed in the analytic process, influenced by (a) the repressed contents of consciousness; (b) subsequent happenings that are similar in form or content; (c) the words and phrases used by the analyst in eliciting and commenting on the early memories as they emerge; and (d) the language choices made by the patient as he tries to put his experience into words. The past, always in flux, is always being created anew. (1982, p 93)

Thus, repression is perhaps *primus inter pares* in truth distortion, but a host of other largely nondynamic factors must also be given their due. Additional truth-falsifying complications as well as those cited above are listed. The patient may concur that a false interpretation is a valid memory for the sake of social acceptability. The transference is considered only as a distorting force rather than as projecting the past through encounters that have some memory content at their core. Countertransference is noted as an obvious source of bias, as are the elastic standards that satisfy analysts in obtaining confirmations of their interpretive conjectures. Spence's doubts do not lead him to temporize or defer to Freud's opinions as earlier generations of analysts often did, and he particularly decries Freud's archeological model where "the past is prologue and discovery is the key." Spence criticizes Freud's (1937) final

paper on constructions in psychoanalysis because Freud obstinately maintained his "pertinent faith in the possibility of uncovering the past, a faith in
the idea that psychoanalysis is an archeology of memories" (p. 176). Freud's
inferences in the Wolf Man case, said by some to be the epitome of his
psychoanalytic interpretations, receive rough treatment from Spence, who
finds several of Freud's conclusions unwarranted on the basis of the evidence.

Spence applauds Freud's apparent giving up of the infantile seduction
theory as a matter of his coming to his senses in regard to the possibility of
infantile memory distortions, but he also notes that Freud's attitude in infantile seduction was not consistent and that occasionally, as in the Wolf Man
case, Freud would relapse into "what might be called a state of rather naive
credulity" (p. 125). To summarize Spence's skepticism in one sentence: It is
hard to remember at all; it is even harder to remember under the conditions
imposed in the psychoanalytic session; and it is impossible to remember
events from early childhood where visual images predominate. Thus the "kernel of historic truth" that Freud thought lay hidden somewhere in the partially
predetermined word and actions of the present moment are, for Spence,
either undecipherable or nonexistent.

If analysts don't recover memories, what do they do? Trends presaged in
the previously discussed ideas of Schafer and Leavy are given a somewhat
different emphasis. Like those theorists, Spence discusses therapy as narrative and dialogue, but he is more interested in the record of the text of the
analytic session. Major influences on Spence's critique are not so much
linguistic as literary, combined with contemporary views on the philosophy
of science. The *text* of a psychoanalytic session would not be complete until
it was "naturalized" by the analyst. To bring about naturalization, the analyst
would be required to provide a gloss of his own unspoken thoughts, images,
hypotheses, and similar mentations in reaction to the symbolic meanings that
patients produce, and these observations are interspersed with the record of
the oral dialogue. As with reaching the goal of a precisely true memory, a
completely naturalized text appears to be an impossible ideal. But Spence is
skeptical of attempts to attain the former while he encourages attempts to
attain the latter.

Since memories are so specifically excluded as valid items in the interpretations that the analyst makes to the patient, it might be supposed that, ideally,
therapy should concentrate almost exclusively on interpreting current actions.
This is not so, however, as is indicated in part by the desirability of obtaining
"naturalized" texts. Such texts are, in one sense, the attempt to create fault-
less historical records that can be put to practical use. The history of the
therapeutic process can be salvaged even if the life history that it presents is
faulty. Moreover, somewhat flawed reconstructions are often found to be
effective in psychotherapy. How can this be? Spence faces up to the fact that
specifying criteria of coherence, convergence, and similar vague generalities is
an insufficient explanation. His two major reasons for therapeutic effectiveness are that interpretations can function both as esthetic experiences and as
pragmatic statements. Neither of these beneficial attainments requires eviden-

tial truth: "Once we have moved into the esthetic domain, it becomes less important to ask about the historical truth of the interpretation, just as we would hardly think of asking about the historical 'truth' of a painting." And, "how it is said may be just as important—or more important than—its message" (p. 269).

An example of the efficacy of a pragmatic statement is the politician who, in order to persuade voters who are still in doubt, says he is going to win. An interpretation is "first of all, a means to an end, uttered in the expectation that it will lead to additional, clarifying clinical material." When both criteria are considered together, the effectiveness of the therapist's speech acts are what is at issue. "Once we give up the concern for historical accuracy, we cannot only abandon the archeological model but we can also become more comfortable with the flawed nature of the clinical data. We no longer need to be embarrassed by our 'archeology of descriptions' " (p. 276).

To date, Spence represents the extreme, at least in explicit expression, that has thus far been reached in detaching psychoanalytic therapy from dependency on the recovery of personal memories. Although many of his criticisms have been borrowed from disciplines outside psychoanalysis, and some of his specific points (e.g., condemning Freud's deductions in the Wolf Man case) have been made often by non-analysts, until recently such a lengthy and integrated negative argument could not have been mounted from within the psychoanalytic fold. When memory recovery is forsworn, the developmental determinism of infancy and early childhood on later life—a *sine qua non* of psychoanalytic theory—becomes somewhat problematic. For where most analysts would stress the memory components in the transference and free associations, Spence finds only causes for distortion and misinterpretation. What is ironic is that such strict and literalist criteria are being applied at a time when academic psychologists have greatly relaxed their exacting standards. Formerly, the nonsense syllables found in the experimental laboratory were considered "memorized" only if each letter in a syllable was recalled correctly. Nowadays recall of approximate schematic visual or aural forms is deemed to represent considerable retention, as is recalling the verbal "gist" of prose passages. Within the Freudian canon such concepts as "deferred action" and the possibility of multiple memory impressions of the same activity would seem to argue for memory content as inherently inexact but still meaningful. Though memories are condensed, telescoped, and elaborated, they, like infantile fantasies, can still be acknowledged as memories, though incomplete and distorted. And Freud argued that the greatest distortion of all, the strong positive assertion by a patient of the lack of any memory, usually meant that the denied memory content had been retained in some form. The novelty of Spence's position within psychoanalysis is that, rather than seeking to enlarge the range of memory claims, he greatly constricts it by specifying extremely rigorous criteria. To qualify as a *memory*, retained content must be exact, inclusive, and untransformed. Yet he recommends a number of psychoanalytic procedures that usually are thought to pertain to the "historical approach" emphasized by earlier analysts.

A Hermeneutical Approach to Memory

A sampling of current psychoanalytic memory theorizing would be incomplete without a description of the approach taken by the contemporary philosophical school of hermeneutics to Freud's ideas about memory. Hermeneuticists have, in general, shown little interest in psychoanalysts apart from Freud or empirical results that bear on Freudian theory.

A brief note is in order to explain why psychoanalysis should be an object of interest for hermeneutic philosophers. Hermeneutics began as a scholarly field in the eighteenth century with the attempt to gain unifying principles for the exegesis and philological analysis of the Bible and classical manuscripts. This field had broadened by the beginning of the twentieth century to focus on the study of epistemological problems dealing with the ascertainment of reliable knowledge. A one-line description of current philosophical hermeneutics is that it is a metatheory of life-experiences as they are given in linguistic expression (Howard, 1982). Recent hermeneutic philosophers have written fairly extensively on Freud in an attempt to describe the presuppositions and meaning structure of his writings (Habermas, 1971; Ricoeur, 1970, 1981). An important motive for these philosophers is that, to a considerable extent, Freud's psychoanalytic techniques, e.g., dream interpretation and free association, are seen as constituting a method for obtaining reliable knowledge through "self-reflection." Thus it can be claimed that, by means of a hermeneutic interpretation, Freud's writings yield unique and important knowledge not obtainable by either idealistic introspection or empirical data gathering. An irony is that, according to prominent hermeneuticists, Freud was clearly mistaken in claiming that psychoanalysis was an empirical natural science when, in fact, it is a foremost example of a hermeneutical science.

The French philosopher Paul Ricoeur, more than any other hermeneuticist, has been influential with contemporary analysts, including several of the theorists discussed earlier in this chapter. Of especially wide influence has been his treatment of the psychoanalytic situation as bringing about an intersubjectively constructed "text" of the patient's life history to be scrutinized in terms of its narrative structure.

From the hermeneutical standpoint "texts" that are either found or constructed are the fundamental data for interpretation. Following this precept for psychoanalysis, Ricoeur states, "the analytic experience selects from a subject's experience what is capable of entering into a story or narrative. In this sense, 'case histories' as histories constitute the primary texts of psychoanalysis" (1981, p. 253). Freud, as Ricoeur recognizes, never advocated this restrictive viewpoint, but Ricoeur claims it is Freud's ideas about memory that warrant it, although Ricoeur's evidence on this point is minimal. Ricoeur writes: "This 'narrative' character of the psychoanalytic experience is never directly discussed by Freud, at least to my knowledge. But he refers to it indirectly in his considerations about memory. We may recall the famous declaration in *Studies on Hysteria* that 'hysterical patients suffer principally from reminiscences.' " However, citing Freud's best known memory maxim as evidence for the fundamental nature of narrativity is less than convincing; the five case histories in *Studies on Hysteria* could easily be used to argue for narrativity's superficial contribution. These case histories mostly describe the repression of traumatic incidents and resultant conversion hysterias where psychosomatic causality is expressed with such directness that, even granting Freud and Breuer's skill in written presentation, story elements appear inconsequential. The essential causality chain, whether considered as explanation or description, seemingly could just as well have been expressed in the bare-bones style of the ordinary nonpsychiatric medical case history. On the other hand, perhaps Ricoeur is making a stronger claim that any causal relation that can be put into words illustrates the necessity and power of narrativity. Thus the scope of narrativity is all-encompassing!

For Ricoeur, the psychoanalytic conception of memory that presumably justifies the primacy of narrative is a global category that includes all the functions pertaining to memory activity.

> But what is it to remember? It is not just to recall certain isolated events, but to be capable of forming meaningful sequences and ordered connections. In short, it is to be able to constitute one's own existence in the form of a story where a memory as such is only a fragment of the story. It is the narrative structure of such life stories that makes a case a case history. (1981, p. 153)

Thus memory functioning is at two levels; there is what one traditionally designates as memory ("memory as such"), and there is also an encompassing, more global memory, which performs editorial functions, but *only* as they are expressible in language (visual and other types of imagery are omitted).

How does one build the macro memory-narrative from micro remembrances? It is largely by the interplay of two functional mechanisms of large scope, "deferred action" and "working through." In regard to deferred action, Freud's controversial Wolf Man case is a prime example, immediately followed by the less controversial generalization that "numerous repressed memories only become traumas after the event." Ricoeur equates the working-through process directly with narration. "We may even say, then, that the patient is both the actor and the critic of a history which he is at first unable to repeat. The problem of recognizing oneself is the problem of recovering the ability to recount one's own history, to continue endlessly to give the form of a story to reflections on oneself. *And working through is nothing other than this continuous narration*" (1981, p. 268; emphasis added). Thus narration achieves its theoretical centrality by fiat not by evidentiary argument. (It will be recalled that Novey, together with many other practicing analysts, characterized working through as "largely nonverbal." Granting the necessity of some verbal contribution, only Ricoeur finds the working-through process nothing but narration.)

Not only does the activity of memory confirm the narrative character of psychoanalysis but, according to Ricoeur by a bit of reciprocal reasoning, the postulate of the "narrative function of existence" implies the memory activity that makes narrative possible. "Here we see that we are far removed from the notion of a memory which would simply reproduce real events in a sort of perception of the past; this is instead a work which goes over and over extremely complex structuralizations. It is this work of memory that is implied, among other things, by the notion of the narrative function of existence" (p. 254). In the hermeneutic scheme of things the recovery of memory content is not a distinct act but a continuing indefinite process of tailoring material to narrative structures. There is a notable lack of concern regarding techniques that encourage memory recovery, an ignoring of the content—let alone form—of subject matter actually remembered, and a disregard of patients' emotional and other responses on the occasion of the initial revival of specific memories. Even the ways in which fantasy intermixes in memory constructions, a major problem for Ernst Kris and other traditional analysts, is at too fine-grained a level to deserve consideration. "Editing" appears to be the only process of interest once the notion of the narrative function of existence is postulated.

Something more can be said about the working-through process. "It is in the process of working through," Ricoeur writes, "that Freud discovers the subject's history does not conform to a linear determinism which would place the present in the firm grip of the past in a univocal fashion." Are we to infer that Ricoeur or Freud is being naive here? Empirical reports are all in agreement that most people cannot order the events from their past in a linear deterministic manner. Several of the concepts of Freudian theory in themselves preclude this form of representation, for example, childhood amnesia. As detailed earlier in this chapter, Schafer condemned the presentation of unproblematic case histories in linear time as untrue to psychotherapeutic procedure, but even these deprecated case histories were the labored outcome of a long period of psychoanalytic discovery rather than a record of the patient's recalls. And there also is the testimony of oral historians, to be considered in Chapter 9, who find that the typical narrative style is that of anecdotal theme and variations, a style that almost always takes precedence over linear cause-and-effect narration. Representing one's life story or fragments thereof in a nonlinear fashion is typical rather than being predisposing to therapy.

Ricoeur's spartan program of concentrating on the psychoanalytic end-product, the verbal text produced by interchange in the psychoanalytic situation, has something rather old-fashioned and belletristic about it. Instead of attempting to modify Freud's theories through later theoretical or cultural developments, Ricoeur returns to the classical rhetoric of Aristotle and considers the verbal tropes in which personal narrative is expressed to be of high importance. Adolf Grünbaum has appropriately characterized Ricoeur's approach as encasing psychoanalysis in a "verbal straitjacket." The distinction between oral and written reminiscences is ignored, and there is not even the slightest hint that for most people narrative today is dominantly structured by television and films rather than by writing. A complete omission from the narrative record of nonverbal stimulation or nonverbal responding obviously also renders difficult the theoretical description of affects. A possible niche can be suggested for this solely verbal analysis in a specialty that has shown much recent growth, therapy by telephone. The increasing number of practitioners in this field can find a rationale tailored to their communication mode in Ricoeur's completely verbal psychoanalytic prescriptions.

Hermeneutics is much more than just a systematic philosophical orientation engaged in interpreting psychoanalysis. A goal within hermeneutics is to differentiate itself from a subjective phenomenological approach. Consonant with this standpoint is the ignoring of events proximal to the actions involved in remembering. Thus while the phenomenologist Merleau-Ponty (cf. Chapter 2) was concerned with minimizing the role of memory and maximizing that of perception, the hermeneutic philosopher prefers to take an opposite tack in considering perceptual phenomena unimportant while making distinctions of meaning paramount. These important meanings are derived from the constructions of memory, but it is a garrulous, yet emaciated "memory" which excludes sensory, perceptual, and many cognitive manifestations.

With a better claim than most, the psychoanalyst who follows Ricoeur's procedures can compare himself to a historian who interprets larger meanings from kaleidoscopic events. But the hermeneutic view of memory neglects two crucial tasks of the historian, a concern for obtaining all relevant evidence and assessment of the validity of the evidential building blocks that make up these larger meanings. Hermeneutic categories as enumerated by Ricoeur are at such a global level that they are unsuitable for accomplishing such tasks; basic data must be accepted or rejected on other grounds. Thus Ricoeur accepts the entire corpus of Freud's case histories without pointing out any possible errors (a scientifically gullible stance according to Grünbaum and others, including many adherents of psychoanalysis). To look to the future, it is likely that the interpretation of narrative constructions will continue as a useful approach to analysis, but the rationale that hermeneutics attaches to it will be discarded as a form of special pleading that narrows the investigatory terrain without producing compensatory advantages.

A wide sampling of psychoanalytic views was represented in this chapter, although no attempt was made for completeness. The pervasiveness of psychoanalytic ideas is not completely covered by citing the views of theorists who have accepted or modified Freud's concepts. In Chapter 6, the views of three memory theorists are described who are highly critical of Freud, yet make important use of psychoanalytic concepts. In many ways, psychoanalytic ideas tend to set the agenda for the study of memory that is *biographical* for the therapist, but *autobiographical* for the patient.

To give a more complete picture, however, mention should be made of several ongoing trends in the practice of psychoanalysis that tend to weaken interest in the psychoanalytic approach to memory. These trends include broadening psychoanalysis to encompass child clients and patients suffering from psychoses; memory recovery and reconstructions are of minor importance in the therapeutic techniques used with both of these treatment groups. An additional point is that memory recovery procedures are very time consuming so that they must be dispensed with in shortened forms of psychotherapy. Economic pressure for brief therapies has been intense in recent years, since health insurance, employee health plans, and other third-party payers have become the main financial providers of mental health services. These factors illustrate that in psychoanalysis, as elsewhere, not all the pressures for change and revision in theoretical applications come about because of competition from rival theories or lack of logical coherence.

6

Some Psychoanalytic Offshoots

Many ideas about personal memories that have some Freudian genealogy have been applied in unchanged or modified form by therapists who are not themselves psychoanalysts. In this chapter I first present the views of Alfred Adler regarding autobiographical memory, followed by two examples of how seemingly minor and even discarded ideas in Freudian theorizing have been enlarged upon and made more consequential than they ever were in psychoanalytic theory. The two psychiatrists, D. Ewen Cameron and William Sargant, who evolved these enlarged Freudians concepts concerning personal memory, are themselves more than a little critical of psychoanalysis, with their criticisms of interest as representing novel viewpoints. The latter part of the chapter, dealing with the contents of Chapters 3 through 6, offers a summarizing assessment of some past and present trends in psychoanalytic theorizing regarding autobiographical memory.[1]

THREE NOVEL VIEWPOINTS
Alfred Adler

Alfred Adler's school of individual psychology was the earliest clearly separate and systematic schism from psychoanalysis. Although Adler died in 1936, his school has persisted, maintaining a clearly formulated core of theoretical doctrines with active clinical practitioners who have applied his tenets in varying degrees through the practice of Adlerian psychotherapy. Adler's views on utilizing personal memories in psychotherapy are not as well known, to non-Adlerians, as his concepts of inferiority complex, style of life, family constellation, and masculine protest, among others. But Adler did hold distinctive ideas about personal memories, many of which are discussed in a post-Adlerian book edited by H. A. Olson, citing a variety of clinical applications (Olson, 1979). The chief emphasis of Adler and Adlerians is on obtaining a patient's first or earliest memories. (Adler himself called these memories *earliest,* but nowadays with greater grammatical precision, since several memories are invariably obtained, Adlerian practitioners call them *early* memories—abbreviated ERs, for early recollections.)

Asking someone for his or her first memory is such a common procedure that it may come as a surprise that a considerable theoretical apparatus has become attached to it. Not only is eliciting the first memory the commonest of all questions in psychological questionnaires pertaining to personal memory, but it is a fairly frequent feature of the Sunday supplements for journalists to probe celebrities regarding their ERs. In comparing the views on memory of Adler and Freud, Heinz Ansbacher (1947), a leading spokesman for the Adlerian viewpoint, emphasized that the early recollections that Adler found "particularly illuminating" were not given any special mention by Freud, whereas Freud stressed infantile amnesia, a concept that Adler never mentioned. Current Adlerians find appropriate acknowledgment of Adler's theoretical priority in a conclusion drawn by Ruth Munroe in her wide-ranging survey of *Schools of Psychoanalytic Thought* (it was used as the epigraph for Olson's book). ". . . Adler's routine request for a first memory was actually the first approach toward the *projective*-test method now so widely used. . . . His first memory technique was not only unique as a quasi-test device but at its inception unique in the theory that loosely governed conscious production may be used *systematically* to reveal deep personality trends" (1955, pp. 428–429n).

Putting Adler's viewpoint concerning early memories under the category of a projective technique indicates, of course, that truthfulness of content is a secondary issue. Rather, such a "memory" is an encapsulated miniature, diagnostic of the patient's present situation—the style of life. Adler states:

> What is altered or imagined is also expressive of the patient's goal, and although there is a difference between the work of fantasy and that of memory we can safely make use of both by relating ideas to our knowledge of other factors. Their worth and meaning, however, cannot be rightly estimated until we relate them to the total style of life of the individual in question, and recognize their unity with his main line of striving towards a goal of superiority. In recollections dating from the first four or five years we find chiefly prototypes of the individual's life-style, or useful hints as to why his life-plan was elaborated into its own particular form. Here also we may gather the surest indications of self-training to overcome the deficiencies felt in the early environment or organic difficulties. In many cases, signs of the person's degree of activity, of his courage and social feeling are also evident in the early recollections (1937).

The question can be raised again about the extent to which obtained memories are *true* memories. Adler does not seem very hopeful. "Many [memories] are even fancied, and most perhaps are changed or distorted at a time later than that in which the events are supposed to have occurred; but this does not diminish their significance." Nonetheless, Adler's statements may be interpreted as indicating that just as recollections of early fantasies or unconscious wishes must be in one sense *memories* since they date from the period of infancy, so too a rehearsed or distorted memory has what Freud termed a "kernel of truth" in it. One does not obtain representative instances solely by projecting current problems and aspirations backward in time. Although Adler is less concerned than Freud with the literal truth of infantile memories, Adler and Freud are alike in believing that some important memory contents can be recovered directly, which distinguishes them from the later psychoanalysts whose views were spelled out in the previous chapter.

Adler also emphasized that there are no nonsensical recollections; we forget "all those events which detract from the fulfillment of a plan" and "every memory is dominated by the goal idea which directs the personality-as-a-whole." An interesting theoretical point here is that Adler, unlike other early analysts, is particularly known for his emphasis on the social side of life, with the goal of replacing competitiveness by mutual cooperation. Yet, somewhat surprisingly, Adler sees one's life plan as diagnostically revealed by the nature of infantile memories. Particularly in view of Adler's disagreement with Freud over his emphasis on infantile sexuality, one might have expected that crucial aspects of socialization and social adjustment could not be diagnosed at such a young age. But Adler states that one's first memories (presumably at an age subject to childhood amnesia according to Freudian theory)

> help us to see the kind of world which a particular person feels he is living in, and the ways he early found of meeting that world. They illuminate the origins of the style of life. The basic attitudes which have guided an individual throughout his life and which prevail, likewise, in his present situation, are reflected in those fragments which he has selected to epitomize his feelings about life, and to cherish in his memory as reminders. He has preserved these as his earliest recollections (1937).

Characteristically, Adler places little emphasis on what early memories can reveal about repression. Instead, emphasis is given to what is sensed in these memories as dangers to be avoided. Dangers may be represented overtly or through rather transparent symbolization. A contemporary Adlerian has claimed that early recollections "prophesy" whether the life-style is durable or has a "weak link" that may give way under stress. "It is no wonder then, that in the outbreak of a neurosis, we so frequently see in the situation a repetition of the situation pictured in the first recollection. Such recollections have usually become a sort of warning signal for the individual. They are symbols of a defeat which he wants to avoid in the future. . . . When the allegory of a recollection is understood, the parallel between the momentary attitude of the individual and the resolution he produces can always be recognized" (Plewa, 1935).

The themes that earliest memories disclose are, not surprisingly, interpreted as exemplifying the main theoretical concepts of individual psychology: sibling rivalry and displacement by the birth of a younger sibling; situations of danger when fears are an important part of one's style of life; interactions with the mother, particularly when the remembering person has been a "spoiled" child. Some of the double-edged deductions that critics of psychoanalysis are always quick to note also appear in the memory interpretations of individual psychology. "If the mother does not appear in the early recollections that, too, may have a certain significance; it may for one thing, indicate a feeling of having been neglected by her" (1937). Another type of personal problem is indicated by earliest remembrances that "disclose an interest in movement, such as travel-ing, running, motoring or jumping" that Adler claims indicate "individuals who encounter difficulties when they find it necessary to begin work in sedentary occupations." Here, as elsewhere, Adler's abbreviated and popular style of presentation—a style that has done so much to undercut his credibility as a theorist with later generations—results in an example so apt and simplistic that it verges on self-parody. A neurotic young man's earliest memory was of "run-ning around the whole day in a kiddy car." After treatment, "he was taken back into his father's office, but he did not find the sedentary life there to his liking. He finally adapted himself to life as a traveling salesman" (1937).

The idea of a screen, or concealing, memory receives no acceptance from Adlerians. Fitting the description of an infantile memory into the broad cate-gory of style of life can always assist in understanding an individual's personal strivings and goals without any resort to an interpretation in terms of layered meanings. Rather, the apparent compression and simplicity of earliest recol-lections often makes them easier to interpret than other memories in terms of personality assessment. In this vein an Adlerian analyst (Rom, 1965) has discussed a widely cited short paper by Freud (1917) concerning one of the German poet Johann Goethe's earliest memories. In this paper Freud quotes from Goethe's autobiography, where Goethe remembers himself as a very small child throwing crockery out of a window into the street below. In the recollection, smashing of the family dishes was much encouraged by some adult neighbors. For Freud this apparently simple description was merely a screen for the infant Goethe's wish to get rid of ("throw out") a newborn rival, a baby brother. As Rom points out, limiting interpretations to the theme of sibling rivalry, even though a cardinal concept of Adlerian analysis, leaves out much of the richness of Goethe's reminiscence. From a style-of-life standpoint the early recollection "reveals an interest in delighting an audi-ence, and emphasis on visual, auditory, and kinetic activity, all of which seem quite consistent with the life of the great poet, statesman and dramatist" (1965). Perhaps there is too much consistency, as with those analytic psycho-historical reconstructions that find a causal connection between early psy-chosexual experience and just those biographical events that are best known.

Finally, going well beyond giving no credence to the repression of memo-ries, Adler did away with drawing any theoretical distinction between per-sonal memories that are retained and those that are forgotten and difficult to recover.

> Looking back, everybody remembers important things, and indeed what is fixed in memory is always important. There are schools of psychology which act on the opposite assumption. They believe that what a person has forgot-ten is the most important point. But there is really no great difference between the two ideas, for even when a person can tell us his conscious remembrances, he still does not know what they mean. He does not see their connection with his actions. Hence the result is the same, whether we empha-size the hidden or forgotten significance of conscious memories or the impor-tance of forgotten memories. . . . Both conscious and unconscious remem-

brances have the common quality of running towards the same goal of superiority. It is well, therefore, to find them both if possible, for both are in the end about equally important, and the individual himself generally understands neither. It is for the outsider to understand and interpret both of them. (Adler, 1929)

D. Ewen Cameron

A theorist who was not a psychoanalyst but who made use of psychoanalytic concepts in an empirical, eclectic approach to memory was the Canadian psychiatrist D. Ewen Cameron. In his monograph on *Remembering* (1947) he claimed that a distinctive feature of Freud's memory theorizing was not simply multiple registration of the same event by young children, as has been previously discussed, but that "Freud was forced to postulate a sort of double life for 'memories' " (1947, p. 101). Memories for the same occurrence existed both in the "original, basic, unchanged form, and that which had undergone secondary elaboration and condensation." Cameron asserted that it was necessary that memories be unchanged from their inception if Freud were to preserve his deterministic theory of behavior, but Freud was too "astute" not to notice that there was often rapid modification of memory content. (Cameron cites no specific references for this assertion, but such a conclusion can be inferred from Freud's writings, particularly from some of the case studies.) Cameron himself felt that the postulate of unchanging memories was in error and had led some psychopathologists to the mistaken credo that "everything that has been experienced has been remembered, even though they allow that it may not be possible to bring much of it back into full consciousness."

Cameron liked to foster an independent and somewhat iconoclastic outlook, thus he found passé "an exceedingly widely used psychopathological concept . . . the conception of the conflict—new a few decades ago but already an obstacle to progress" (p. 102). Specifically in regard to memory,

> where the difficulty arises is in the fact that the older psychopathologists, being committed to determinism, see this conflict as taking place in an unchanging system. For them it is quite essential that one or other participants in the conflict be dealt with and overcome. The conflicting 'memories' must be removed, repressed or one must be vanquished. The newer conceptions of emergent evaluation render this quite unnecessary, the whole setting is shifting and changing and in many instances the conflict disappears in the process. (pp. 102–103)

Partial acceptance and reasoned modification of psychoanalytic ideas is not, however, what marks Cameron as a distinctive memory theorist strongly influenced by psychoanalytic concepts. Rather, it is the extensive use he makes of the psychoanalytic concept *secondary elaboration*. In Freud's early theorizing, secondary elaboration (or alternatively, secondary revision) was part of the distorting dream work, "the attempts on the part of the ego to mold the manifest dream content into a semblance of logic and coherence"

(Brenner, 1973, p. 167). The ego tries to make the manifest dream "sensible," just as it tries to "make sense" of the impressions that impinge on it. Secondary elaboration was soon extended in Freud's theorizing well beyond dream formation. By the time *Totem and Taboo* was written (1912–13) he found that secondary elaboration figured in the formation of systems of thought such as those manifested in phobias, obsessive thinking, and paranoid delusions. Secondary elaboration was claimed to be "an intellectual function in us which demands unity, connection and intelligibility from any material, whether of perception or thought, that comes within its grasp; and if, as a result of special circumstances, it is unable to establish a true connection, it does not hesitate to fabricate a false one" (1912–13, p. 95).

To elucidate the critical role played by secondary elaboration in remembering, it is helpful to give a brief outline of Cameron's views. He stressed that memory concerned *reactivity,* in which the actual memory content is just one part of the total reactivity. The registration phase that he called the *primary reaction* occurs while an incident is taking place. The legacy of a strong primary reaction is a tensional endowment that persists. The tensional endowment concept does not relate to conscious volition or effort but rather borrows from the well-known Zeigarnik effect, which refers to the generalization that tasks which are not carried through to completion will later be better recalled than similar completed tasks. This superior recall was attributed to the tension an individual retained for tasks still "in progress." According to Cameron, the fact that the incidents with which psychoanalysts characteristically deal have strong tensional endowments is another reason they claim that nothing experienced can ever become completely lost, since "reaction tendencies with marked tensional endowments rarely disappear."

The second phase of memory in Cameron's theory is that of *integration,* occurring between the primary reaction and recall reactivation. It is here that secondary elaboration comes into its own with extensive ramifications since

> a secondary elaboration, not only of the action tendency but of its relations takes place. This expanded application of the term secondary elaboration is important. It has long been used to indicate that the action tendency undergoes modification within itself. Here we are pointing up the fact that its relationship, its integrations with other action tendencies, with indeed, the total potential activity, may also undergo secondary elaboration. (pp. 66–67)

Cameron includes in his category of secondary elaboration both the occasions when there is conscious representation, reminiscence, memory reviews, and the occasions when there is no conscious reaction at all. The practical outcome of secondary elaborations may be either harmful or helpful to the individual, depending on such factors as content and timing.

That therapy carried out early in the course of the traumatic anxiety state is apparently much more effective than therapy carried out later is a phenomenon that Cameron attributes to a curtailing of secondary elaboration by the early application of therapy. Here he cites the relatively great psychiatric success enjoyed during World War II when anxiety patients were immediately sedated, as compared with World War I when therapy was only instituted after a return to base. This comparison is illustrative of the good level of success achieved when secondary elaboration is not allowed to flourish. But he applies this thesis to civilian traumas also, citing in particular the tragic Cocoanut Grove nightclub fire in Boston in 1942, where those "who lost consciousness early and whose period of unconsciousness lasted at least an hour showed a much lesser incidence of anxiety states after the event than those who remained conscious throughout" (p. 66).

In themselves these examples would seem unconvincing as evidence for the role played by secondary elaboration, since a number of alternative explanations could be given for why immediate treatment is superior to delayed treatment. But Cameron viewed his emphasis on elaboration as complementary to the study of memory change by interference (particularly so-called retroactive inhibition, where there was a fall off in retention by the insertion of intervening material to be learned or dealt with in some other way). However, interference theorists had not concerned themselves with meaningful content changes produced in the individual's remembrance of the originally learned material. (In fact at the time Cameron was writing (1947), they could not do so in any useful way since they worked principally with arbitrary and meaningless materials. Cameron conceded that some earlier investigators, Frederic Bartlett in his study of folk stories and William Stern in his study of testimony, were to some extent dealing with secondary elaborations, but he faulted them for neglecting intervening processes, at most giving the duration between original learning and reactivation while ignoring what happened qualitatively during the retention period.)

Cameron claimed that in certain circumstances the secondary elaboration of memories can have an adaptive function. It can be recalled (cf. Chapter 4) that in the 1890s, before a mechanism of secondary elaboration was identified, Freud had described the useful "wearing away" of unpleasant memories by the process of association. Cameron saw secondary elaboration not so much as a "wearing away" of memories but as a mechanism for memory transformations. Therefore the failure to reduce the emotional content of traumatic or shame-provoking events can be described either as a failure to achieve complete repression or a failure to change recollections into an innocuous, or at least endurable, form by means of secondary elaboration. It is Cameron's claim that *significant* memory contents are more frequently transformed than altogether forgotten.

The memory integration phase is followed by the *reactivation* phase, in which the specific evocation of the remembered material is only a part of the total activity. Cameron combined results obtained by Hermann Ebbinghaus and other early experimental psychologists with the psychoanalytic concept of repression to reach the following conclusion:

> It appears that action tendencies which have been long repressed undergo little modification, but that once reactivated, and especially when they achieve complete representation in consciousness, modification starts in

again with full intensity. . . . This, of course, is not true of rote learning where, through frequent rehearsals, an attempt is made to ensure a precise recollection. It is true, however, of the reminiscent, reverie type of recollection, where recall is carried out under various circumstances. (pp. 90–91)

As one seeks to modify a patient's mental representations, the most favorable time for forgetting and therefore for therapeutic modifications is immediately after the primary reaction.

The individual's own actions, what psychoanalysts consider as attempts at memory "suppression" or manipulation, receive both good and bad marks from Cameron, but the fact is inescapable that people do it.

A great deal of the protection of the individual against the development of persistently deviated action tendencies is achieved during the period when the individual relives in memory the painful happenings of the day. For while it is true that "brooding about things," "stewing over things," "being burned up about things" may be unsuccessful in dealing with them and the disturbing action tendencies may be unmodifiable, nonetheless the process is primarily preventive and therapeutic. This fact emerges with special clarity in those individuals who have developed an enhanced capacity to suppress painful action tendencies, to "put things out of their minds," to refuse to deal with disturbing reality situations. Here a steady accumulation of painful action tendencies goes on until the capacity to manage day to day affairs becomes clearly impaired, and this inability becomes expressed in symptoms. (1947, pp. 86–87)

Another topic pertaining to ordinary living considered by Cameron is the importance of reactivation in the presence of another individual, "unburdening" oneself, the value of which, as Cameron notes, has been known since the earliest times. Although the popular media have made much mention of the need for "rapping" as therapeutic for Vietnam veterans and the need for confessionally "unloading one's problems" is a perennial favorite of "advice" columns, Cameron's 1947 statement still holds: "The mechanics of this process is not well understood." What is being referred to here comes close to the historical concept of *catharsis*. Early psychoanalysis, of course, elicited cathartic responses and codified them as abreactive responding when appropriate associated emotions were evident. But this conceptualization dealt with an almost mechanical release of tension and anxiety. Later formulations complicated this explanation since they described unburdening as a problem of social communication in which the ability to trust the listener plays a key role. No theory has yet satisfactorily explained the common need for everyday disclosure and the satisfaction obtained therefrom.

Cameron believed that much of what happens in unburdening oneself of memory content can be stated in terms of group formation. An assimilation with the point of view of the listener can produce a fertile field for modifying the action tendencies of the speaker, while when the listener assimilates his point of view to that of the speaker, this tends to strengthen rather than modify action tendencies and greatly increase the speaker's feeling of security.

(*Action tendency* is Cameron's term for comprehensive reactivation, not just of words and descriptions but also of attitudes, emotions, and behaviors.)

As with anxiety situations, so also with more ordinary "mulling things over": *when* such reactivation occurs is germane to whether the insidious effects of secondary elaboration are likely to take effect. "Where the action tendency has recently been set up, rumination, 'turning the matter over in one's mind,' 'getting burned up about it,' may be of value in effecting modification and preventing the establishment of an undesirable action tendency" (p. 94). Where the action tendency is long established, it is more likely that reminiscence promotes elaboration. In turn this process may lead to obsessive thinking. But Cameron believed that what results usually is not a true obsessive-compulsive neurosis but what he would prefer to call "topicalized thinking," where thinking is dominated by a very few topics of major concern.

Cameron recognized that the "vastly greater part of what we experience is never reactivated," including those action tendencies that were shielded by repression. But of those contents that are elaborated, timing is almost always a key concept. In particular, as has been described, Cameron repeatedly emphasized distinctions that can be made according to whether memory elaborations occurred immediately, soon, or long after initial content registration. This obvious variable is often neglected because it is only occasionally susceptible, on a realistic basis, to either clinical or experimental study. It is not accidental that the best controlled evidence for its importance comes from the military situation, wherein both time of trauma and treatment are part of an objective record. Consideration of the course of memory elaborations is neglected for more theoretical reasons by those therapists who believe manifest, worked-over memories are too consciously accessible to aid in the charting of any important motivational dynamics.

It can be seen that the "secondary elaboration" mechanism espoused by Cameron is wonderfully inclusive and open-ended, as indeed it was for Freud. But even loosely defined, it brackets real phenomena. The concept of "elaboration" has recently been used more and more in experimental psychology memory experiments. Under this aegis the concept is more restrictive but nevertheless vague. A useful commentary in terms of the information-processing approach is given by Fergus Craik (1979). "The terms *elaboration, breadth,* and *spread* of processing, and *richness* and *extensiveness* all seem to refer to greater amounts of processing of the same general type. As such, the concept differs from 'depth,' which refers to qualitative changes in encoding" (1979, p. 449). (The basic idea of "depth of processing" put forward by Craik and Lockhart [1972] is that there are different levels of dealing with memorable material; the *deepest* is the semantic level of processing, which tends to produce the most tenacious retention.) According to Craik, *elaboration* and its multiple synonyms are like depth of processing in that they "describe the operations carried out during encoding." Secondary elaboration as used by Freud, and especially in Cameron's applications, is not limited in occurrence to the time of encoding of events and tends to produce distortions *after* initial registration. In fact, it is difficult to imagine how experimentalists using *mean-*

ingful material could themselves design procedures that might limit elaborations solely to the encoding phase of memory.

William Sargant

Another eclectic theorist who reacted both favorably and unfavorably to psychoanalytic doctrines concerning memory functioning is the British psychiatrist William Sargant. Even more than Cameron, he was influenced by the brief but often successful battlefield psychotherapeutic treatments of World War II. Sargant, in a return to the earliest era of psychoanalysis, argued most strongly for the reality and efficacy of Breuer's "hypnoid state" theory described in Breuer and Freud's *Studies on Hysteria.* There Breuer had theorized that unresolved traumas were especially likely to be registered and retained in the semitrance, sometimes twilight states of consciousness he designated as "hypnoid" (hypnotic) states. In particular, in these states painful experiences are preserved with strong affect because connections are lacking between the sometimes borderline pathological hypnoid states and ordinary states of consciousness. But from time to time hypnoid contents penetrate into more normal states "like unassimilated foreign bodies." In the 1890s Freud had accepted this theory along with his own theory of repression (defense) but later dropped it as a supernumerary hypothesis.

While Sargant argued strongly for the reality and far-reaching importance of hypnoid states, he also fully accepted the concept of repressed memories, and abreaction to these memories was a vital element in obtaining cures. He argued that soldiers suffering from battle neurosis in World War II best relieved their suffering by trying to relive their traumatic experiences and placing them in the "present tense" with appropriate accompanying affect.

> It was this verbalizing and emotional re-creation of a harrowing past experience which both Freud and Breuer had insisted was the essential curative agent of the abreactive process. For it enabled repressed and highly traumatic memories to flood back into the patient's normal stream of consciousness, instead of being isolated and shut off from it, perhaps even totally forgotten, but still existing in the patient's subconscious mind and causing disabling symptoms. (1975, p 4)

Sargant noted that abreactive procedures often produced quick and lasting results, although good results were not achieved if the soldier had been neurotic or deeply depressed before his breakdown.

What causes hypnoid states to occur? Sargant claimed that periods of high stress and intense fatigue were predisposing. Noncombat examples of stressful and enervating emotional phenomena, often partially self-induced, that tend to produce hypnoid states include religious ecstasy and demonic "possession." Physiologically, hypnoid states were equated by Sargant with Pavlov's cerebral *transmarginal or ultraboundary inhibition.* (Sargant, however, was primarily interested in the behavior that accompanies this inhibition, and he noted that Pavlov's explanatory brain physiology was outdated in that it focused exclusively on the cerebral cortex.) Different behaviors are correlated with each of the three phases that Pavlov attributed to transmarginal inhibition. In the first phase, called the *equivalent* phase, when strong stresses occur followed by subsequent fatigue, stressed persons cannot respond differentially to strong and weak stimuli, nor are they able to experience emotions appropriately. When even stronger stresses occur, the second or *paradoxical* phase can occur, in which weak and formerly ineffective stimuli produce more responsiveness than stronger stimuli that, in fact, increase inhibition.

In regard to remembering, Sargant assimilated the occurrence of the "effort paradox"—the harder you try to remember something the less you succeed—to this paradoxical inhibition phase. (In contrast, Dunlap [Chapter 2] found the inefficacy of effort not at all special but part of the usual state of affairs.) A third phase of transmarginal inhibition is the *ultraparadoxical,* wherein conditioned positive responses and behavior suddenly start to switch to negative ones, and negative ones become positive. All these phases of transmarginal inhibition are thought to function as a "protective inhibition," in that stress and fatigue have placed the brain in a position where it can no longer react with normal responsivity. Although the biological inhibition model was developed through Pavlov's experimentation with dogs, Sargant equates transmarginal inhibition with "a state of brain activity which is similar to that seen in human hysteria." In this regard, stress-induced transmarginal inhibition "can produce a marked increase in hysterical suggestibility (or, more rarely, extreme counter-suggestibility) so that the individual becomes susceptible to influences in the environment to which he was formerly immune" (1975, p. 13).

On a behavioral level, as already intimated, Sargant is in almost perfect agreement with the much earlier conclusions of Breuer and Freud that hysterical symptoms can be ameliorated if the patient will accompany his detailed description of the event that provoked the hysterical symptoms with appropriate affect. In other words, cathartic treatment is the therapy of choice. But there is an important emendation to Breuer and Freud's description, a crucial one from the perspective of interest in memory phenomena. The tensional release or abreaction in successful treatment does not always require that patients recall the specific incident that precipitated the breakdown.

> It was often enough to create in them a state of excitement and keep it going until the patient finally collapsed; he might then start to improve very rapidly. Imaginary situations might have to be invented or actual events distorted, especially when the patient, remembering the real experience which had caused the neurosis or reliving it under drugs, had not reached the transmarginal phase of collapse necessary to disrupt his morbid behavior patterns. (Sargant, 1975, pp. 16–17)

In these instances it would appear that memory recovery defers to the shock aspect of treatment by accepting a gilding of the truth, but illustrative examples were also given by Sargant of cases in which true traumatic memories elicited abreaction. None of the memories that Sargant describes are traced to infantile experiences, and he agrees with Breuer that many of the instances of hysterical breakdown and dissociation have nothing to do with sex.

The three theorists discussed in this chapter were each in his own way highly critical of psychoanalysis. Yet each adopted a basic tenet of Freud's treatment of personal memories and elevated it well beyond the uses that Freud had found for it. Thus Alfred Adler asserted that what were claimed as early childhood memories were projections of the present into the past, as well as the past into the present. D. Ewen Cameron believed that secondary elaborations not only invalidated memory accuracy but also, through interaction with other action tendencies, could distort the wider context in which a particular memory was embedded. William Sargant restored the discarded Freud and Breuer concept of hypnoid states with abreaction to a position of great therapeutic importance, while pointing out the tendency for inadvertent hypnoid state induction to lead to undesirable patient indoctrination. Considered together, these avowedly independent (and even idiosyncratic) theorists offer a good illustration of how Freudian concepts, whether accepted or rejected, have for so long been at the center of theorizing about personal memories.

All in all, Sargant is generally critical of developments that occurred in psychoanalysis after the dissolution of Breuer's collaboration with Freud. Traumatic memories are implanted when the brain is in a suggestible hypnoid state. The explanation is found in the occurrence of stressful situations and resulting changes in brain physiology much more than in the extended life history of the individual. An assertion more denigrating to psychoanalysis is that

> if any patient is subjected to repeated abreactions on the couch, as in psycho-
> analysis, and if this occurs over a period of months or years, he often
> becomes increasingly sensitive and suggestible to the therapist's suggestions
> and interpretations of symptoms. A hypnoid state of brain activity may
> result. . . . Quite bizarre interpretations are accepted and false memories
> are believed as facts if they fit in with the analyst's own beliefs. (1977, p. 16)

There is thus some irony (if not theoretical ultraparadox) in that the largely rejected early psychoanalytic doctrine of hypnoid states is thought to be valid and important in short-term therapy and, at the same time, too often unwittingly invoked in the course of long-term treatment as an obstacle to psychotherapeutic success.

MEMORY CONCEPTS: PSYCHOANALYTIC SUMMARIZING TRENDS

A large number of psychoanalytic concepts have been discussed in Chapters 3 through 5 and in the first part of this chapter. Choices have been made regarding which concepts should be represented and which omitted. And in some instances limited evaluations have been given in reference to the generality and importance of a particular concept. In concluding my discussion of psychoanalytic concepts relating to memory, I present a more comprehensive classification. This classification represents my evaluation of current conceptual usefulness, rather than depending on historical or authoritative commentary. A point that cannot be emphasized too often in considering *any psychoanalytic classification* is that autobiographical memory can include both what Freud termed conscious "recollections" and "repetitions" without conscious awareness. Recently the awareness dimension has also been reinstated in academic psychology, with a partially parallel differentiation made between "explicit" and "implicit" memory. With either classification, whether we consider memory without awareness as *repetitions* or as *implicit memory,* the scope of autobiographical memory must include much more than individual self-reports.

Freud's Theorizing

More evidence has accumulated around Freudian theory than most others, and therefore I am more confident in assessing concepts that largely originated with Freud himself than in evaluating post-Freud psychoanalytic doctrines. In the discussion that follows, Freudian concepts are sorted into four categories, each of which is followed by a brief justification. In discussing concepts put forward by more recent psychoanalytic theorists, however, the assessments made are more tentative. The four Freudian concept categories are these: Potentially Fruitful Concepts, Vaguely Defined or Inadequately Stated Concepts, Currently Deemphasized Concepts, and Later Freudian Concepts.

Potentially Fruitful Concepts

Multiple registration
Sensory and motor registration in memory representation and imagery
Deferred understanding
Memory for fantasy vs. real events
Place of association in memory

Both *Multiple registration* and *Sensory and motor registration in memory representation and imagery* deal with possibilities in memory registration, contradicting the common assertion that Freud was concerned solely with forgetting and not with the registration of events. It is the case, however, that Freud seems to have written only one paper concerned exclusively with memory registration, "A Note upon the 'Mystic Writing-Pad' " (1925).[2] *Deferred understanding* (or "action"), in Freud's theorizing, hinged largely on the uprush of new sensations and experiences occurring at times of sexual concern that especially gave rise to sexual reinterpretations—for example, the period of Oedipal conflict resolution and puberty. However, in his Wolf Man case, Freud himself invoked "deferred action" to imply delayed understanding of past events at a still very young age. This view can be contrasted with Piaget's treatment, in which the idea of distortion of retained memories (sometimes resulting in increased content accuracy) occurs throughout childhood as a result of the attainment of new knowledge structures. The deferred understanding concept is now often generalized to mean any memory that is experienced as more painful a considerable time after an event than it was near the time of its occurrence.

Opinions concerning *memory for fantasy vs. real events* vary among psychoanalytic practitioners, and Freud came to no firm conclusions about whether retention of fantasies was different from retention of real events. Perhaps when formulated in regard to infants, the question is not answerable. Although one would suspect differences in retention for older children, no evidence is available, as virtually nothing is known about the course of fantasy retention at any age. Some study of memories of avowed fantasies is needed before the infiltration of fantasies into memories can be understood. Freud's ideas about *place of association in memory* phenomena were by no means limited to the manipulation of the "free association" technique, as is well illustrated earlier in this book (see under "Subjective Descriptions and A Functional Association Memory Model," in Chapter 4) with material drawn from some of Freud's earliest psychoanalytic writings. But even for free associations to be as revelatory and determinative as claimed, they must, in the final analysis, be dependent on more encompassing associative principles. Freud sometimes asserted that he emphasized contiguity as an associative principle, but commentators have remarked that in actuality he made much more use of similarity. Of great interest was the consideration that associations were far from being exclusively verbal. There were also associative and often symbolic sensory, motor, and symptom representations. Where Freud varied most from his turn-of-the-century contemporaries was in describing several converging chains of associations that could lead to a summation or overdetermination of a specific type of action.

Vaguely Defined or Inadequately Stated Concepts

Everything is remembered
Childhood amnesia
Traumatic memories

Everything is remembered. Freud's statements supporting an affirmative answer to the proposition that everything is remembered in some form must be balanced against statements that there are no memories without distortions. When affirmative statements that Freud made late in his life are cited, a reminder should also be given that this affirmation occurred when he was also asserting the much more radical idea of archaic memories. In discussing motivated activity, Freud's frequently expressed formulation of a "kernel of historic truth" discernible in ongoing actions does seem to imply an almost universal expression of memoric content. This phrase is sufficiently vague, however, to still grant that any expressed memoric content is inevitably distorted. In any case, to assume that Freud was using "everything" as a logical universal quantifier is a bit pedantic, since what the word "remembered" can refer to is never defined and is unlikely to be agreed on.

Childhood amnesia. Childhood amnesia, or "infantile amnesia," seems to be a blanket term applied in a much looser way than is commonly supposed. Freud himself qualified the phenomenon, giving variable ages for its appearance and asserting that it did not occur in "primitive" societies. (Here, as elsewhere, Freud's use of the strong term "amnesia" to describe an inability to remember personal happenings does not seem appropriate. One wonders if such a usage was not a carryover from his earlier research on aphasia.) For a time, early childhood amnesia was closely tied to the Oedipal complex and its resolution through the formation of the superego. But this interpretation was weakened by Freud when he suggested that superego repression should not be overemphasized as the concept of organic repression was of equal or greater importance. Kris's interpretation, that only memories with a personal reference were repressed while the preschool child retained other important memories, was an ingenious attempt to preserve part of the original doctrinal force of the childhood amnesia concept. But there is nothing conceptually surprising in the fact that infants progress rapidly in language and motor skills in which remembering is "in the use," while at the same time they can only haphazardly conceptualize memories for events. Recent views emphasize the young child's lack of capability for prolonged retention rather than repressive counterforces.

Traumatic memories. A description of a *single* traumatic incident with a subsequent repressed but disturbing memory often figured prominently in the cases described in the early Breuer and Freud collaboration *Studies on Hysteria*. With the exception of the frequently cited Wolf Man case, later descriptions of such "turning point" instances do not occur. In the monograph on Leonardo da Vinci, in which a psychoanalytic *explication de texte* is applied to a memory recalled as a one-time event, no claim is made that an early amalgamation of several events or several retellings may not have occurred. For Freud, possible amalgamations and retellings did not necessarily detract from the diagnostic significance of the recall. At the least, an important early memory-cum-fantasy can represent a "mnemic symbol" specifying emotional content. With one's earliest memories, Freud's perspective is that one is in the present recovering the past, not as with Adler, that one projects from the present into the past with the selection from the past diagnostic of present interests.

Currently Deemphasized Concepts

Regression and fixation
Recovery of early memories by means of dream analysis
Hypnoid states

Regression and fixation. Kris and others followed up on Freud's concept that frequently a developmental regression with an ensuing fixation at an earlier period of one's life made some childhood memories newly accessible. This explanation can be viewed as a first cousin of the discarded hypnoid state hypotheses, in that one's subjective mental state must be specifically appropriate to the state of the retained memories, and this occurs only under special circumstances. Note also that this is to some extent the converse of some of the theories (other than Freud's) that account for childhood amnesia by finding a *mismatch* between present and earlier states of understanding. Presumably, after regression the enabling state of the individual matches the registration state at the time of the original occurrence. Unfortunately, explanation in terms of a process of regression tends to be applied only after the fact. No independent criteria seem to have been established to certify when regression has occurred. Childhood memories, singly or in groups, can be claimed as recovered either with or without regression.

Recovery of early memories by means of dream analysis. I have previously quoted Freud on the validity of treating a memory disclosed in a dream as the equivalent, and on occasion the superior, of memories recovered by other means. But in Freudian theory, memory content in dreams is of two kinds, those depicting temporary recent events, the so-called day residues, and the less transparent and more disguised memories that originate in early childhood. Nowadays, with interest flagging in the recovery of specific memories, few analysts seem to undertake the double translation from manifest to latent dream content and thence to interpreting such content as representing a much earlier event lived through by the dreamer.

Hypnoid states. Breuer's theory of hypnoid states was pretty much discarded by 1910. Thus it may have seemed odd that I discussed it earlier in this chapter in presenting some of Sargant's ideas. But I believe that the idea of special memory sensitivity at particular times is one that will always be with us. Commonly associated with the idea of a special state, both for registration and recovery of memories, is the imputation that receptivity is greatest when one's condition is more "primitive" and constrained than normal. Thus not only are ecstatic religious experiences and hypnosis likely candidates, but also states of intoxication, fatigue, and, as noted, the presumed reinstatement of childishness brought about by age regression. Also, there seems to be a new willingness to recognize a diagnosis of hysteria, though frequently in the qualified form "hysterical personality." It is not the case, as often intimated a few years ago, that hysteria, like smallpox, can no longer be found. A diagnosis of hysteria manifests as one of its symptoms dissociation, with special proclivities for memory receptivity as well as memory encapsulation. In fact, the first psychoanalytic case, the case of the hysterical and hyperamnesic Anna O., led to Breuer's formulation of the hypnoid state hypothesis.

It is obvious that I do not believe that the three currently "deemphasized concepts" of Freudian theory just discussed have been invalidated. Future novel methodologies may yet return to them some explanatory as well as descriptive power.

Later Freudian Concepts

Aggression as a primary drive
The role of the superego
Preconscious functioning
Defense mechanisms other than repression

An obvious, and in large part noncontroversial, task that Freud's psychoanalytic followers and successors assigned themselves was to elaborate on Freud's later theoretical concepts. Some of these concepts had implications for autobiographical memory, implications that Freud himself had not spelled out. The four concepts described in the paragraphs that follow were introduced in 1920 and after. They are particularly pertinent because they deal with fundamental considerations.

Aggression as a primary drive. I have documented how aggression, which was treated only indirectly in the earlier theory of Freud, came eventually to be seen as a basic concept in formulating the Oedipal situation theoretically and in activating repressions. This explanatory dominance given to aggression was foreshadowed by the motivations behind the parapraxes described earlier in the *Psychopathology of Everyday Life,* where sexual motivations had been explicitly (though apologetically) excluded. Around that time, and for some years later, it was rather lamely asserted that, in any event, aggressive motives were always tied to sexual ones. But modern analysts find aggression everywhere, hiding, distorting, and occasionally disclosing memories, with minimal reference to any sexual linkage.

The role of the superego. The superego, with its dual function of conscience and ego ideal and its dual state of being both conscious and unconscious, remains somewhat enigmatic within the general theory of psychoanalysis. When a role is accorded the superego in memory functioning, it usually is not clear-cut either. Depending on circumstances, the superego can either aid or hinder remembering. On the one hand the stern superego may assist by demanding that memories be produced, while on the other hand the superego, performing the role played by the "censor" in early Freudian theory, blocks unpleasant memories from consciousness. Perhaps some theoretical clarification will come through approaches that do more than lump together all disturbing motives as guilt or anxiety. Here a longstanding point of controversy is the role played by "shame" as distinct from other sources of guilt. An interesting recent attempt to give shame distinctive motive power is found in the theoretical writings of Helen B. Lewis (1981). To the disgust of Freud, the prominent psychologist G. Stanley Hall, Freud's host on his only trip to

America, had much earlier strongly advocated the major importance of shame in successful psychoanalyses.[3]

Preconscious functioning. Along with Freud's structural tripartite division of ego, superego, and id came a growing emphasis on preconscious functioning. Although the distinction between conscious and preconscious had been discussed in *The Interpretation of Dreams* and subsequently, the new identification of preconscious mentation with the ego (and to some extent the superego) required more exact specification of preconscious activity. The ego analysts specifically recognized this possibility with their concept of a conflict-free sphere of ego activity as a ground for preconscious functioning. Both Lawrence Kubie and Ernst Kris emphasized preconscious functioning as a locus of creativity. In memory functioning, Kris hypothesized that, by means of preconscious functioning, memory recovery can often take place in a more gradual way than by the sudden release granted by the lifting of a repression. Such a concept allows memory retrieval, like other learning (or learning-to-learn), to possess a cumulative aspect. Making preconscious mentation a way-station on the road to conscious memory recovery is, in the present state of theory, hard to either verify or contradict. Here Kris's hypothesis that memories that rise no higher than preconscious existence are available to recognition but not to recall could prove useful.

Defense mechanisms other than repression. That repression can act to deny memory contents access to consciousness is an axiom of psychoanalysis. However, under the broad interpretation that Freud gave to repression, other mechanisms—mechanisms ostensibly different from repression as usually defined—also adhere to the criterion of preventing mental contents from becoming conscious. Near the end of Freud's life, Anna Freud (1936) codified the full array of ego defenses. Kris and others pointed out *denial* (or *negation*) and *isolation* as two mechanisms that frequently prevent conscious realization. In this vein, the mechanism of repression was seen as never acting alone except in cases of pure hysteria—which were for a time scarcely recognized as existing. In breaking the monopoly of repression on the forgetting of tendentious material, theorists recognized that there are other claimants besides orthodox defense mechanisms as causes of forgetting.

Over the span of nearly a century of psychoanalytic theorizing, changes in terminology have inevitably taken place. What makes for a good deal of ambiguity is that some of the important early concepts have acquired meanings that extend far beyond their original connotations. A further complication is that some terms can be used either in a narrow sense, close to Freud's original meaning, or in the changed and usually wider sense that has since developed. As noted, in regard to memory phenomena this is particularly the case for the concepts of *screen memories* and *repression*. Another example, cited by Samuel Novey, was that of *acting out,* in which a pejorative implication has largely replaced the original more neutral meaning. And *deferred action* is now being invoked for instances well beyond Freud's usage. There is nothing peculiar to psychoanalysis in this pattern since frequently used concepts from any school of psychology invariably seem to generalize with great rapidity to a host of related phenomena.

Psychoanalytic Conceptions in Regard to
Personal Memory after Freud

Developments since Freud cannot easily be described by identifying the fate of discrete concepts. Instead of taking such an approach, I will summarize what can be considered two opposing trends in theorizing about memory recovery and interpretation. One trend considers memory recovery feasible, often important and pertinent to therapy. I have argued that this is a position close to that held by Freud. But later theorists sympathetic to this persuasion acknowledge additional memory complexities and the need for innovation in memory interpretations that go well beyond Freud's original theories. The opposing trend, to some extent active during Freud's lifetime, lays stress on the practical difficulties and theoretical irrelevance of recovering personal memories. I label this trend "negative" not in a pejorative sense but because it is, in general, pessimistic concerning memory recovery or importance. A theorist can, of course, hold ideas that are congruent with both trends. For this reason, and because the current scene is still open, I prefer to describe these two trends in terms of idea clusters rather than in terms of specific theorists. To conclude, I argue for investigation of the autobiographical memories obtainable in middle and late childhood.

The Negative Trend

In recent years there has been a strong emphasis on the fallibility of memory in general (including sources of distortion commonly studied in academic psychology). The complications inherent in the screen memory concept have been extended to all personal memories. According to one line of reasoning, it is not even of prime importance whether the memory being "covered," or screened, is itself identified and described. What is of greater importance are motivational presuppositions and frameworks that may never have been concretized in specific memories. Undistorted memories of any sort—emotion-laden or otherwise—are seldom obtainable from human beings. Critical factors are found in unconscious fantasies and compulsive and peremptory behaviors. Actual infantile memories may be thoroughly intermixed with these fantasies, which are of a primitive, fixated character saturated with misunderstood body and body-function imagery and magical causation. Determining the memory component of free associations or transference is not paramount, since current modes of acting and defending against anxiety are emphasized. Repression often acts in concert with other mechanisms so that the lifting of repressions is only a minor therapeutic goal compared to a successful analysis of transference. With a weakening of interest in historical causation, aggressive motives seem to be emphasized more than sexual ones that tend to have an infantile basis.

A prominent rationale for ignoring the techniques or modes of memory recovery is the adoption of the hermeneutic perspective, with its emphasis on an exclusively verbal methodology. Major concern is with evaluations of the patient's pieced-together narrative in terms of coherence, cohesiveness, plot-making narrative logic, and other features of story-telling. Although this approach claims somewhat spuriously that the necessity for a narrative end-product is justified by Freud's views about memory, it is unconcerned with "memory as such" in the apparent belief that, for a particular individual, a solely verbal "working-through" process will, in the end, lead to a therapeutically adequate life-story.

Modern analysts accept much of the theory Freud derived from recovering what he believed to be his own and his patients' early memories. Nevertheless, it is not necessary to take this laborious road to obtain therapeutic success; there are alternative therapeutic methods that have a better probability of success with the majority of present-day patients. The recovery of early memories might serve as some verification for psychoanalytic theory, but this process is redundant since the theory is no longer in need of verification. It is therefore quite wasteful and unnecessary to make every patient serve as a test case. In principle, it is not of great importance whether early memories obtained in the psychoanalytic sessions are true or not, as the patient's "sense of conviction" of the validity of the memories incorporated into the interpretation is what is important. Memory reconstructing can more appropriately be manipulated for pragmatic effects and considered as an esthetic experience rather than be viewed as a series of attempts to make true statements about the past. From this standpoint there would seem to be no theoretical objection to the Adlerian practice of regarding early memories as a "projective technique," although the rationale and interpretation of obtained results would be rather different from those advocated by Adler.

The Positive Trend

In large measure what is "positive" is not so much a greater confidence in and dependence on memoric products but the belief in an enlarged range of memory phenomena. Thus on the debit side, there is acceptance that individuals rehearse and condense retained material, telescope earlier contents with later contents, and produce admixtures of fantasy and memory in such a fashion that most items cannot be directly related to originating events. Offsetting this, a wide range of inexact paraphrase in attempted recall is considered basically memoric in origin. This acceptance leads to an interest in a large array of rhetorical and prosodic devices, from metaphor and symbolic expression to synecdoche and synonymy. Recently there has been an emphasis on fitting autobiographical memories into a *pattern* or *narrative structure*. This approach allows logical inferences to be drawn about merely probable past events, even when there is no precise memory of such events. (But when itself suggests, there is some possibility for modification in the structure of the schemes. For example, differentiation of a thought structure can occur when one attempts to understand a new situation. Both assimilation and accommodation are continuously involved in mental processes, but they may be quite unequally represented. When there is a tilt toward the active-imaginative, as in dreams and children's play, assimilative processes are dominant. When there is a tilt toward the passive-realistic, as in imitative behavior and image formation, accommodative processes are dominant. It might be thought that memoric processes would be exclusively accommodative, but some assimilation is always present with accommodation. A particular form of assimilation may even serve memoric functions, namely reproductive assimilation, where young children attain functional mastery through repetition. Nevertheless, it is the accommodative pole that commonly shapes memoric functioning to a greater extent.

For Piaget, ordinary forgetting does not come about through schemes being forgotten. The schemes themselves are the embodiment of what Piaget terms *operatory intelligence,* the potential to perform constructive and transformational actions (real or potential) such as causality, additivity, identity, and transitivity, among others. Usually, concepts embodied in schemes are not forgotten, although infantile schemes are supplanted by developmentally more mature ones. The doctrine of not forgetting important childhood achievements was previously met with in describing Ernst Kris's ideas (see Chapter 5). Unlike Piaget, however, Kris argued that memories with personal content become inaccessible through repression. For several reasons, including what Piaget considered Freud's postulation of a precocious maturity on the part of infants, Piaget finds special memoric treatment on the basis of personal content mistaken. The psychoanalytic accomplishment Piaget finds most praiseworthy is its delineation of infantile and childhood affectivity. Piaget is sympathetic to Freud's claim that early childhood affectivity passes through well-defined stages and yet possesses an underlying continuity. He believes that there is a good complementary fit with his own delineation of childhood stages in attaining a higher-level operatory intelligence propelled by the acquisition of intellectual schemes.

How does childhood forgetting come about according to Piaget? There are two sorts of forgetting, everyday forgetting of concrete facts or events and repression. Piaget takes an interest in the first kind of forgetting only to the extent that it reflects the progressive growth and differential operations of intelligence. More interesting from the present standpoint is Piaget's unexpected acknowledgment that the concept of repression is important, although only in a descriptive sense, since he gives repression a causal mechanism completely different from that assigned by Freud. This must be so, of course, since Piaget neither accepted a separate dynamic unconscious nor made use of association principles. His explanation of repression is bound up with the inherent tendency that schemes have to assimilate one another, whether wholly or in part. Where such assimilation is impossible and schemes are incompatible, they tend to exclude each other. This exclusion is particularly likely with affective schemes, but Piaget has also suggested that intellectual cognitive repressions are also possible. In any case, the dominance of a specific affective scheme with the concomitant exclusion of rival alternative schemes is Piaget's explanation of "Freudian" repression. Lack of awareness in repression does not relate to containment of unconscious stirrings but "derives entirely from this primacy of assimilation which in extreme form limits all accommodation, thereby excluding consciousness of the ego and awareness of the assimilating mechanisms" (1951, p. 205).

Piaget's view of affective retention as in some ways analogous to the idea of a *mémoire affective* was presented in Chapter 2. For Piaget, there is also something like a *logique affective* that regulates the affective schemes, but the basis is immaturity rather than the distinctiveness of affective content. He calls this affective logic a "pre-logic," by which, as he makes clear, he means a rudimentary kind of logic that can give a descriptive account of some of the Freudian representational mechanisms.

> A system of affective schemes is comparable to a system of intellectual schemes, if it is true that they are complementary aspects of a single total reality, the system of schemes of real or virtual actions. It has not been sufficiently emphasized that, in spite of its apparent lack of coherence, symbolic thought contains an element of logic, a pre-logic of a level comparable to intuitive pre-logic except that there is free assimilation and no adaptation. Thus two basic processes "condensation" and "displacement," which according to Freud are constituents of the unconscious symbol, represent on this plane the functional equivalents of the generalisation and abstraction involved in concepts. (1951, p. 210)

Piaget contrasts affective with conceptual logic and finds the former treating only of particulars, and not general concepts. But for very young children there is no difference in their logical treatment of affective and intellectual content. They are incapable of generalizations since their representations occur only by imagining, not by forming concepts. Another form of specificity or logical particularity is noted by Piaget in his claim that the psychoanalytic concept of *identification* is "nearer to a kind of pre-logical participation than to abstract conceptual assimilation" insofar as "the scheme of affective reactions assimilated to feelings connected with the father is more closely related to the particular scheme of this father than is a logical concept to the scheme which gave rise to it" (1951, p. 211). Note that Piaget interprets identification as well as repression in terms of schemes. This is true for other Freudian mechanisms as well, since there is a blanket exclusion of dependence on unconscious personal memories, for "there is always a scheme not merely reduction to unconscious memories."

There remains a major body of evidence attesting to Freudian repression that must be accounted for by any non-Freudian explanation. These are the alleged products of repression, the representational compromise formations and distortions that occur both in dreams and in waking life—in other words, the Freudian symbols. Piaget's point of view is that (unconscious) symbolism acceptance of a plausible narrative becomes paramount, with little or no check on factual validity, such free-ranging, rhetorical constructions become part of the negative trend.)

Dialectical interchange through patient–analyst dialogue can be helpful in eliciting useful memories by joint constructions, an outcome that would not have been possible in the earlier years of psychoanalysis when the analyst was typically less of an interactive participant. It would seem that, in part, the advantage that dialogue has in activating true-to-life, if not literally true, past occurrences is often dependent on the usual superiority of recognition over recall memory. For example, the analyst can bring up aspects of the past that can be either accepted or rejected by the patient without the necessity for the patient to evoke the material. Analysts, however, do not often emphasize this aspect of dialogue. The description of systematic techniques of probing, "cueing," and otherwise elucidating memory contents that can lead to joint constructions are, to a surprising degree, absent from the psychoanalytic literature. Pehaps like hypnosis in former days, such techniques smack too much of the "mechanistic."

Ostensibly on the positive side has been the acknowledgment by some analysts of the incorporation of early memories into the relatively permanent character structure of the individual. At a minimum there is some acceptance that early memories are historically causal. The determination of the actual events making up these memories is so inferential, however, that they can scarcely figure importantly in the analysis of so-called character disorders.

The Present and Future

Although in the past a major theoretical emphasis in psychoanalysis was infantile memory recovery, this is no longer the case. The link between infantile and early childhood repression and resolution of the Oedipal complex has greatly loosened. Thus the theoretical necessity to penetrate the veil of childhood amnesia for crucial incidents is no longer so pressing, particularly since the "amnesia" is not often conceived of as an inescapable developmental deficit. Psychoanalytic case studies, classical and contemporary, are far from being exclusive in the age periods they tap for significant memories. Many useful memories are drawn from the period spanning ages 5 or 6 to 11 or 12. Initially this was the sexually inactive "latent period" in psychoanalysis so that little theoretical significance attached to the memories stemming from the events of this period, practically useful as such memories might be. (Nowadays, of course, no one believes in *latency*.) Even so, memories from this period in Freud's classical case studies were sometimes found to be critical and troublesome enough to be repressed; for example, memories from a younger age could screen unwelcome memories of events that had occurred at an older childhood age. It also seems likely that considerable "deferred action" takes place during this age period well before the onset of puberty. However, psychoanalytic interest in memory recovery during middle and late childhood is strongly discouraged by the theoretical doctrine that memory recovery during this age period is of minimal importance for therapy (see Chapter 10). Autobiographical memory researchers in academic psychology have neglected this childhood period as well.

There are psychoanalytic theorists of various persuasions who have recognized the theoretical claims of later childhood, notably Harry Stack Sullivan and Erik Erikson. Both men in different ways have emphasized the integrative personality synthesis that occurs at this period, sometimes never to be achieved again. Neither Sullivan nor Erikson, however, showed much interest in theorizing about children's personal memories. Study of the organization and systematization of autobiographical memories deriving from the middle and late childhood period is the arena that can most profit from future theorizing and empirical research on the part of both analysts and academicians. Obviously the study of memories recalled part way to adulthood would also aid in elucidating the pathways, narrow and dead-end though some may be, that early preschool memories take before—in some way or other—becoming incorporated into adult retrospection.

7

Developmental
Memory Theories

Theoretical ideas about development of children's personal memories are by
no means monopolized by psychoanalysis and related theories. As to the part
such memories play in the normal socialization of the child, questions arise
that scarcely occur when psychotherapy is the goal. In nonanalytical approaches, however, concepts descriptive of memory functioning tend to be
fragmented and less central to overarching theory. This chapter samples concepts from three important theorists independent of the psychoanalytic tradition: James Mark Baldwin, Jean Piaget, and Pierre Janet.[1]

Psychologist–philosopher James Mark Baldwin emphasized the social nature of early memory formation in the child. Although critical of data from
autobiographical memory as extraneous to his major enterprise of building a
genetic epistemology, Jean Piaget not only gave a trenchant critique of major
Freudian memory (and forgetting) concepts but, of equal importance, sketched
out how his own theory would handle the phenomena Freud describes. Finally,
psychiatrist and psychologist Pierre Janet developed an innovative concept of
memory as a form of social communication by means of recall that is structured
as narrative. A clear distinction should be made between the therapeutic autobiographical life-narratives discussed in Chapter 5 and Janet's "narrative behavior" concept. For Janet, narrative memory is a spontaneous mode of recalling,
not always strictly autobiographical, but at least encompassing personally experienced past events. One tends to reconstruct many events in this narrative or
anecdotal form, which is the form they will have when transmitted to others.

The lives of these three theorists were contemporaneous, although they
were of different generations; in theorizing about children's memory development, Piaget and Janet included some appreciative citation and corrective
emendation of the other's concepts, while Piaget was influenced by Baldwin
in his early theorizing.

Autobiographical Memory in the Developmental Theory of
James Mark Baldwin

In the first decade of this century James Mark Baldwin, who like William
James was both psychologist and philosopher, published extensively on his

theory of knowledge based in considerable part on his ideas about child development. Although Baldwin had founded several experimental psychology laboratories, his most original insights were contained in theoretical hypotheses not bolstered by experimental data. His theoretical ideas about childhood memory were put forward in his formulation of what he was the first to call "genetic epistemology," a term later attached by Piaget to his own copious theorizing. Many of the questions Baldwin posed and attempted to answer are similar to those asked by philosophers, examples of which were given in Chapter 2. The major difference is that, rather than depending on adult introspections, Baldwin, working from his own observations, theorized about how the young child comes to distinguish memory experiences from perceptions and fantasies and what makes the child believe that personal memories are valid. When philosophers ask the same kinds of questions they tend to seem contrived, for they require a false naiveté, a setting aside of knowledge that adults have long possessed. An example of this strained rhetorical approach is given by the philosopher Ludwig Wittgenstein. "Would this situation be conceivable; someone remembers for the first time in his life and says "Yes, now I know what 'remembering' is, what it *feels like* to remember."— How does he know that this feeling is 'remembering?' " Baldwin thought that any meaningful answer must pertain to the cognitive development of the child, not to the adult feigning ignorance.

Baldwin placed heavy emphasis on the child's subjective experiencing since Baldwin, unlike Piaget, stressed the development of the self and self-awareness. In this regard his approach antedates but bears a similarity to the development of the autonomous ego in some later theories of psychoanalysis. Two of the major themes of this book, the subjective experiences associated with having or expressing memories and the development of memory functioning, are exemplified in Baldwin's writings. His memory theorizing mainly concerns itself with the preschool and early school years, although a frustrating aspect of his presentation is that he nowhere identifies the ages at which different behaviors originate. Because of the young ages that are implicated in his descriptions and his special concern with self-consciousness, many of his ideas can be applied to autobiographical memory, even where such a connection is not directly drawn. Indeed, the questions of memory origin that Baldwin asks rarely arise when one is concerned with pedagogical and factual learning at older ages.

What is Baldwin's developmental answer to Wittgenstein's question, what does it feel like to remember? The answer can be considered in two parts. First, there must be an advance in mental functioning adequate to permit memory experiences to occur. For Baldwin, the necessary biologically based precursor of memory was imitative behavior. "The effect of imitation, it is clear, is to make the brain a 'repeating organ,' i.e., to secure the repetitions which on all biological theories the organism must have if it is to develop" (1920, p. 251). The earliest form of imitation is what Baldwin called the "circular reaction," a form of imitation characterized by a muscular reaction that reinstates the same stimulating condition that triggers the reaction in the first place, say a motor movement that continually centers a visual stimulus (in principle an activity not unlike the actions performed in many arcade computer games). Imitation is not subsumed by memory because memory is more consciously representing; memory stems from prior perceptions, whereas imitation is brought about by actions that produce no representations. In memory, although the recalled object is itself absent, appropriate movement reactions come about just the same; early memories are in sense simply more sophisticated "circular reactions."

The second part of Baldwin's answer to Wittgenstein's question would stress the feeling of control involved in memory experiencing. For the young child, perceptions have a degree of "stubbornness" in that they cannot easily be changed. But with a well-formed memory image, there can be some shifting back of the memory image toward the prior perceptual experience. This cannot go all the way, but it can be sufficient to ensure that a memory is not confused with a fantasy. Overall, there is a feeling of manipulability in the memory that is absent in the perception. Baldwin argued that the felt experience of potential memory control is a unique qualitative feeling and not simply a quantitatively weak percept-like experience, as some older philosophers stated. Thus Baldwin claimed to some degree to have categorized the introspective will-o'-the-wisp, the "memory mark."

As noted in Chapter 2 (see under Memory for Emotions), Baldwin believed in the direct retention of emotions and in an associated affective logic. Affects built up from isolated motor tendencies could be grouped and patterned by what he termed "affective generalization." These emotional patterns furnish a basis for designating and communicating about emotions, since emotions, unlike cognitions, lack schematic organization. It is through a projection of these patterns that the child comes to attribute the general form of hope or fear, impulse or desire to others (cf. Sartre's concept of affective empathy in Chapter 2). Emotions and cognitions are not retained and verified in the same way, because cognitions must be preceded by classificatory generalizations while affective experiences are singular and unique. Emotions are immediate while cognitions are mediated. Baldwin adhered to the older sense of recognition as the identification and awareness of memory content as such. Full recognition is only possible for cognitive representations, not affective or conative expressions. Early memories are of entire happenings, but much early progress is made through the individuation of memories and through making them "detachable." Of special interest for autobiographical memory is that social interactions possess priority in retention over either memory of persons or perceptual events.

In most cases, in order to persist, memories must have occasional verification, or at least a possible claim to validity. For cognitions, memories can be verified by (1) perceptual reinstatements; (2) social interchanges, e.g., a child asking his parents about events; and (3) psychical confirmation, mostly by means of additional recalls and memory reexamination. Affective memories can only be verified by the revival of inner experiences, not by perceptual and social confirmations. This is also the only means of confirmation for memories of imagination and memories of other memories. In spite of the presence of more paths to verification, cognitions have numerous sources of memory distortion. For example, the young child has insufficient experience to exclude memories because of grotesque content, and memory and imagination may be mixed together in a context that the child comes to believe solely because of its plausibility. In attempting social confirmation, the child, without intent to deceive, may appropriate the experience of others and merge his own experience with that of others into a larger context. The young child can become "credulous and suggestive to a scandalous degree."

Early in life the distinction for the child between subjective representations and external objects is still indistinct. For this reason the young child does not possess a correct understanding of what should be classed as memory. Representations that can be validated and are instrumentally satisfying to the child, whether perceptions or memories, are grouped together and categorically opposed to other images and memories that were found to be ineffectual, fragmentary, and incapable of validation. *Verified* memories, as well as perceptions, are classed as external, whereas ineffective and fragmentary memories are classed with imagination as internal. It is only later that the child is able to ignore pragmatic utility and group both helpful and extraneous memories together by appreciating their common memoric function. Also, consonant with the theories of Bergson and Ellis presented in Chapter 2, there is the possibility that memory and perception can occur at the same time. Thus an object can be simultaneously perceived and remembered, sometimes leading to confusion about whether one is dealing with a perceived event or a remembered one.

In conclusion, Baldwin's views, a mixture of trends prevalent in his era, are enriched with some unique insights. His sensationistic, introspective analysis resulting in the concepts of a memory mark and an affective logic was typical of the psychology of his time, although these were minority positions. Also current was his linking of repetitive motoric actions to a biologically based reflex, but he was original in viewing motoric actions as the precursors of memory. Typical of the times, he was thoroughly functionalist in outlook; memories must be useful (i.e., at least potentially capable of validation) or they will lapse. Even the child's failures can be functional. For instance, the first separation between internal representations and external objects is abetted by the child's *failed* imitations, since imitative actions and representations do not yield the expected duplication of external objects or events. Although Baldwin might seem old fashioned and occasionally adultomorphic in outlook, he was well ahead of his time in believing that "important questions in epistemology could be elucidated by examining the knowledge origins of the child." (Obtaining empirical data on developmental epistemological questions had to wait for Piaget.) A distinctive feature of Baldwin's theorizing was the strong emphasis he put on the social shaping of cognitive functions. He claimed that memory functioning, through social exchanges, enters into the early classification of the self as distinct from others, the separation of the internal from the external world, and the extent to which the memories of is a general function of early childhood far more pervasive than could be accounted for by repressions. Instead, symbolism constitutes the "elementary form of consciousness of active assimilation."[4] Since so-called unconscious activity is mainly an inability or an ignorance to attain the more complete understanding accruing to full conscious knowledge, Piaget finds the whole concept of censorship particularly mistaken. He even makes bold to suggest that in this case Freud may have the conscious–unconscious relationship backwards. In Piaget's view, Freud found that "censorship is a product of consciousness, and symbolism a product of unconscious associations which elude censorship." Piaget claims the reverse to be more likely, "censorship being merely the expression of the unconscious uncomprehended character of the symbol, and the symbol itself being the result of a beginning of conscious assimilation, i.e., an attempt at comprehension" (p. 191). It should be emphasized that in Piaget's reformulation of Freudian concepts, his objection to the "unconscious" had less to do with the semantic slipperiness of the concept than with an unwillingness to accept the doctrine of two largely independent centers of thought.

Piaget adduces several examples where symbolism extends well beyond repression and conflict situations, for example, hypnagogic imagery that appears in the half-waking state and the occurrence of functional symbols that participate in thought rather than merely fulfilling a representational function (so-called "material" symbols). A more unusual example is the existence of what Piaget terms "transparent" dreams, that is, dreams that are symbolic but whose symbolism is immediately comprehended on waking. This surprisingly introspective argument about occurrences that are unlikely to be met with in children would, Piaget admits, probably not be convincing to Freudians, who could either diagnose a failed case of censorship or claim that such transparent dreams were incompletely interpreted. In any case the argument is symptomatic of the rational stance Piaget assumed against much of Freudian theory.

Several examples of phenomena that Freud attributed to the special nature of the unconscious Piaget explained on the basis of the young child's mode of thinking by means of symbolism. There is nothing unusual about this mode since "it follows the same laws as thought in general, of which it is merely an extreme form, being an extension of symbolic play in the direction of pure assimilation" (p. 212). Examples include images in which a part represents the whole, images in which there are logical contradictions, and images in which a thing represents its opposite. More related to the previous discussion of psychoanalytic views of autobiographical memory are multiple-image encodings, "two distinct images for the same signified object or event."

The surprising extent to which James, Titchener, and Freud invoke association explanations in spite of their wide theoretical differences has been described (in Chapter 2 for James and Titchener and Chapters 3 and 4 for Freud). In contrast, a notable feature of Piaget's theory is that it dispenses with all forms of associationism. Thus it is quite natural that Piaget sees associationism as the major prop in Freud's mistaken theory of memory: "Freud was trained in an atmosphere of classic associationism, and although the technique he invented was such as to make a restatement of the idea of association possible, he remained much too dependent on it" (p. 189). Notwithstanding the grudging admiration Piaget expresses for Freud's ingenuity, Piaget condemns associative explanations, which he finds central to Freud's strategy for maintaining that "the whole of the past is preserved in the unconscious." The correct view for Piaget is that memories are present constructions in which judgments, logical relations, and other aspects of intelligence must intervene. Freud's theory stands convicted of guilt by (the theory of) association.[5]

Piaget's perspective is that "with regard to the spontaneous, non-directed thought which is freed by the technique of psychoanalysis, it is obvious that what are called 'associations' are assimilations. These are affective rather than logical, but are none the less active, which means that construction does take place." Piaget admits that in psychoanalytic practice this change in perspective might not be important, but he claims that there is considerable theoretical gain because "it leads to the essential conclusion that in the analysis of a dream, the 'free associations' of the subject are not confined to the topics and meanings which gave rise to the dream. Of necessity they go beyond the dream and form a new system of assimilations which merely integrate the earlier ones" (p. 190). At first this argument might seem to be a rather narrow one hinging on Piaget's pointing out that the Freudian interpretation of *association* was mistakenly based on a belief in key causal associations. The argument, however, takes on more interest in a hypothetical test experiment proposed by Piaget.

> Instead of a dream, any news item from a paper could be taken as the starting point for "associations." The spontaneous assimilations of the subject would then make him give a symbolic meaning to every detail, as though he were dealing with one of his own dreams. . . . The experiment would definitely prove that it is a question of active assimilations, and not of an automatic associative mechanism making contact with the one that gave rise to the dreams. (p. 190)

As far as is known, the experiment remains unperformed.

The rationale for Piaget's conclusion is straightforward: an individual's system of mental schemes with their assimilative tendencies can be probed equally well regardless of where the system is entered. There is no need to give special pride of place to some thought product deemed to be *relevant*. One is reminded of Freud's own historical progression in giving up relevancy in therapeutic encounters that probed the past, first by dropping hypnotic suggestion, then by discarding the "pressure" method where the patient concentrated on personal difficulties. Piaget goes a step further by claiming that there is no need for initial subject matter produced by the patient; the structure of the individual's schemes is the same from any angle of approach, personal or impersonal.

The assertion that memory content is continuously undergoing reorganization makes assessment of autobiographical memory theoretically difficult from the Piagetian standpoint. In particular, occasions when awareness occurs are a frequently appearing index that a reorganization has taken place. Claiming to be in agreement with the psychoanalyst Erik Erikson, Piaget wrote: An individual's affective present is indeed determined, as Freud showed, by his past, but the past itself is constantly reconstructed by the present. Now, that is profoundly true of cognitive systems, and that is why "becoming conscious" is always in part a reorganization and not simply a translation or an evocation. (1973, pp. 257–258). More analogically, the memory works like a historian who reconstructs the past, in part deductively, on the basis of documents which are always to some extent incomplete. The idea of reorganization through awareness also suggested to Piaget the concept of catharsis. This process of awareness of becoming conscious cognitively recalls what psychoanalysts have described under the name of *catharsis*—simultaneously a "becoming conscious" of affective conflicts and a reorganization which permits them to be overcome. (1973, p. 257)

It is possible to establish a rough chronology of expanding memory competency in terms of Piaget's description of the memory capabilities of the young child. During the first two years of life only recognition can be performed; thus autobiographical memory is not possible since the child is without recall capability. (At this juncture the human infant is no more advanced than other species.) Recognition memory at this early age is not yet dependent on images but rather on schemes of action that can later become images. "The baby recognizes an object or a person insofar as he is able to react to them, and it is these sensory-motor schemes which become memory images . . ." (1951, p. 188). Later on there is a "transposition of active recognition into representative evocation," but this organized memory can only be achieved when speech and systems of concepts exist. In a more speculative vein, Piaget acknowledges that at a very young age (he gives no age range) there is a kind of rudimentary thinking and representation that is consonant with some psychoanalytic descriptions. At this level of thought, representative exemplars are not imagined directly, but "they are assimilated to imaged signifiers of some kind, of whose meaning the subject is unaware" (1951, p. 211). This vague "unconscious" type of thinking occurs only when the assimilation process is completely dominant. It can manifest itself in dreams, certain types of play, and sometimes in completely relaxed thought. At older ages recall memory is added to recognition memory. (Piaget's term is "evocative memory" to indicate a retention capability broader than mere verbal recall.) But, as previously noted, the achievement of some degree of recall memory is not sufficient to establish autobiographical memory competency without an understanding of seriation that can order memories appropriately.

A clear difference between Piaget and other theorists of memory is the importance he places on *reconstructive* memory, not simply as a general description of memory functioning that contrasts active retention with passive retention, but as a specific mode of remembering acquired by children at around the age of four. The order of acquisition of memory modes, to at least a moderate degree of mastery, is recognition, reconstruction, recall. Piaget conceives of the reconstruction mode as primarily a kind of reinstatement by actions that are easy to perform and therefore occurs developmentally prior to recall, with its necessity for the coordination of images to mediate absent objects or events. A four-step scale is given for reconstruction, with a progression from "sensory-motor" imitation to the highest type, actions that form part of representational schemes tied to previous occurrences. A complication in defining reconstruction as a separate memory mode is that material objects have to be present to permit reconstruction to occur. This allows recognition memory to operate to an unknown extent, so that the specific "reconstruction" component is difficult to isolate. Difficulty in evaluation does not detract from Piaget's major point that reconstruction mirrors the order of acquisition, the action (overt or imagined) being performed first, followed by the more difficult activity of scheme formation. Subsequently an image develops from the scheme that can "recall" a memory. But this is a more difficult feat, not simply because it is more "abstract" with no object present but because the original order of acquisition is reversed in that schemes precede actions. Piaget did not work with reconstructive memory at older ages. (It seems a feasible hypothesis that some of the advantage accruing to reconstruction may well disappear when the child subsequently becomes more facile in recall during the age period 8 to 12.)

Age 2 to 5 is the range within which most people date their earliest memory. Empirical results suggest that age $3\frac{1}{2}$ is a good approximation and, interestingly, this age does not seem to vary much as a function of the age of the person who is attempting the recall.[6] Piaget has called the period from 2 to 4 years of age the *preconceptual stage*. During this period the first form of conceptual thought superimposed on "sensory-motor" schemes are the "preconcepts," which are defective as concepts since they are not determinate enough to pertain exactly to either the individual object or the general class. Reasoning also is in an indefinite state, proceeding neither by deduction nor by induction, but "transductively" from instance to instance without regulating guidelines. Typical memories from this period are consonant with this style of thinking in that they are isolated fragments with no continuity, frequently containing strong sensory content. What has often confounded expectations, however, is that strong affect might also be expected, but, in fact, memory content is usually surprisingly neutral in this regard. (Freud's concept of "screen memories" was in part meant to handle this seeming discrepancy.)

The period from age 4 to age 7 or 8 has been designated by Piaget as the *stage of intuitive thought,* a period when imagination and imitative tendencies are maximized. At first, imagination draws heavily on memoric images while yet gaining some freedom from perception. This reproductive imagination or interior imitation expresses itself in symbolic play and drawings. For Piaget, it should be emphasized, the drawings of young children are always attempts at representation. However, Piaget agrees with Baldwin that children are highly suggestible at this period. In part this is owing to their egocentricity, the inability to differentiate their own point of view from that of others. This blurring of point of view is in fact greatest during the years when the child is most imitative. In several ways this period would appear to be favorable for the formation and retention of autobiographical memories, even though, as judged by real-world standards, memory content might not be very accurate. The child is capable of retaining figurative content for scene and event detail, while complex symbolic transformations and operations on mental content have not yet been mastered. At older ages the child can be expected to be more selective in separating essential features from irrelevant detail, but possibly to the detriment of exact, literal retention since many figurative details will be omitted.

Around the age of 7 or 8, at the beginning of what Piaget terms the *concrete operatory stage* (ages 7–8 to 11–12), the child is able to perform seriation tasks adequately. Although such tasks are often nonmemoric in nature, the presumption is that memory ordering is correlated with performance on these tasks. But for adults as well as children, many memories can be approximately ordered by considering only relative dating; that is one can determine accurately which event occurred earlier and which later (or before and after). It is likely, nonetheless, that a reliable narrative pattern cannot be given to memory self-report until the concrete operatory stage is reached. What I am arguing for is that memory for isolated incidents can be well established during the intuitive period but that a consistent chronology from the standpoint of linkages through connected meanings and external dating can only be established later. When objections are made that childhood memories are not "real" because they have been rehearsed and subsequently altered, it is probable that the ordering and narrative structure have been relearned and revised much more than the initial content. As an example, when "coherence" and "consistency" are found in the narratives given by psychoanalytic patients, it is likely that the narrative framework is, to a considerable degree, a product of middle childhood. This need not, however, invalidate the authenticity of the recalled events.

In concluding the discussion of Piaget's theory, three interrelated topics can be highlighted in contrasting his position with Freud's—permanence of memories, memory registration, and repression. Because Piaget believed that early behavior is not maintained by memory but only by actions, even those contents that appear to be memoric must be preserved through usage. The extent to which Freud believed all memories are preserved in unchanged form has been exaggerated, but he did opt for a high degree of permanence. Piaget stressed developmental changes in memory capability that were reflective of the child's changing mental structure. Although Freud acknowledged memory cover-up, disguise, and distortion, the only change that could be considered strictly a developmental advance was the rather special case of "deferred action."

The two theorists differ in terms of the extent to which initial registration or encoding of memories rather than subsequent memoric processes can be held accountable for memory inaccuracies. With Piaget, faulty registration appears to be the dominant error source. His memory experiments are often the vehicle for expressing conceptual inadequacies, though, to be sure, such experiments are not concerned with personal life-events. For Freud, the situation is more complex. With young children there can be multiple registrations of the same event that give both true and false representations. There can be veridical registrations that remain repressed or screened, and there can be registrations in primal repressions that continue to distort later after-repressions. On the other hand, as Piaget also acknowledged, some early retentions can become commingled with ways of acting so that they form permanent character tendencies and are lost to memory.

In briefest compass, repression for Piaget was based on an inevitable process of development in which there was a kind of survival, if not of the fittest mental structure, at least of a *single* mental structure. In contrast, for Freud, repression established a permanent adversarial system between conscious and unconscious that divides, deflects, and rigidifies thinking. (The paradoxical footnote has sometimes been added that repression can frequently be less handicapping, because less adversarial, if it succeeds completely rather than only partially.)

This highly critical critique of Freudian theory was Piaget's view in the late 1940s, but by the 1970s an appreciative and even genial rapprochement was suggested. In his 1973 monograph, Piaget kept his structural explanations intact but allowed that "though conscious awareness is easy in most instances, there are cases where it is opposed by an inhibiting mechanism that we could compare to affective repression (a notion which is one of the great discoveries of Freudian psychoanalysis)" (p. 253).

But more than a tribute was essayed.

> . . . we find ourselves in a situation very comparable to that of affective repression: when a feeling or an impulse finds itself in contradiction with feelings or tendencies of a higher rank (emanating from the superego, etc.) they are then eliminated, through one of two processes, a conscious suppression or an unconscious repression. In the cognitive field we now observe an analogous mechanism, and it is indeed unconscious repression we are dealing with. In effect, the child has not first constructed a conscious hypothesis and then set it aside. He has, on the contrary, avoided a conscious awareness of the schema. That is, he had repressed it from conscious territory before it penetrated there in any conceptualized form (and we will see in time that there is no other possible form in which it might penetrate, since even a mental image refers to a concept). This mechanism of cognitive repression, moreover, is without doubt more general than the area of becoming conscious of actions (that is of sensorimotor schemes). (1973, p. 253)

This description comes close to Freud's later (1915a) definition of repression as not limited to the forceful action of resistances but, in fact, being equated with the broad function of any keeping of material at a distance from consciousness.

It can be noted that this proposed duality of repressions, affective and cognitive, does not really characterize Freudian repression accurately, as Freud's theory is not a theory of direct affective repression but is, as was true for Piaget, primarily a theory of cognitively mediated repression. Freud did, to be sure, emphasize that affects distort cognitive content such as memories that otherwise would remain essentially veridical, whereas Piaget stressed that children have inadequate cognitive means to register, appropriately classify, and subsequently recover memories. It was Piaget's hope for the future that there might be a "general psychology which would bear simultaneously upon the mechanisms discovered by psychoanalysis and upon the cognitive processes." This project might well render unto psychoanalysis the affective side of life, but one could be sure that cognition as described by Piaget would have foremost pride of place.

> Certainly, affectivity or its deprivations may be the cause of acceleration or retardation in cognitive development. Spitz has demonstrated just that in his celebrated analyses. But this does not mean that affect engenders, or even modifies, the cognitive structures, whose necessity remains intrinsic. In fact, the affective and cognitive mechanisms always remain interrelated though distinct, which goes without saying if the first are based on energies and the second on structures. (1973, pp. 260–261)

Narrative Memory According to Pierre Janet

The once-prominent French psychiatric theorist, Pierre Janet, a contemporary of Freud and in some ways a rival, put forward his views concerning personal memory in a series of lectures delivered in 1928. Although not mainly concerned with development, he gave some consideration to memory development, particularly in elaborating his best-known memoric concept, "narrative behavior." Some of the evidence for Janet's views was drawn from Piaget's early empirical studies. At a later date Piaget (Piaget and Inhelder, 1973), in turn, partly allied his idea of "reconstructive memory" with Janet's theoretical stance. There was some exaggeration in Piaget's description of Janet's position in that Janet was said to "assume that all acts of recall are direct reconstructions of material facts." This outlook was cited as antipodal to the theories of Freud and Bergson who, in the view of Piaget, believed that the entire past of an individual was recorded and conserved in the unconscious. Between these extremes, Piaget noted, "every conceivable hypothesis" could find room. Piaget makes it abundantly clear, however, that in the geographical plotting of memory theory his own position is closer to Janet than to Freud.

Janet's position vis-à-vis Freud is a highly critical one. Emphasis is put on synthesis of mental functioning to achieve recall, in contrast to Freud's emphasis on mental conflict that prevents recall. As one somewhat typical example, Janet asserts that we do not fail to recall dreams because of "abominable repressions." Rather, the reason there is little accurate recall of dreams is that dreams are at a level in our mental economy that lacks a facility for memory. We do not know how to make a veridical post-dream recitation because we are simply unable to encode and construct our dream experiences into satisfactory narratives. For similar reasons, accurate personal memory retention is even less likely with young children. Memory functioning demands the ability to deal with mental events at a level of some complexity. Janet points out that the mention of "childhood amnesia" presupposes a person capable of memory. With young children up to the age of 3 or 4, and sometimes with very old people, however, there is an "absence of memory." For this malady Janet coined the term "amnemosynie."

Given the above considerations, it is not surprising that Janet does not believe that the kind of memory performance he is concerned with can be found in animals. Hence Janet states: "the act of memory is a human invention," and it is social since "memory is a social reaction in a condition of absence." For Janet, the origins of memory begin with the descriptions of objects. Humans find it a necessity to attempt to make absent objects present, and in this endeavor they have used signs, gestures, movements, dance, chanting, and the mimicking of objects to encourage the pretense that missing objects continue to persist. Narration is a more advanced form of memory that describes events, not objects. It is less utilitarian than the memory for objects in that it describes events as they were witnessed. Events, much more frequently than objects, are likely to have altered or even to have ceased to exist after the passage of time.

Janet asks why narrative memory with its predilection for inaccuracy has become the dominant form of human memory. The reason, according to Janet, is that there are always two aspects of any human action, the act itself and sentiments and emotions associated with that action, particularly if it was a successful one. The essential goal of retention and remembering is not limited to recounting actions; rather, it is to bring hearers to an experience of the sentiments they themselves would have had if they had been present at the events. Event narration is primarily a social function. The beginning of narrative memory formation can be dated from the occasion when the young child utters what Janet terms the classic phrase of infancy: "I will tell it to mama." The emotional component that is most important to transmit is expectancy. For Janet, *expectancy* is not just an aspect of attention but a pervasive sentiment tinging desires and emotions such as joy, triumph, and hope with a predisposition to believe. At bottom, particularly for the child, the cognitive components of narrative memory play only a strong supporting role for the engendering and transmission of affects.

Obviously Piaget has oversimplified Janet's theoretical position by characterizing him as believing that *all* memory is a total reconstruction. And Piaget has ignored Janet's important emphasis on the social transmission of emotions. Nevertheless, in citing Janet's theory, Piaget does raise an important if unresolved question: To what extent is memory directly imprinted and given back in discrete and largely unchanged form, and to what degree is it reconstructed in terms of "narrative behavior?" Or, alternatively, in popular terminology: Which memories receive only a limited amount of processing and which receive a great deal? Certainly in myriad ways personal memories are a mixture of literal and reconstructed memories. For Piaget, this problem can be further subdivided since there are two major but distinct types of memory reconstructions. One is reconstruction in Janet's sense of narrative behavior; the other is deductive or operatory reconstructions that result from the translation of memory schemes into actual figurative forms (memory schemas). Although it is apparent that Piaget regarded narrative reconstructions as more complex and thoroughgoing than deductive reconstructions, his research efforts stopped short of investigating this level of complexity.

This chapter has described childhood memories in terms of their formation and development. This outlook, considering memories from the child's point of view, contrasts with the dominant perspective in psychoanalysis that considers personal memories primarily from the standpoint of adult recall. The theoretical clash entailed by this shift was most apparent in Piaget's sharp critique of Freud's description of childhood memories that he had based on the analysis of adult patients. Although psychoanalysis, by analysts other than Freud, has undertaken the direct study of children since the 1920's, memory recovery has never played an important role in the analysis of children (see Chapter 10).

Chapters 8 and 9 present an abrupt change from the developmental emphasis of the preceding chapters, insofar as memory functioning is described within naturally occurring social contexts. An emphasis on social-historical memory means that descriptions are at a more global level and memory data are less reliable than that which can be obtained by questioning children or administering psychotherapy. There are compensations for the weakness inherent in dependency on social observations compared to performing controlled experiments, as, for example, enhanced possibilities for the wide generalizability that can occur when the same results repeat themselves across varied natural contexts.

8

Sociological and Historical Perspectives

In considering the complexities of autobiographical memory, the point of view that restricts itself to the study of single individuals at one point in time has definite limitations. Previous chapters have dealt only indirectly with the social interactions between child and parent and between patient and psychotherapist, both societally ordained relationships, and the main concern has been the manner in which social contacts help or hinder individual memoric endeavors. This chapter and the next deal with larger societal perspectives. However they are restricted, out of necessity, to only a limited sampling of theoretical ideas about personal memory in extended temporal contexts. Most of the ideas discussed are meant to supplement concepts and theories already presented.

This chapter enlarges the context of remembering and suggests that disciplines with a broad social base as their purview can challenge and extend current psychological theories about personal memory. In the social realm the disciplines of sociology and history not only afford different perspectives than those provided by traditional psychology, psychotherapy, and philosophy, but they can contribute ideas and theories about forms and expressions of memory that would not naturally occur when the individual is studied in isolation. In the discipline of sociology the views of the French sociologist Maurice Halbwachs, whose emphasis on memory as a central concern was (and is) unusual for a sociologist, are presented in some detail. Sociologists have, of course, made frequent use of psychoanalytic and psychological ideas, but even when adverted to, memory has not been a focus. Several ideas concerning memory put forward by the contemporary American sociologist Edward Shils are described briefly. Shils, while less concerned with memory than Halbwachs, nonetheless conceptualized the intentional and unintentional actions of human memory as crucial to a sociology intimately involved in tracing historical continuity.

In comparing history and memory the focus becomes more precise than with the presentation of sociological views about memory. Though potential topics of interest, neither historical conceptions of memory nor the conceptions of human memory that historians themselves have held are discussed.

Nor is consideration given to determining what critical judgments would be entailed in invoking the frequently mentioned but often vague simile that therapists, or psychologists, or patients themselves must sometimes act like historians. Instead, the discussion focuses on the criteria of validity for historical truth compared with the criteria for memoric truth.

History and personal memory have in common that they both try to determine which facts and events are true. We can if we wish label history as "objective" and memory as "subjective," but these labels are relative at best; there are many parallels and much remains only probable in validating the contents of either. From the wide array of thoughts on this topic presented by historians a number of ideas from the French historian Marc Bloch can be recommended as most pertinent and least arcane. To demonstrate that the problem of truth verification continues at the forefront of historical concern (with resolution to the problem paralleling some recent theorizing in psychoanalysis), an essay by the prominent contemporary American historian William H. McNeill is also considered later in this chapter.

Sociological Descriptions of Memory

It is a truism that personal memory can be influenced by group identifications and currents of social thought. But is it possible to go further and take the sociological dimension as the exclusive explanatory perspective on individual memory? It is this task that the French sociologist Maurice Halbwachs set himself in a book titled *The Collective Memory,* which was published posthumously (1950). This work was a theoretical continuation of a book Halbwachs had written a quarter of a century before titled *The Social Framework of Memory* (*Les Cadres Sociaux de la Mémoire,* 1925). The earlier work, whose point of view was similar to the later one, was discussed at some length by Frederic Bartlett (1932/1961, pp. 294–296). Halbwachs's ideas were recognized by Bartlett as showing that "social organization gives a persistent framework into which all detailed recall must fit," and these ideas were than used as a point of departure for a discussion of whether there is a group memory apart from individual memories. Bartlett was surprisingly open-minded on this question, asserting that "a literal memory of the group cannot, at present at least, be demonstrated. Equally it cannot be disproved, and consequently must not be dogmatically denied" (p. 298). Unfortunately, as pointed out by the anthropologist Mary Douglas in the introduction to the reissue of Halbwachs's 1950 book, Bartlett's discussion seems to have left the mistaken impression among English-speaking psychologists that Halbwachs equated "collective memory" with a "group mind" memory. Halbwachs can somewhat justly be accused of having a single-track perspective on memory phenomena, but his theory definitely did not argue for retention by means of a superordinate "group mind."

Nonetheless, Halbwachs's theory of memory is unique in that it combines dogmatic suppositions and quite ordinary memoric observations with some unusual and potentially valuable insights. It is these insights that I will attempt to highlight in my outline of Halbwachs's leading ideas. Halbwachs was a disciple of the eminent French sociologist Emile Durkheim, who scarcely admitted that the psychological level of analysis, located between the physiological and sociological, was of the slightest use in describing social phenomena. Halbwachs supported Durkheim by producing his theory of "collective memory" in which he took particular pains to contradict Bergson's intuitional approach to memory. Part of the dogmatism in Halbwachs's theorizing comes not by asserting that social influences are prominent in shaping memory content, or that they are the major influence, but that *all* memory content is socially determined. Not even 1 percent of memories are, strictly speaking, individual, since remembrances that one might presume to be "individual" are always at the intersection of collective influences. Similarly, in the temporal dimension he postulates "collective durations as the sole basis of so-called individual memory."

The "wild card" in making collective memory a universal attribute of all memories is Halbwachs's elastic definition of the term *social group*. "When I speak of the individual making use of the group memory, it must be understood that this assistance does not imply the actual presence of group members. I continue under the influence of a group even though I am distant from it. I need only carry in mind whatever enables me to gain the group viewpoint, plunge into its milieu and time and feel in its midst" (p. 118). Thus when a critic suggested that purely individual memories must play a part when a young child is alone and lost, Halbwachs rebutted this assumption by asserting that it is the "familial responses" in the mind of the child that determine the meaning of any memories that are invoked. This test case example, it should be added, is not typical in that Halbwachs's main concern was with the memory of adults. In fairness, it also should be acknowledged that he is, in general, referring to real groups, even if transitory, rather than the retained memoric residue of some previous social encounter. Up to now it would appear that Halbwachs's ideas could not be very promising because many of his conclusions are assumed in his strong premises. But Halbwachs also put forward several ideas that are thought provoking, even provocative, and in some cases open to empirical observation.

One major idea is the postulation of a built-in bias that groups exert on memory content—groups can be familial, social, religious, military, political, etc. "What strikes us about this collective memory, however, is that resemblances are paramount. When it considers its own past, the group feels strongly that it has remained the same and become conscious of its identity throughout time" (p. 85). The meaning of this conclusion is spelled out in greater detail.

> The collective memory is a record of resemblances and, naturally, is convinced that the group remains the same because it focuses attention on the group, whereas what has changed are the group's relations or contacts with other groups. If the group always remains the same, any changes must be

imaginary, and the changes that do occur in the group are transformed into similarities. Their function is to develop the several aspects of one single content—that is, the various fundamental characteristics of the group itself. (1950, pp. 86–87)

In this way the group seeks to maintain its identity. If a sufficiently disruptive event were in fact to occur, then another group would arise with its own collective memory. Halbwachs acknowledges that "the group is undoubtedly under the influence of an illusion when it believes the similarities more important than the differences," but "what is essential is that the features distinguishing it from other groups survive and be imprinted on all its content" (p. 87).

Halbwachs wishes to draw a strong contrast between the collective memory of groups, which favors resemblances, and history, which emphasizes differences. "History is a record of changes" and has little interest in those intervals where few changes occur. Because of this bias, history is discontinuous in its emphasis and encompasses long time-spans so that even slow changes can be detected. History views events from the outside, while the collective memory views the group from within over a time-span usually shorter than a human life. The group is provided with a "self-portrait that unfolds through time, since it is an image of the past, and allows the group to recognize itself through the total succession of images." Memory of distinctive differences is emphasized in the collective memory principally by concentrating on the features that make a particular group distinctive from other similar groups or organizations. Thus a written history of a family representing the collective memory (rather than the historical memory) would have major importance for the kin group itself "only by providing clear proof of its own almost unaltered character, distinctive from all other families."

In a descriptive, subjective vein, waxing somewhat poetic, Halbwachs suggests that groups from which we are long separated, or broken away from, or whose members have died may be recalled with a kind of *blurred unity:* "So much so that we sometimes imagine the oldest remembrances to be the most immediate; or, rather, they are all illuminated in a uniform light, like objects blending together in the twilight" (p. 87). Thus Halbwachs links the "telescoping" of memories, so frequently mentioned in psychoanalytic descriptions, to the similarity predisposition inherent in collective memories, and especially to memories generated by groups at some temporal distance from the rememberer, groups that perhaps no longer even exist.

Elsewhere Halbwachs cautions that the frequent feelings of apparent unity in our remembrances are themselves often illusions that hide multiple influences (causes) acting in concert—"since the remembrance reappears owing to the interweaving of several series of collective thoughts, and since we cannot attribute it to any single one, we imagine it independent and contrast its unity to their multiplicity" (p. 49). But the diversity of memory influences may express itself less by content than by loss of personal control in bringing about memory recurrences. This lack of control manifests itself in the undoubted fact that many personal memories seem to occur by chance rather than by intent. "We must wait for the various systems of waves (in the social milieus where we move mentally or physically) to intersect again and cause that registering apparatus which is our individual consciousness to vibrate the same way it did in the past" (pp. 48–49). Complete determinism for *all* memories is asserted, a more Freudian-then-Freud hypothesis. There are *no* accidental or random memories. "Chance" recalls, i.e., those that are sporadic and uncontrollable, are neither undetermined nor overdetermined but are instead multiply determined beyond human power to discern. And, as just described, this multiplicity is often subjectively masked by an illusion of apparent unity in memory content.

We also possess memories that we ourselves can invoke on command. These memories are "preserved in groups we enter at will and collective thoughts to which we are closely related." Other memories, although collectively determined in origin, are our personal concern alone. These more exclusive possessions tend to lack reliable group supports in that collective influences are intermittent and at a greater distance. Thus the more ostensibly "private" a memory is the more unstable it is. Even with easily controlled memories, there are inevitable differences from one person to another since each personal memory is only one viewpoint derived from the collective memory. In any case, relative ease of accessibility never bears on the question of the collective nature of memory. "It is always necessary to revert to a combination of influences that are social in nature" (p. 48).

Perhaps a bit oddly for a sociologist, Halbwachs reinforces his argument for the collective determination of memory by the use of introspective metaphors. He states that there is a descriptive truth to William James's "stream of consciousness" metaphor. Memory as experienced is, however, in direct opposition to the "stream" since it stops, cross-cuts, shifts, and dams the flow of mental events. A kind of dualism is postulated between the flow of passive perceptions and socially caused, hence memoric, thoughts. We can "distinguish the current of impressions from the current of thought (properly so-called), or memory. The first is rigidly linked to the body, never causes us to go outside ourself, and provides no perspective on the past. The second has its origins and most of its course in the thought of the various groups to which we belong" (p. 126). Just as groups impose on the individual the bias of emphasizing similarities, so also it is the nature of collective memory transmitted to the individual to foster the illusion of "stopped" time.

> Past time (a certain image of time) has to exist immobile in each collective consciousness and endure within given limits, which vary by group. . . . Every group—be it religious, political or economic, family, friends, or acquaintances, even a transient gathering in a salon, auditorium or street—immobilizes time in its own way and imposes on its members the illusion that, in a given duration of a constantly changing world, certain zones have acquired a relative stability and balance in which nothing essentially is altered. (p. 126)

Halbwachs is opposed to a sensational or intuitionist conception of time, since collective time is constituted solely by memoric content. For when we probe the past we find that: "Beyond this moving fringe of time or, more correctly, of collective times, there is nothing more, for the time of the philosophers is an empty form. Time is real only insofar as it has content—that is, insofar as it offers events as material for thought" (pp. 126–127). For Halbwachs, since time can be subdivided in any way whatsoever, every memory event can be assigned a place within it. But the boundaries of group recall are not solely dependent on the temporal dimension. The variation among groups according to how far back their collective memories reach depends both on the degree of group participation that constitutes a given thought and on the age of the group.

Must experienced time be thought of as collective? Are there not obvious exceptions? In an argument (not unlike one by Wittgenstein) Halbwachs considers *pain* as a good example of an experience that would seem to exist in private time yet is subject to a collective time even when it does not relate to any sensational reality. An "objective representation" of a pain is given under any of three contingencies: our pain is caused by a physical action (external or organic); we are only imagining a pain; we think others are experiencing or could experience the same pain. It therefore follows, according to Halbwachs, that "Since that [objective] representation's very character derives from being common to more than one consciousness, since it is collective only to the extent that it is objective, must we not think that our previous concept of the pain (which is all that is retained in the remembrance of it), if not the pain itself, could only be an incomplete and truncated collective representation?" (pp. 96–97). The answer is affirmative for collective time because the memory of a pain is more like other memories than it is like its private sensational onset. It is sufficient for Halbwachs that if we relegate pain to a "common domain and restore its collective and familiar character," we must "discard the hypothesis of purely individual and mutually inaccessible durations" (p. 97). Importantly, the more general conclusion is drawn that if pain and its experienced durations are collective, this must be the case also for other affects, "for affective impressions tend to blossom into collective images and representations" (p. 98).

The most common application of collective time is that it allows events to be dated. Although any simple attempt at dating a personal remembrance may be very approximate, a framework of events can often produce surprising accuracy. Halbwachs gives the example of recalling a trip by the following kind of bracketing: "For instance, it took place before or after the war, when a child, youth, or adult, in the company of a certain friend who was himself a certain age, during a specific season of the year, while engaged in a certain piece of work, or when some famous event was in the news. A series of reflections of this kind very often enables one to substantiate and complete such a remembrance" (p. 98). If nothing else "the fact that it [a memory] belongs to a different period from the other remembrances localizes it after a fashion" (p. 99). Dating a memory may occur either after a memory appears or, more commonly, when we traverse the framework of time and retrieve the image of a past event.

Halbwachs stresses that spatial stability complements temporal immobility in collective retention. This emphasis is, in part, an attempt to refute the exclusive concern with the temporal dimension found in Henri Bergson's theorizing. The spatial dimension is relevant to remembrances in two ways. The first is the focus that the actual physical locating of events gives to memory organization. Collective thought "has the best chance of immobilizing itself and enduring when it concentrates on places, sealing itself within their confines and molding its character to theirs." But collective space, like collective time, has immense variety since "there are as many ways of representing space as there are groups" (p. 156). The second need for spatiality is in imagery. Halbwachs holds that "feelings and reflections, like all other events, have to be situated in some place I have resided or passed by and which is still in existence, . . . it is the spatial image alone that, by reason of its stability, gives us an illusion of not having changed through time and of retrieving the past in the present. But that's how memory is defined. Space alone is stable enough to endure without growing old or losing any of its parts" (p. 157).

Previously it was suggested that Freud's strong theoretical emphasis on the importance of personal memories was well in accord with, if not actually influenced by, his own exceptional memory. Does the same type of putative correlation apply to Halbwachs as an advocate of collective memory to the exclusion of any autonomous "individual" memory? It is not clear what kind of personal memory performance might be thought to be in harmony with a strong belief in collective memory. One guess might be that since it takes a number of years *to socialize* the child, a believer in collective memory might well be a person who had difficulty in eliciting his own earliest memories. In particular, the age at which an earliest memory could be elicited might be older than usual. If we were to reason in this *ad hoc* way, we would not be disappointed in Halbwachs, since by his own report his earliest childhood memory did not occur until the remarkably late age of ten-and-a-half (p. 36).

On the other hand, it could be the case that a person as sensitive to memory nuances as Halbwachs might have set an unusually strict criterion for himself as to what constituted a first memory. The necessity for careful discrimination is acute, because Halbwach's theory suggests that socially determined memories are particularly liable to be confused with social attitudes. This is so because the thesis that memory content is determined by social frameworks implies that there is a built-in indeterminacy as to memoric figure (actual event) and memoric ground (ambient social ideas). Thus the *specific* memoric event does not possess a sharp outline but a smudged chiaroscuro shading. Bartlett captures this idea in commenting on Halbwach's earlier book. "It may be that we have occasion to recall some event or other of our family life which is 'engraven upon our memory.' If we then try to cut out all those traditional ideas and judgments which are a part of the family proper, practically nothing remains. Or rather, try how we will, we cannot make this kind of dissociation. We cannot distinguish, in our remembering of the particular event, between 'the image which has but one place and time' and the notions which reflect in a general way 'our experience of the manner of life of our parents' " (1932/1961, p. 295). Note that there is a kind of rough parallel between the developmental theory previously cited of early childhood memories lost by incorporation in character structure and Halbwachs's theory (as described by Bartlett) that other early memories are badly blurred, if not altogether lost, by reason of their affinities with those social attitudes that, in fact, shape those memories. Both theories stress that many individual memories are irretrievably blended with ongoing actions.

One of the few contemporary sociologists with an interest in the societal functioning of human memory is Edward Shils. In his book *Tradition* (1981), Shils sought for a general theory of "tradition" as it impinges on both the individual and the group. While other scholarly works have examined *specific* traditions in detail, Shils makes an innovative attempt to describe the "nature of tradition" independent of particular content. He gives important consideration to memory among several powerful mechanisms that structure traditions. A strong emphasis is a concern with those memory contents that form a crucial part of one's self-identity. These contents—family, social class, religion, race, etc.—are the result of early indoctrination rather than learning through experience.

> Memory is furnished not only from the recollection of events which the individual has himself experienced but from the memories of others older than himself with whom he associates. From their account of their own experiences, which frequently antedate his own, and from written works at various removes, his image of his "larger self" is brought to include events which occurred both recently and earlier outside his own experiences. Thus, his knowledge of the past is furnished by the history of his family, of his neighborhood, of his city, of his religious community, of his ethnic group, of his nationality, of his country and of the wider culture into which he has been assimilated. (p. 51)

Shils directs our attention to categories that are nearly inescapable for everyone, even though the contents of those categories are rooted in one's prenatal past. He grants that these factual memory contents may not have quite the efficacy possessed by events recalled from personal experience, but they are still potent, not the least reason being their shaping of a category of *pastness*.

> The individual's experiences of his ancestors—his biological ancestors, and the ancestors who were earlier members of the collectivities and aggregates of which he has become a member—usually hold a less salient position in his memory than at least some of the immediate experiences of the individual's own lifetime. Nonetheless, a sensibility to past things and, more deeply, a category of pastness, is nurtured in the mind by all this unwritten and written history which is presented to the person growing into society. (p. 51)

Three aspects of Shils's viewpoint can be particularly noted. Developmentally, one's penumbra of identifications is acquired very early; specific facts, however, are not usually acquired on a single occasion; and, more generally, one's "sense of the past" includes much more than the personally experienced past. Precise accuracy is not demanded, however, since Shils postulates a universal human craving that establishes a "sensibility which is usually content with a very small measure of precision but it requires its objects in the past."

Sociologists have mostly been content to theorize about attitudes, identifications, and sociological variables such as socioeconomic class, while taking for granted the memory functions that undergird these variables. It is instructive to compare Shils's views with those of Halbwachs. Their emphases are different but not contradictory. While Halbwachs claimed that group membership influenced memory in a major way, Shils stressed that society must be constituted by perpetual reenactment guided by memory.

> A society to exist at all must be incessantly reenacted, its communications must repeatedly be resaid. The reenactments and the resayings are guided by what the individual members *remember* about what they themselves said and did before, what they perceive and *remember* of what other persons expect and require of them; they are guided too by what they *remember* is expected and required of them, what they *remember* to be claims which they are entitled to exercise by virtue of particular qualifications such as skill, title, appointment, ownership which are *engrained in their own memory traces,* recorded in writing and in the correspondingly recorded qualifications of others. (italics added; p. 166)

As with Freud, Shils defines memory so broadly that awareness is not required. "Memory is more than the act of recollection by recollecting persons. Memory leaves an objective deposit in tradition. The past does not have to be remembered by all who reenact it; the deposit is carried forward by a continuing train of transmissions and receptions. But to become a tradition, and to remain a tradition, a pattern of assertion or action must have entered into memory" (p. 167). Thus, memory transmission, though neglected in society, Shils considers a constituting principle of any society: ". . . we are in fact saying that a society is more than an instantaneous synchronic phenomenon. It would not be a society if it did not have duration; the mechanisms of reproduction give it the duration which permits it to be defined as a society" (p. 167).

A comparison of the ideas of Halbwachs with Shils also raises a theoretical question about where we draw the boundaries of memory. For Halbwachs and Bartlett, social attitudes are to be differentiated from autobiographical memories. Insofar as early development is concerned, this is not the case for Shils, who emphasizes that we retain attitudes about our identity along with lived memories from our earliest years. The extensive narrative framework of Shils's "larger self," like Ernst Kris's "personal myth," includes both sorts of memory content. Furthermore, to a considerable extent, Shils makes common cause with those phenomenologists who claim "pastness" is a necessary concept by which to orient ourselves and place personal memories in an appropriate context. Halbwachs takes the opposing position that we know the past solely through content; hence his emphasis on the spatial dimension in memory.

Neither similarities nor differences in content origin yield theoretical certainty regarding where we should draw the demarcation line for "memory." Nor should we cast such a wide net that we equate the fact of continued existence with memory. My suggestion is that we study delimited phenomena in the borderlands of memory for their own sake without concern for conceptual labels. A precedent is this regard occurred previously in psychology when the information-processing point of view broke down the categorical distinction between perception and memory for many short-duration cognitive activities.

History and Memory: Some Ways of Comparison

When we consider the past and its assessment, it is natural to turn toward the discipline whose focus is on accurate interpretations of the past. One would not want to press the analogy too far between personal history and professional or "real" history, but some provocative parallels can be drawn. Personal history is, of course, not solely the embodiment of personal memory, but remembrance is the key subjective component. Similarly, the preference of professional history for written documents does not allow it to evade consideration of the frailty of human memory. The particular virtue of the historian is the necessity of taking a stand. The historian does not have the liberty of the skeptical philosopher of doubting all factual claims; the historian must sift the evidence and come to some conclusion. Like the psychotherapist, historians take an external approach to assessing validity, but they have a burden that psychotherapists seldom have (except in training) of always exposing to peer review both the conclusions reached and the reasoning invoked.

I emphasize a few insights about history and its methodological problems made by the French historian Marc Bloch in his short, posthumous and unfinished book *The Historian's Craft*[1] (1953). A major point for Bloch is the impossibility of knowing exactly what an historical event meant and implied at the time of its occurrence. To interpret a past event correctly, we would have to become acquainted with a wide and always partly unknowable swath of the past in addition to the specific historical occurrence under consideration, and still many uncertainties would remain. The center of attention of societies shifts over time, making interpretation difficult. But even more important, what is feasible for historians, and what they are most skilled at doing, is fitting newly obtained facts to current historical theories. The theories are of a different nature than those held by the society under study at the time the events were occurring. Over time, historians' theories also exhibit changes in their focus of interest. Inescapably, it is given to any historian to understand the past only through the present. In fact, sometimes knowledge of the present is more important than historical sensitivity: ". . . the scholar who has no inclination to observe the men, the things or the events around him will perhaps deserve the title, as Pirenne put it, of a useful antiquarian" (pp. 44–45).

Bloch's viewpoint here is not universally accepted. A segment of the American legal profession has suggested that the past can best be understood and interpreted correctly by taking into account the suppositions and beliefs held by the individuals who participated in the events under study. In the most publicized example, in the 1980s United States Attorney General Edwin Meese and others espoused the "doctrine of original intent" in regard to the legal interpretation of the Constitution of the United States. This doctrine implies that, to a considerable extent, it is possible to know what the eighteenth-century framers of the Constitution "had in mind" when that document was written, and that these "intentions" ought to have precedence over subsequent court interpretations. To this theoretical belief, Bloch supplies a cautionary note.

> How then are we to believe that we understand these men, if we study them only in their reactions to circumstances peculiar to a moment? It would be an inadequate test of them, even for that particular moment. A great many potentialities, which might at any instant emerge from concealment, a great many more or less unconscious drives behind individual or collective attitudes, would remain in the shadows. In a unique case the specific elements cannot be differentiated; hence an interpretation cannot be made. (1953, pp. 42–43)

Intensive scholarly study on the part of doctrinal adherents, it has been argued, would overcome all potential difficulties. Nevertheless, this doctrine of "original intent" in the strong form in which it has been advocated as to what facts are obtainable by historical analysis is obviously a clear contradiction of Bloch's viewpoint, and probably that of a majority of historians.[2]

How, then, are we today to feel ourselves continuous with the past? Bloch takes a middle position in answering this question. "With some reason, perhaps, the man of the age of electricity and of the airplane feels himself far removed from his ancestors." Nonetheless, Bloch emphasizes, it is a mistake for modern man to think that the past does not influence him. At a minimum some continuity is given by the fact that undergirding human actions there is a "permanent foundation in human nature and in human society, or the very names of man or society become meaningless." From this conceptual plan, however, the older political theorists and historians, e.g., Niccolo Machiavelli and David Hume, drew too strong a conclusion—there is "at least something which is changeless: that is man." Bloch believed, to the contrary, that the human species cannot remain a constant in history when everything from hygiene and diet to mental climate and modes of perceiving have changed.

Bloch asserts that not only people and theories but also methodological trends change over time. A strong trend in the twentieth century has been the increasing reliance of historians on *indirect* evidence. The information gained from indirect evidence may not always be true, but, according to Bloch, this kind of evidence is valuable because it has "not been specially designed to deceive posterity." This deceptiveness is less often a kind of deliberate falsification than the distortion produced by the climate of opinion and prejudices contemporaneous with the historical event itself. Bloch takes as an example Roman history. Nineteenth-century historians relied almost exclusively on classical Roman historians in constructing their own accounts, but twentieth-century historians supplemented and corrected those accounts with the study of inscriptions, papyri, and coins. Documents are, to be sure, the very stuff of history, but even with them the indirect approach is often valuable. "Because history has tended to make more and more frequent use of unintentional evidence, it can no longer confine itself to weighing the explicit assertion of the documents. It has been necessary to wring from them further confessions which they had never intended to give" (p. 89).

Some parallels in the study of personal memory are evident. Early in this century Freud's probing of memory relied increasingly on indirect methods, going from hypnosis, the pressure method, and concentration on a troubling past event to-be-recalled, to the analysis of free associations and the transference. In Freudian theory, more and more confidence was placed on what Bloch termed "the evidence of witnesses in spite of themselves." Psychoanalysts since Freud's death have tended to criticize and seek alternatives to Freud's belief in the massive retention of early childhood memories in substantially unchanged though often inaccurate form. The usual argument against this doctrine is that it is factually mistaken. But the more subtle argument, similar to Bloch's, is also made that we would have to understand the contextual world of the child if we were to know the meaning of a specific retained event. At a given temporal point we cannot do this adequately for childhood in general, nor for the individual child, and not even for ourselves. Just as society shifts its focus of attention so does the developing individual so that an autobiographical event may acquire a new and expanded meaning only later through Freudian "deferred action" or, as Piaget alleges, through the development of more mature cognitive structures.

A second and related major conclusion for Bloch also touches on the central idea of the meaningful interpretation or patterning of historical facts. From the standpoint of the historian, the descriptions of an important historical event and of its immediately antecedent events are invariably incomplete and inaccurate, but not to the extent that valid interpretations cannot be obtained. "It is only the most immediate antecedent causes which are frequently rendered uncertain by the psychology of evidence" (p. 103). Bloch is explicit that it is for this reason that historians need not be psychologists, even though he gives full credence to the psychologists' findings of frequent memory distortions in witnessing and reporting events. At the same time, he makes the point that when it comes to evaluating past events, historians were ahead of psychologists in taking testimony as a field of study, and just possibly, it is implied, this sustained interest may have endowed historians with some greater expertise. But according to Bloch the chief focus of the two disciplines differs; the psychologist is concerned mainly with distortions of attention and perception, whereas the historian's goal is to understand the meaning of events and not the concrete events themselves.

Important events, Bloch stresses, have complex and multiple causation.

Thus inaccuracies in putatively key events and the events immediately prior to them can to a degree be corrected by an abundance of partially overlapping and redundant evidence. (One is here reminded of Freud's preference that patients *not* record their dreams, since the important topics were always among those that would eventually be remembered.) On this point it is of interest to contrast Bloch's outlook with that of Halbwachs, both of whom stress the actuality of multiple causation in human affairs. Halbwachs stresses that for the individual, multiple causation makes the occurrence of some personal memories appear as chance events, while Bloch emphasizes that in history multiple causation gives good hope for gaining valid understanding. These two viewpoints are only apparently contradictory. Halbwachs is referring to the view of the immediate moment from the inside, the psychological and subjective standpoint. Bloch is concerned with the objective view of the historian from the outside, a scholar who can achieve distance from particular events by taking a long temporal perspective in tracing out movements and trends. History, Bloch assures us, is not afraid of multiple causation, and he quotes Voltaire approvingly: "What is most profound is most certain."

The orientation of many psychoanalysts mirrors some of these ideas from historical studies. In early psychoanalysis, emphasis was put on the recovery of infantile memories, whose recall was resisted but once obtained could be directly understood (a theme of several movies of theoretically laggard Hollywood as late as the 1950s and beyond). In actual practice this sudden cure by means of regaining a traumatic memory did not occur often. More complex therapeutic procedures were necessary. The psychoanalyst and the practitioner of other forms of psychotherapy where the patient history was consequential assigned themselves a theoretical role not unlike the privileged position of the historian. The patient can relate events, some true and some distorted, but only the therapist has the skill to detect the true, discard the false, infer the implied event and weave these events into a pattern encompassing a long timespan in the patient's life. By taking the long perspective, the most probable pattern can be detected, and partially false memories can be made to yield true meanings. Commensurate with Bloch' view is the idea that the memories that are truthfully maintained are at the same time hidden and often presented symbolically, so that only the analyst can give a meaningful and, allowing some latitude, invariant interpretation.

In designating parallels between Bloch's reflections on the "nature and uses of history" and personal memory I would mention several additional ideas. One is concern with the interplay between past and present in the researching and writing of history. In general, Bloch believes that the direction for historical investigation tends to be backward, from the present to the past. The main reason for urging this directionality is that it allows one to proceed from what is relatively clear to what is less clear. There are exceptions; more is known about some earlier periods than some later periods, say the Roman era as compared to the tenth century. But within the period that the historian selects for study it is rare that the most certain anchor of fact will lie in the most remote period. By reading history backwards it is not that effect becomes cause but that light precedes shadow. If one goes back to the most remote period and immediately searches for origins "the beginning or causes of phenomena may turn out to be somewhat imaginary." Furthermore, we need to understand the present to obtain a sufficiently broad vista to understand how the past can be interpreted. The present even with all its unknown biases is what we know best, or at least could know. Bloch adds that it is a cliché to say that we can't understand the present without the past, but it is also necessary to add the point that we can't understand the past without the present—in particular, the past on our own terms, which is all that we are capable of understanding.

In regard to autobiographical memory, because the individual is always rooted in the present, even when striving to recover a memory, such an emphasis on what Bloch calls the "prudently retrogressive method" would seem to be inevitable. However, with those psychological theories and therapies that posit developmental universals, a retrogressive sequence is usually dispensed with. The past is queried directly to give answers for use in the present. Classical psychoanalysis is not alone in this regard; other theories that posit critical developmental periods also tend to focus on development somewhat discontinuously. Events occurring in the time-spans intervening between these periods can largely be omitted. The prudently retrogressive method is, of course, also ignored on those occasions when individuals attempt to recall their earliest memories. Adlerian theory rationalizes such attempts by asserting that reputed memories from one's earliest past where, as Bloch states, "phenomena may turn out to be somewhat imaginary," can be interpreted as an index of current personality trends.

There appears to be good agreement between history and psychology on one aspect of what can make for difficulty in remembering. As Bloch puts it, the most familiar objects or events are those of which it is subsequently most difficult to get accurate descriptions; "familiarity almost always breeds indifference." Since the commonplace is dismissed as unimportant background, it tends to disappear from history. (Bloch gives an example from French history.) An example from American history that is sometimes offered notes that no accurate description exists of how the famous and often mentioned Confederate Civil War battle cry, the "rebel yell," really sounded. Yet only a generation ago veterans of this conflict were still alive.[3]

In academic psychology many textbook examples have been given of frequently performed real-life activities or objects in common use that people can mostly not reproduce or even accurately identify. (Adherents of the psychological learning theories of the 1950s argued: because frequently repeated events could not be well described a law of frequency or exercise was ineffective in the absence of rewards.) In the last few years a particularly popular demonstration has been the inability of students to identify correctly the "true" Lincoln-head penny when drawn in a recognition format with false alternatives. Most people have no firm conviction as to which direction Lincoln's head is facing and what words are inscribed where. This doubtless sensible failure to register and retain nonessentials has its counterpart in autobiographical memory with the added dimension of temporal confusions, e.g., confusions that ensue when near-repetitive events such as the celebration of annual holidays is involved.

The idea that the "fish cannot know water" also has been used to explain why our most intimate feelings and emotions remain so amorphous they cannot be retained or communicated. Philosopher Susan Langer has been particularly eloquent on this point.

> It may seem strange that the most immediate experiences in our lives should be the least recognized, but there is a reason for this apparent paradox, and the reason is precisely their immediacy. They pass unrecorded because they are known without any symbolic mediation, and therefore without conceptual form. We usually have no objectifying images of such experiences to recall and recognize, and we do not often try to convey them in more detail than would be likely to elicit sympathy from other poeple. For that general communication we have words: sad, happy, curious, nauseated, nervous, etc. But each of these words fits a large class of actual events, with practically no detail. (1967, p. 57)

In discriminating the true from the false, Bloch gives special importance to the double-edged role of similarity. He speaks, particularly in regard to historical documents, of "the similarity which vindicates and that which discredits." Documents and historical items in general must be similar to or in the style of better verified items in order to be relevant. At the other extreme, exact similarity between two or more allegedly valuable items spells intentional imitation and even forgery. In history a further reason for discounting the full truth value of documents can be excessive detail and elaboration. Bloch gives the example of medieval chroniclers who, in the guise of first-person reports, presented complete and overly detailed descriptions of events that occurred amidst stress and confusions. These alleged eye-witness reports from memory exceeded the credible bounds of human retention—at least of anyone living today.

Equivalent distinctions can be made in the area of personal memory. It is the exactitude and clarity claimed in the preservation of early childhood memories that many find difficult to accept in Freud's theory. Freud asserted in his early theorizing that the return of memories from which repressions had been lifted could sometimes even provoke surprise in the person experiencing the memory because of the vivid "hallucinatory" qualities of the memories. These memories were suspected of revelatory significance, as indeed were some screen memories, since they were too clear, too "fresh." The need others have found for indirect strategies in deciphering the residues of memory content has led many analysts to doubt whether any childhood memories exist in such mint condition. As previously noted, D. E. Cameron suggested that, although Freud's texts fail to show it in an explicit statement, Freud actually believed in the dual existence of early memories in both an unchanged and a changed state. (Freud's concept of multiple registrations of early life events furnishes important support for Cameron's claim.) Nowadays, however, perfect memory preservation is not often claimed. It has been my hypothesis, nevertheless, that there are some important motivational and conative memories that remain in at least partially recallable form, though without clear cognitive representations, after their formation and calibration by early life events.

Too much precision in recall for too many events on the part of the individual is thought to denote rehearsal and memorization rather than spontaneous recall. Such overlearning in regard to selected personal events makes up an anecdotal part of every autobiographical memory, although it is often the least revealing part. Substantive importance is even more discounted when lengthy word-for-word repetitions reoccur. Indeed, it is a known stratagem of lawyers to ask witnesses for oral repetitions which when too exact suggest practiced rehearsal and therefore collaborative testimony. But exactness of memory is also often noticed and at least implicitly interpreted in social conversations. Too many accurate details in recall, say for precise facts and figures, is thought to indicate a special and therefore non-neutral interest in a topic.

Another kind of similarity is the occurrence of *coincidences* in life events. Bloch says that many historical events have to be determined by a weighing of probabilities, although historical facts are too diverse for the direct application of mathematical probabilities. Some knowledge of mathematical probability might be helpful, however, when it comes to evaluating coincidences. Historical scholars, according to Bloch, are often loathe to admit that coincidences do sometimes occur by chance, certainly more frequently than most people, including historians, tend to think possible.

A related idea when considering the probable is the range of what is considered possible. Because we are all experienced in human social relations and performance potential, such as the capacity of human memory, the range of possibilities is quite narrow; we are realistic! Most people are much less able to draw realistic limits to geographical and scientific possibilities. For example, concepts relating to health and nutrition are notoriously unbounded. In the past this inability to draw limits was even more true than it is today. Bloch gives the example of European travelers during the Middle Ages who gullibly accepted fantastic tales of plants, animals, and topography, while detailing human social relations in terms that we would find wholly acceptable today. Numerous writers have pointed out that the young child, in contrast, is often at sea in locating boundaries for the expectable in human conduct. Thus, as Baldwin stated, what is adopted by the young child as memory content is not excluded by reason of bizarreness.

Exceeding the bounds of the probable has been given as the historical reason for Freud's ultimate rejection of the "seduction hypothesis"—that neuroses, particularly hysteria, had an invariable link to childhood sexual abuse. Hysterias presumably occurred too frequently and in too many varieties for such a monocausal explanation to be true. So runs the received, and on the whole rational, version of psychoanalytic history promulgated by Ernest Jones and others who have put on the historian's hat. This historical interpretation is now under attack, with the alternative interpretation substituted: that Freud's change of mind came about because he gave in to self-serving motives (see Chapter 3). But might an oversimplification be occurring with either interpretation in that a mixture of motives is involved? Bloch thought one of the two besetting sins of historians was that after taking great pains to verify events, they attributed overly simplistic motivations to explain why the events had occurred. This is, of course, a common charge against psychohistorians; perhaps it also applies to the narrower field of psychoanalytic biography—an irony, indeed, when we consider that mixed motives are the centerpiece of psychoanalysis. The other near-universal error that Bloch attributed to historians was that they believe there was more intentional planning before events occur than, in fact, ever took place. (In psychology some applications of theories of decision making to memory retrieval appear to succumb to this temptation.)

Bloch's remarks appear not to have become dated in the light of recent statements on historiography. What is of special interest is that, at the level of stating aims and goals, similar almost interchangeable critiques often obtain for historians and those who theorize about recovering personal memories. A representative statement in this vein is the 1985 American Historical Association presidential address by William H. McNeill. The idea that it is the pattern of events not the individual happening that requires understanding is one that McNeill finds congenial and in the mold of endeavors in natural science. Pattern finding is what historians do, whether they know it or not. However, paralleling statements in psychological apologetics, McNeill notes that the task of the historian is harder than that of the natural scientist because of the "greater complexity of the behavior the historian seeks to understand." He also points out that the most difficult problem in all interpretive pattern recognition of this sort is selecting the essential facts from the clutter of inessential material that must be relegated to the status of background noise. The situation is further complicated by the fact that criteria of "truth" change over time. Nevertheless, McNeill finds that this is a reason for some optimism, since "historians' truths, like those of natural science, evolve across the generations, so that versions of the past acceptable today are superior in scope, range, and accuracy to versions available in earlier times" (1986, p. 19).

McNeill emphasizes the limited and relativistic nature of historical truths by coining the word "mythohistory," which he used as the title of his presidential address. "Eternal and universal truth about human behavior is an unattainable goal, however delectable as an ideal. Truths are what historians achieve when they bend their minds as critically and carefully as they can to the task of making their account of public affairs credible as well as intelligible to an audience that shares enough of their particular outlook and assumptions to accept what they say. The result might best be called mythohistory perhaps (though I do not expect the term to catch on in professional circles), for the same words that constitute truth for some are, and always will be, myth for others, who inherit or embrace different assumptions and organizing concepts about the world" (p. 19). McNeill emphasizes that historians' hopes for obtaining unsullied truths were very high at the end of the nineteenth century. But the then new "scientific history" proved disappointing in this regard, although it was not without beneficial effects. In recent years there has also been a diminishment of expectations in psychoanalysis. One example of the critical reassessment that is taking place involves denial of the possibility of recovering theoretically useful early memories. Perhaps the recency of this disenchantment accounts for an outlook calling for a number of retrenchments. In contrast, in spite of admitted limitations, McNeill shuns any false modesty for the history profession: "Pattern recognition of the sort historians engage in is the chef d'oeuvre of human intelligence."

Reference to the "mythological," with its ambivalence and possibility of combining truth and error, occurs frequently in psychoanalytic writings. During the early 1960s, in the first flush of enthusiasm over the newly minted discipline of psychohistory, it was claimed that psychoanalysis had the special virtue of eliminating the mythological. "Freud's philosophy of history is a powerful searchlight turned on the tunnel of human development, both individual and social . . . it marks in the best sense of that word an *historical* rather than a *mythical* explanation of man's past; and that, after all, is the triumphal point to which all explanation called 'historical' seeks to raise itself" (Mazlish, 1963, p. 12). Some years before, however, Freud, in his letter of reply (Freud, 1933b) to the question "Why war?" put by Einstein in a letter to Freud, had taken a contrary tack in suggesting that not only psychoanalysis but all other scientific theories are in the last analysis only a form of myth. "It may perhaps seems to you that our theories are a kind of mythology. . . . But does not every science come in the end to a kind of mythology?"

Conceptual Summary

In Halbwachs's view all memory is collective memory owing to the influence of group membership, e.g., family, religion, vocation, etc., and group identifications.[4] Groups exert a built-in bias on memory contents in that any group feels strongly that it has remained the same, unaffected by the passage of time. To maintain this illusion and foster group identity, groups emphasize similarities at the expense of differences, with particular emphasis on what distinguishes them from other groups. History, which views events from the outside, has the opposite bias. It emphasizes differences. Halbwachs says that memories stemming from groups now nonexistent or occurring in a now distant past may sometimes be recalled in a telescopic fashion with a feeling of "blurred unity." Other feelings of apparent unity in our remembrances are even more illusory because they mask multiple influences. Regardless of subjective feelings, loss of intentional control is often a clue that converging series of thoughts are at work, as is apparent randomness in recall. Memories that are private in nature are more unstable than others because they lack reliable group supports, but they nonetheless possess a certain collective character.

For Halbwachs, James's "stream of consciousness" refers to a flow of passive perceptions that can be cut across and shut off by memories, leading to the illusion of "stopped time." This illusion, fostered by every social group in its own way, imposes the feeling of suspended duration on the members participating in a group. Degree of group participation is a variable in recall, as is the time elapsed since an event occurred. But time itself is collective and constituted by memory contents. As a test of the limits of collectivity, Halbwachs argues that remembered *pain* occurs in collective time rather than private time because the objective representation of pain is a collective representation, though truncated and incomplete. The memory of a pain is more like other memories than it is like the originating sensation. For like reasons, pleasurable as well as disagreeable affects, are also considered to be collective in nature. Collective time is involved in dating events, which is usually performed by bracketing known remembrances. Collective space, because of its localization possibilities and stability, aids in the retention of imagery even for feelings and reflections. Halbwachs is sensitive to the possibility that specific memories can become confused with social attitudes acquired from one's family.

For Shils not only early indoctrination but also things that one is "born into," such as ethnicity, religion, and nationality, are inescapable and produce memories, although no specific personal experience is recalled. These formants of personal identity help shape a "sense of the past" for every individual. A penumbra of information is acquired through early multiple reiterations and helps each person construct what Shils terms the "larger self." Shils finds consideration of memory important for sociology because the existence of society requires perpetual reenactment, particularly through the carrying forward of traditions, which as assertions or actions can only be maintained by memory.

Bloch is concerned with the method and goals of professional historians. The modern historian's understanding both of facts and theories and of methodological trends differs from that of historians of previous generations; even human nature is not constant but changes over time. It seems doubtful that a concept such as the "doctrine of original intent" in regard to the Constitution of the United States (i.e., the concept that Constitutional interpretations should to a great extent be based on the authors' intentions and societal understanding at the time of authorship) would be upheld by any historian of Bloch's persuasion, since adequate knowledge of this sort is not recoverable.

In the twentieth century historians have put great emphasis on indirect evidence as more objective for present historical concerns than interpretations contemporary with past happenings. These older interpretations were formed in a climate of opinion and prejudice peculiar to their own times; they were inevitably limited and were partially mistaken, even when there was no intent to deceive. A parallel can be found in psychoanalytic theory which, as it developed, came to rely more and more on indirect memory representations. According to Bloch, that psychologists demonstrate faulty witnessing and the unreliability of memory testimony need not unduly worry historians, because psychologists are concerned with distortions of attention and perception in relation to perceptual memory, while the historians' task is to understand the meaning of events, not their concrete representations. Understanding meaning is abetted rather than hindered by the complication of multiple causation of events.

Other comparisons can be drawn between Bloch's ideas and the recovery of veridical memories. History, like psychology, finds that the most familiar objects or events are the ones most apt to disappear from consciousness since "familiarity breeds indifference." In philosopher Susan Langer's view, a major reason for a similar inaccuracy in retention of intimate personal feelings is that the immediacy of familiar events allows for no symbolic mediation; hence these occurrences assume no specific symbolic form that can be remembered or communicated. Frequently, the historian works in progression from what is factually clearer to what is less clear, which means traversing a temporal sequence from the present to the past. This procedure can be somewhat abridged by psychotherapists, for if they posit developmental universals, it is less important to trace an unbroken retrogressive sequence. In the attempt to recover autobiographical memories in psychotherapy, backward sequential searches are seldom undertaken. Rather, certain meaningful childhood memories or remembered fantasies are directly sought.

Exactitude in remembering can discredit content as representing a practiced performance or well-learned anecdote. Bloch thinks that historians underestimate the frequency of the type of similarity generally seen as "coincidence." For this reason, wrongful discrediting of true coincidences sometimes take place. Historians also evaluate whether an event is in the range of likely occurrences. Travelers in the Middle Ages were quite gullible in believing absurdities when events were outside their range of experience. The same thing can happen to today's young children when they assess which of their memories pertain to their own experience. The assessment of normal likelihood can also enter into theoretical changes as part of the estimation of the validity of events. According to Bloch, the historian fails most frequently by oversimplifying motivations and overestimating the amount of pre-event planning. Perhaps psychologists do the same.

Additional parallels between the interpretation of historical facts and the interpretation of personal memories can be based on the ideas of historian McNeill. A good example is the claim by psychotherapists that personal memories, though often individually indeterminate, can nevertheless be fitted into useful behavioral patterns. McNeill says: "Pattern finding is what historians do whether they know it or not." The most difficult problem is selecting the essential from an indefinite multitude of facts. A preeminent complication is that, just as with natural science, truth criteria change over time. Even though contemporary truth criteria for history are superior to those of the past, McNeill emphasizes the limited and relativistic nature of current historical "patterns" by calling them "mythohistory." Since historians and their audiences must share some common basic assumptions, at any point in time there are no truth criteria acceptable to everyone. Some have seen psychoanalysis as a tool to separate history from myth, but Freud himself believed otherwise, suggesting that every science in the last analysis is a "kind of mythology."

9

Memory Transmission
and Cultivation

This chapter continues the emphasis of the previous chapter on the social aspects of memory. The central focus is the transmission of memories— communication within society that is linked and interpreted in different ways by the retention capabilities of interacting individuals. Societal contexts are far broader, more representative, and less artificial than the laboratory experiments and psychotherapeutic inteviews that have been central to memory theorizing. In the past, memoric factors in societal interchanges have more often been assumed than studied by humanists and social scientists, but interest in formal study has been increasing in the latter half of the twentieth century. My selection of topics is intended to demonstrate the diversity of problems and theories that have been discussed within and between a variety of academic disciplines that ordinarily have minimal communication with each other. Overall, by displaying how memory functions, we learn to some extent *what memory is*.

Problems and possibilities in the transmission of memories can be considered in some detail by describing ideas arising from the study of nonliterate societies. The anthropologist looks at the few such societies in today's world, while the classicist studies the functions of human memory in the ancient world and "survivals" from the past in today's world. From pedagogy to jokes and anecdotes, there are many messages in today's "advanced" world that are transmitted orally, and every literate person starts life by living in an oral culture. As part of their investigation of the shaping of the present by the past, oral historians and folklorists have recently alerted us to a variety of memory-transmitted functions in contemporary societies. Even psychologists have contributed their mite by studying repeated memory recalls in laboratory settings. All these methods of analysis have some value because they seek more than descriptions of "lawful" functional relations that hold good only under highly artificial conditions. The results, however, can sometimes appear too information-centered, devoid of those emotional shadings that lead us at times to cherish our memories. I attempt to fill in this omission by concluding the chapter with a short discussion of that emotionally double-edged product of memories we term "nostalgia."

Oral Tradition and Oral History

Some approaches to history relate the capabilities and limitations of the individual human memory more directly to information production than ordinary historical studies do. One such approach is the scholarly study of *oral tradition* and the diverse techniques of personal interviewing about past events that have collectively been called *oral history*. It is ironic that, just as societies that are dependent primarily on oral traditions have all but disappeared, the study of oral tradition as a process in its own right has come in for much scholarly attention. The case for the study of oral traditions does not rest just on the current existence of a few totally nonliterate soceities. As recently as the nineteenth century all societies, though many were partially literate, depended strongly on oral traditions, and considerable dependence on oral traditions still occurs in the majority of third-world countries.

Anthrolopogist Jan Vansina, an authority in the field of *oral tradition,* defines it as the study of oral verbal messages that are reported statements from the past that derive from previous generations. Since individuals from at least two generations must be involved, concern with current information dispersed through gossip and rumor is excluded from study. At the same time it is *not* a requirement that an oral tradition pertain to past events. Vansina believes that all memory is collective, and that memories transmitted through oral traditions are especially so; he mentions specifically that Halbwachs's thesis of a "collective memory" is completely justified. Furthermore, Vansina states, "the memory of oral tradition is more dynamic at all times than individual memory." Changes come about constantly through new input and reorganizations. But oral traditions, above all, have the vulnerability that items once lost are lost forever. Especially likely to be forgotten are events that are repeated, since there is insufficient individualization to distinguish separate events that bear a similarity to each other.

Various definitions have been given for *oral history,* depending on whether methodology or retained subject matter is stressed. In Vansina's classification oral history concentrates on relatively recent events, those occurring within the lifetime of the individual informant. In actual practice there is another way that oral history sets itself apart from oral tradition. Since oral history informants are often chosen for achieving some eminence or for knowing events from the distant past, they tend to be well along in years, but this is less the case in assessing oral traditions. (It should be noted that Vansina's definitions of oral tradition and oral history are far from being agreed upon by all scholars in these fields.)

Vansina gives a concrete example of how interpretation differs depending on whether trans-generational oral tradition or same-generation oral history is involved. The example pertains to the findings of *separate but similar descriptions* about the same past event. Vansina reasons that since *oral history* deals with the relatively recent past, descriptions must stem from narrative sources that have not yet become standardized. Insofar as divergent descriptions are overlapping, they can be viewed as confirming, since the sources are at least semi-independent. But with *oral tradition* the case is otherwise. Because of the time-span involved in cross-generational transmissions, similarities in descriptions cannot be interpreted as confirming. Instead, such agreement indicates that the various descriptions derive from a common source. Vansina cites a Biblical example of oral tradition, stating that it is probable that the first three synoptic gospels in the New Testament (and some parts of the gospel of John) stem from "one single oral milieu."

The problem of chronological dating is also rather different in oral history than it is in the study of oral traditions. A number of insights into the problem of event dating are given by oral historians Barbara Allen and Lynwood Montell in their book *From Memory to History: Using Oral Sources in Local Historical Research* (1981). Dates are most frequently associated with personal episodes in the informant's life. Some dates given in this fashion are surprisingly accurate, although others are dismissed as "before my time." Almost invariably the chronological order is scrambled. Commonly, instead of presenting events in linear order informants focus on a topic and then "talk around it," e.g., by relating a series of stories. The crucial order to be preserved is the order that lends narrative drama to the telling. Event dating for main occurrences is often accurate although given out of chronological order.

In *oral-tradition* dating, Vansina notes a specific type of error, a "floating gap," that exists nearly everywhere given the following condition.

> There are many accounts for very recent times, tapering off as one goes farther back until one reaches times or origin for which, once again, there are many accounts. This profile has been compared to an hourglass. At the junction of times of origin and the very sparse subsequent records, there usually is a chronological gap. It is called "floating" because over time it tends to advance towards the present, that is, the oldest accounts of later times tend to be forgotten or else amalgamated with later or earlier materials. (pp. 168–69)

In considering personal memory, one situation in which a "floating gap" could be sought is the instance where repetitive events occur year after year in only slightly changed form, say annual family celebrations of holidays, like Thanksgiving. Admittedly, this is only an analogue pertaining to individual remembering of what is a group phenomenon in the cross-generational time spans of oral tradition. Two questions would be pertinent. Is the hourglass configuration found, indicating that relatively early and quite recent memories are best retained? (From the standpoint of academic psychology, these would be chronological primacy and recency effects.) Assuming this result, does the memory gap "float," i.e., does it track recent holidays with the result that near-term holiday memories consistently go back only three or four years?

All information is not acquired with the same degree of concern about ultimate retention. Some ideas and descriptions are intentionally learned as "memorized speech" and therefore are retained more exactly than information that has not been overtly rehearsed. But, of course, individuals forget and the wording of all remembered material varies over time.

Historically, special linguistic forms have acted as mnemonic aids to retention. For example, the lyrics of songs are usually well retained because the melody serves as a mnemonic device. Because poetry and other forms of set speech are composed they have a definite date of origin, unlike some other forms transmitted by oral tradition. From various extant versions of a given composition it is therefore possible to reconstruct the hypothetical original wording—the so-called archetype—in the same way that is done for a written composition whose original has been lost. Vansina acknowledges epic poems as an interesting exception. They will be treated in some detail in the next section.

David Henige, author of *Oral Historiography* (1983), is somewhat less sanguine than Vansina about the scholar's ability to extract useful information from oral traditions. A chief caution has to do with the nature of societies that give major importance to oral forms of expression. Oral disseminators frequently tend to act as advocates and exhorters because of the innate instability of many of these societies. "Social, economic, and political relationships in oral societies are necessarily in flux since there is no opportunity to categorize them by referring to an accessible fixed body of law. Instead, social equilibrium is pursued by means of constant mediation among interest groups" (1983, p. 78).

Another complication is that in oral cultures the presenting of oral traditions is often part of a performance in which variation is permitted in the text, "for the essence of oral art is the complementary relationship between the artist and his listeners and there is rarely any desire to allow a text to constrain this relationship," even when the audience is but one person. The text cannot safely be isolated from its social setting. Henige contrasts this attitude with that of societies that depend on the written word (such as our own) where "if the performers depart from the text, all know it and seldom approve because the text is regarded as inviolate." In a review of Henige's book a sharp rejoinder is given by Barbara Allen (1984), who claims that *folklorists* (Henige was a bibliographer of African studies) would be able to deal adequately with the problems he raises—both in recognizing "the distinctions that native narrators would be likely to make between traditional fictive narrative and historical narrative" and in assessing "the historical usefulness of personal experience narratives that appear to be polished items in a narrator's repertoire."

Justifications supporting the value and validity of the often rather haphazard procedures used by oral historians in gathering oral history protocols can come surprisingly close to the procedural rationales enunciated by contemporary psychotherapists. In a chapter entitled "Submerged Forms of Historical Truth," Allen and Montell make the case for emphasizing features other than surface textual meanings. "The truth in orally communicated history does not always lie in its factual accuracy. Local historians should look for underlying truths contained in values, attitudes, beliefs, and feelings, as expressed orally in exaggerations, distortions, and seeming contradictions of historical fact. What we *believe* happened is often as important as what actually happened, for people think, act, and react in accordance with what they believe to be true" (p. 89). (If this point of view, with its emphasis on stylistic and prosodic features, prevails in oral history, technological obsolescence appears imminent. Soon the limited tape-recorder must give way to the richer video-recorder, and oral history itself will become audiovisual history.)

Oral Interpretation and Oral Culture

In the study of oral tradition as a distinctive ethos some of the seminal ideas have come from classical and literary scholars. They have put particular emphasis on the concept of "oral culture" as playing a key role in shaping the literature of the past. And they have not hesitated to discuss the ways and means in which mnemonic elements have tailored and maintained these *unwritten* "literatures." Since individuals who lack literacy must "hold in the head" their accumulated lore and wisdom, there is a clear comparison with autobiographical memory, where content is seldom committed to writing. Classical literary theorists have also been more concerned than anthropologists with finding carryovers from oral cultures of the past, not only in literature but also more generally in many sorts of communicative activities.

The basic starting point of this oral interpretation movement was the collaborative research of Milman Parry and his student Alfred Lord, beginning in the 1920s and 1930s. They investigated epic narrative poetry which has a flexibility in wording that sets it apart from other forms of poetry. Their work established for most scholars that the *Iliad* and *Odyssey* of Homer were products of a purely oral culture. Only many centuries later were these masterpieces put into written form. What is of prime interest here is that in Yugoslavia in the 1930s Parry and Lord were able to locate and study living bards (usually self-accompanied on a simple stringed instrument) who were able to recite long cycles of epic narrative poetry indigenous to their culture. These performers were thought to be in the bardic tradition of Homer. Intensive study was made of these performers, including the expressive and mnemonic aspects of their techniques, as documented in Lord's *The Singer of Tales* (1960).

Verbatim memorization and practice by repetition were *not* part of the bardic technique. Instead, the approach to learning was by way of *formulas*, in that the same groups of words were "regularly employed under the same metrical conditions to express a given essential idea." No bard used all formulas or exactly the same ones used by someone else. In addition, a large but limited number of traditional *themes* that referred to the "repeated incidents and descriptive passages" in the narratives were part of the bardic repertoire. Taken in combination, these formulas and themes created patterns that could describe every likely situation in an heroic epic. Lord said of the individual bard: "His art consists not so much in learning through repetition the time-worn formulas as in the ability to compass and recompass the phrases for the idea of the moment on the pattern established by the basic formulas . . . we are dealing with a particular and distinctive process in which oral learning, oral composition, and oral transmission almost merge" (p. 4). It is evident that schemas, as discussed in Chapter 7, are central to the performance of these narratives. (Schemas are purely at the level of narrative description rather than transformative action, as with Piaget's theory.)

What are some implications of bardic performance for understanding personal memory? One peculiarity is that new narratives are learned from a model that is itself evanescent. There is "no idea of a fixed model text to serve as his [the singer's] guide, every time he hears a song sung it is different." Therefore, there is no original version that can be reassembled by diligent effort. And, "it follows then, that we cannot correctly speak of a 'variant' since there is no original to be varied!" In Lord's view, it would also be a mistake to think that a hypothesized ideal form would have meaning. At the same time, "it cannot be said that 'anything goes.' Nor are there changes due in the ordinary sense to failure of a fixed text. . . ." To talk about paraphrase is also irrelevant since synonymy is not definable. But key elements have been retained even though, as Lord describes the outcome, what is retained is in a state of "fluid variation."

It is worth considering that, apart from the performance skills involved, the singer's situation might represent an analogue of what can occur fairly frequently in personal memory. What is innovative in such an analogy is that each personal memory is not necessarily based on an original counterpart event. Consider that the lived-through past is both complex and continuous, beyond human capability to register. Thus there are numerous limited sequences of varying content that can well represent past actions through time. Such a view would make of memory recollections a sampling procedure, for which, as with oral epic poems, multiple interpretations are possible. Personal style can play a role, however, insofar as segments of the past can be reconstructed by means of those formulas and themes (stereotypes and concepts) available to the individual rememberer. This concept of remembering (or reproducing), based on lack of text fixity, is not only far from the laboratory but also far from the implicit psychotherapeutic model of attempted veridical retention modified by distorting factors (e.g., condensation, telescoping, dissociation). I would, however, reinforce a previous strongly emphasized point; alternative memory narratives, unlike multiple versions of bardic tale-telling, are not all equally valid. A variety of accounts can be given, but truth to what happened is the acid test, even where truth measurement is inexact.

Lord describes an unexpected finding that sets bardic performance apart from ordinary verbatim memorization.

> Literates are usually surprised to learn that the bard planning to retell the story he has heard only once wants to wait a day or so before he himself recites it. In memorizing a written text, postponing recitation generally weakens it overall. An oral poet is not working with a text or in a textual frame-

work. He needs time to let the story sink into his own story of themes and formulas, time to 'get with' the story. In recalling and retelling the story, he has not in any literal sense 'memorized' its metrical rendition from the version of the other singer" (p. 60).

I would suggest that with many personal memories, particularly where events and personages are somewhat novel, a lapse of some days can also bring more coherence.

Berkeley Peabody, a student of Lord's, has carried the memoric analysis of epic bards further and added pertinent glosses to Lord's findings in his book, *The Winged Word* (1975). Peabody enlarges on Lord's statement that oral composition is a "technique of remembering rather than memorization" by concluding: " 'Remembering,' both conscious and subconscious, is no more rigorous or deliberate a process than recalling where one was the day before. 'Memorization,' the deliberate act of fixing information in memory, is not needed or found in oral traditions" (p. 430). In other words, oral composition is akin to autobiographical memory. Furthermore, Peabody says that to claim "memorization" is necessary would itself, though an erroneous assertion, illustrate the way in which oral composition functions.

> The person who insists that memorization must be a feature of oral tradi-
> tions unwittingly demonstrates the very mechanisms by which oral composi-
> tion works. That person will deny he memorized his explanation. He will say
> that there is no other mechanism that makes sense, this is not true but it
> illustrates the traditional mechanism: a situation that requires action for
> which only one solution is known to exist. Oral composition sets up a run-
> ning chain of associations that requires action after action for each of which
> only one or two viable possibilities exist in the singer's experience. (p. 430)

It is Peabody's contention that in one way at least the bardic oral tradition is not like a sizeable sector of autobiographical memory, which can be the object of *intentional* recovery searches. Oral tradition, in contrast, is con- strued by Peabody as a form of psychological conditioning. In this regard, Peabody acknowledged that B. F. Skinner gained renown as the foremost "controversial spokesman against the priority of conscious conceptualization and intention" who advocated the view that much thought was simply "condi- tioned behavior." "Whether this position supports the human ego or not, the evidence suggests that in oral tradition this is largely so" (p. 427). This state- ment is a bit unexpected, since "memory" in any of its usual usages along with terms related to "information processing" are excluded from the Skinnerian lexicon. (See Chapter 10.) Peabody's characterization of bardic processes is nonetheless surprisingly consistent with the Skinnerian viewpoint. Not only intentionality is played down but also narrative, which is found to be "not fundamental." ("It [narrative] is a semantic surface, an epiphany of tradi- tional thought but not its substance" [p. 214].) In claiming that conditioned behavior is demonstrated, more than exclusion of possible subjective factors is involved; Peabody asserts that situational strictures can frequently substi- tute for memory retrieval in the usual sense. "The reduction of choice, the increase of redundancy, and the regularization of structures unquestionably have the same effect on a system as memory. An oral tradition does not retrieve actions from the past; it performs actions that were also performed in the past" (p. 430). Thus the ability to perform epics of great length is less indebted to possessing a prodigious memory than it is to one's being immersed in a tradition with but few degrees of freedom.

Stylistically, however, a bardic poet's performance can vary from poor to excellent. In an attempt to suggest a modern-day composition technique parallel to bardic performance, Peabody takes as a counterpart the improvisations that some musicians perform. With both the ancient and the modern improvisational techniques "the number of elements in a set of possibilities is sharply and habitually restricted by tradition or convention, the making of a particular choice under given limiting conditions becomes almost automatically easy or 'natural.' The product of a series of such choices appears as regularity of form" (p. 8). Though modalities differ, techniques for the two kinds of artists are similar. (To illustrate this point one might then consider this dichotomously dissimilar quartet of master improvisers: Homer, Hesiod, Art Tatum, Thelonious Monk.)

Walter Ong in his book *Orality and Literacy: The Technology of the Word* (1982) starts with the Parry-Lord and Peabody findings and goes much further in pointing out the extent to which orally shaped institutions exist in presumably literate Western cultures. Ong discriminates several cultural stages of orality. Historically before general literacy, there was *primary orality,* as in the Homeric period. The subsequent diffusion of literacy proceeded slowly, leaving numerous pockets of residual orality. When printing was introduced, literacy spread faster, but print also produced unique effects pertaining to literary forms and their understanding not found in a manuscript culture. Today there is another kind of orality, *secondary orality,* that has been strongly influenced by the cultural framework of literacy; television produces many examples. With all varieties of orality there is a common trait that performance orientation is dominant over information orientation.

Ong and other students of oral culture have not shown much interest in applying the orality–literacy dichotomy to the ongoing development of the child but the child emphasis is one that I find appealing. Although surrounded by an environment of literacy, preschoolers live in an oral culture in which almost all tutelage is orally expressed. The young child who seeks to verify and maintain memories must do so primarily by oral means. Perhaps, following Ong, this gives one reason for a generational clash in aims. The child favors a performance orientation; the parents favor an information orientation.

Oral cultures possess a number of common characteristics. Remembering puts a persistent strain on the performer, so mnemonic requirements influence syntax as well as meaning. Redundancy must be at a high level in oral communications if misunderstanding is to be avoided. Rhythm and body participation, such as gestures or body rocking, are often practiced as mnemonic aids. A less obvious point that Ong stresses is that "lists" only begin with literacy since there is no true oral equivalent. A bare, unadorned list is too disjointed and abstract for retention and oral repetition. Sometimes there are approximations to lists in ancient oral narratives but these are at best a kind of inventory-taking by means of elaborated descriptions. Ong gives a number of examples that originated in oral cultures and later were written down: the description of the Greek ships and their captains in the *Iliad,* the formulary action-narrative giving geographical relationships in the biblical Book of Numbers, and the genealogies in Genesis orally framed by the "begat" relationships. Ong presents an incisive mnemonically slanted analysis of why the seemingly lackluster genealogies in Genesis are "in effect commonly narrative."

> This sort of aggregation derives partly from the oral drive to use formulas, partly from the oral mnemonic drive to exploit balance (recurrence of subject-predicate-object produces a swing which aids recall and which a mere sequence of names would lack), partly from the oral drive to redundancy (each person is mentioned twice, as begetter and begotten), and partly from the oral drive to narrate rather than simply to juxtapose (the persons are not immobilized as in a police line-up, but are doing something—namely, begetting). (p. 99)

I would comment that the study of memory in psychology reversed the historical process and began with the memorization of lists (lists that usually are presented visually but recited orally). It is little wonder that, though perhaps aligned with certain pedagogical demands, results obtained from this empirical tradition have had little to say about autobiographical memory, in which oral narrative inevitably plays so large a part.

Certain aspects of epic narratives seem applicable to oral transmissions in general. Narratives of any length that must be retained orally are always episodic and full of interpolations and digressions. They lack what Ong calls the "lengthy climactic plot." (Ong states that in the classical world only the drama approached tight plotting; this was because it was for a long period the only performance based on writing.)

> Memory, as it guides the oral poet, often has little to do with the strict linear presentations of events in sequence. . . . Today we like in our typographic and electronic culture exact correspondence between linear order of elements in discourse and the referential order, the chronological order in the world to which the discourse refers. We like sequence in verbal reports to parallel exactly what we experience or can arrange to experience. (1982, p. 147)

According to Ong, the parallelism between narrative and chronological event occurrence "becomes a major objective only when the mind interiorizes literacy," recent somewhat self-conscious, avant-garde efforts to "deplot" (mix up) the order of event occurrence notwithstanding. Since episodes are out-of-order but must be somehow related, skill in handling flashbacks was one of the marks of the accomplished epic poet. If placing a string of events in order is impossible for an oral poet, so too is accurate dating of events. As mentioned above, Allen and Montell in their oral history research found exact chronological ordering with accurate dating very difficult for contemporary oral respondents. In past ages, as Ong points out, people generally lacked even the concept of calendrical dating. "It appears unlikely that most persons in medieval or even renaissance western Europe would ordinarily have been aware of the number of the current calendar year—from the birth of Christ or any other point in the past. Why should they be?" (pp. 97–98).

Ong strongly emphasizes that all oral expression is social. This is not an emphasis on the "social" in the sense of Halbwachs that group membership predicates every action, even if group membership is only implicit. Rather, it is an emphasis on all verbal expression as audience centered; there are no soliloquies. (Ong gives a more extended rationale than the psychoanalysts who reached the same conclusion as discussed in Chapter 5.) "In real human communication the sender has to be in receiver position as well as sender. Even to talk to yourself you have to pretend you are two people. The reason is that what I say depends on what reality or fancy I feel I am talking into, that is, on what possible responses I might anticipate. . . . To speak, I have to be somehow already in communication with the mind I am to address before I start speaking. . . . Human communication is never one way" (p. 175). Thus Ong finds all communication, including self-communication, intersubjective. He puts forth this idea to combat the concept of one-way transmission in human communication, even where it might be thought most evident, namely with printed text. Every writer "conjures up a fictional person or persons"; it is this fictionalizing of readers that makes writing so difficult, since there must be a common tradition for both writer and readers—an intertextuality.

If communication even with oneself has the duality of the individual being both sender and receiver, then there seems no reason that many memory communications one makes to oneself cannot also be considered in the same way. I find this extension appealing; however it goes beyond what Ong himself states. Two objections can be raised against this concept of memory contents as implicit dialogue. First, some memories impose themselves on us as sudden isolated shafts from the past, sometimes almost against our will. But these memories are relatively few in number. A more important objection is that many memories are not verbally expressed or are given only elliptical verbal representation. Even in those cases, however, memory contents can be some-what tailored to anticipate the needs of the individual self as audience. Often a strong part of self-audience demand is to fit content into some narrative incident of the past about oneself. When we can detect such tailoring of memory content, we tend to speak of *biases* and *distortions,* but perhaps some more neutral term would more accurately label this inevitable ingredient of memory construction. For example, it might be construed as a more dialogical and less peremptory type of "secondary revision" than that described by Freud.

Repeated Recalls and Personal Memories

Most memories that become a permanent part of one's autobiographical memory are recalled on more than one occasion, some rather often. Here I am not referring to the repetitions involved in rehearsals intended to lead to memorization but to the occurrence of repeated recalls and references to past life-course events. Unlike the drill procedure with items to be memorized, there is no feedback concerning how well performance checks out against the original event or text, and usually there is no bunching of recalls such as takes place when an exact repetition is intended. A few early memories are fairly often recalled (childhood amnesia notwithstanding), just as was concluded about Leonardo da Vinci's early, presumably prophetic "vulture" memory that Freud discussed at such great length. Purists have claimed that only those contents that have never previously been recalled count as valid, uncontaminated "memories." These virgin "first" memories tend to occur soon after an event; therefore if this criterion were consistently applied, the field of autobiographical memory would be largely reduced to the study of near-term memories. Sensibly, no one who actually studies autobiographical memories has ever adopted such a limiting criterion.

Whether repetitions of a recall are given by different persons, as occurs frequently in oral cultures, or by the same person is an obvious distinction to make in considering the characteristic recall alterations produced by repetitions. Bartlett (1932/1961) categorized between-person repetitions as *serial* reproductions, while repetitions by the same individual were termed *repeated* reproductions. Serial reproductions characteristically produce dramatic and often eccentric changes in prose content. In contrast, repeated prose reproductions tend to fall off rapidly in quantity, but qualitative changes are rather mild. Using visual rather than verbal material, stability is also attained rapidly for repeated reproductions.

The serial repetition procedure more frequently applies to oral tradition (as previously defined) and the repeated repetition procedure to oral history. But can one generalize outside the laboratory, even in regard to the supposedly well-established finding that *repeated* reproductions tend to maintain relatively stable repetitions? Several commentators, indeed, claim that this outcome is far from universal. Henige, like some other theorists, emphasizes mulling over memories, particularly those of greatest emotional interest, as a likely source for reproductive falsification.

> Whether we like it or not memory eventually makes cheats of us all, so that it may not be absurd to suggest that sometimes an individual is not best qualified to remember his own experiences accurately. Oddly, perhaps, this problem stems in part from the fact that we spend too much time thinking about—remembering—the past: The more important or pleasant or unpleasant certain experiences seem to us to be, the more likely we are to dwell on and imperceptibly modify them. The effects of this will vary according to the type of experiences. Facts and events may be remembered but the attitudes we had toward them at the time may have been forgotten and replaced by new viewpoints. And events that were of little interest to us are likely to be remembered more accurately, if less fully, than those in which we were heavily, perhaps emotionally involved. (1982, p. 110)

There is certainly a paradox in Henige's thesis that people are sometimes not the best interpreters of the contents of their own memories. He seems to indicate that there are other agencies that "know better." Wisely, even so, they are not named. It is also suggested by Henige that increased effort in the form of repeating, amplifying, and "studying" one's memories is not only inefficient but positively deleterious for memory accuracy, just as has been noted for initial memory registrations. Looking closely at Henige's assertion, however, self-interest rather than repetitions per se is the major factor in producing distortions. Repetitions are merely the vehicles that allow self-interest free play. Similar ideas were discussed at considerable length in Chapter 6, where D. Ewen Cameron's views on "secondary elaborations" of memory contents were considered.

Further evidence for the notion that reminiscing can change and falsify repeated recollections is given by the results of a small experimental study by John Neuenschwander (1984), one of but very few studies performed by an oral historian to speak to memory methodology. In 1977 Neuenschwander interviewed survivors of the American Expeditionary Forces-Siberia who were in Russia from August 1918 until April 1920. One focus was "whether repeated public reminiscence had created a stylized pattern of recall." Neuenschwander found structural similarities in recall among those men who were frequent reminiscers. Of greater interest, "the relative accuracy of their accounts when compared with the official records of the American Expeditionary Force-Siberia at the National Archives was markedly lower than the accounts provided by veterans who rarely recounted their experiences in public. This result will come as no suprise to those who are old enough to recall how competently World War I service club veterans met the anecdotal challenge but failed in accuracy of recall when newly minted veterans returned at the end of World War II with tales of more recent adventures. Perhaps the moral is that the extrovert who voluntarily regales us probably embroiders more than the somewhat close-mouthed introvert.

Urban Legends: Oral Transmission Today

Other possibilities for commonplace oral interchanges do not fall under either the heading oral tradition or oral history as these areas were previously defined. (It should again be emphasized that the terminology I have cited is far from being agreed to by all the experts in these somewhat heterodox fields.) In any case, the majority of serial reproductions, whether gossip, rumors, or jokes, do not pertain to anything of historical interest and are only incidentally transmitted across generations. The rumor form has been most studied by social scientists. Gordon Allport and Leo Postman (1947), in a pioneering work, considered rumor from the standpoint of social stereotypes and prejudices, applying with some limited success the Gestalt theory of memory to the process of content distortion in serial transmissions.

Here I would briefly consider, rather than rumors, narratives of incidents that people have been told and believe to be true but that either are not true or, if they were ever true for anyone, did not happen to the people alleged in the described incidents. These narratives, typically bizarre but believable, have been dubbed "urban legends" and amusingly described by the folklorist Jan Harold Brunvand in two popular books, *The Vanishing Hitchhiker* (1981) and *The Choking Doberman* (1984). Brunvand mentions numerous urban legends well studied by folklorists, among them, "The Death Car" (smell of death permeates upholstery), "The Runaway Grandmother" (granny's corpse nabbed from auto roof rack), and "The Hook" (maniac's hook hand caught in car door handle and wrenched loose). But there are many others, including, for example, a genre treating a variety of embarrassing "superglue" permanent attachments. Brunvand asserts that the urban legend has "long been second in popularity only to the joke in American oral folklore." Of interest for memory theory is that the central plots of these rapidly and widely disseminated narratives are thought to be transmitted with little change or distortion, even though transmissions are by *serial* rather than *repeated* reproductions. In maintaining their meaning, these narratives are like jokes rather than rumors. Doubtless as with the punchline of a joke, the bizarreness cannot be tampered with and permit the legend to remain viable. In this regard, mnemonicists have pointed out for untold generations that "bizarreness" is in itself an excellent associative crutch for good retention.

Who are the alleged participants in these often cautionary anecdotes? According to Brunvand, "those who accept urban legends as true, then, have for verification not personal experience, nor even a friend's own experience, but only an unnamed, elusive, but somehow readily trusted anonymous individual—a 'friend of a friend' [f-o-a-f]—or, we might say a 'foaf' " (1984, p. 51). Thus identified locales and presumed dramatis personae in one sense change rapidly, but in another sense because of vagueness in identification they don't change at all (perhaps this is a hallmark of *legendariness*). Brunvand notes another claim to validation special to our own time that is sometimes invoked by the believers in urban legends—"I read it in the paper" (abbreviated [r-i-p] "rip" and referring to that ultimate authority, a newspaper article that can never quite be located).[1]

Nostalgia: A Complex Memoric Experience

Sometimes realism is obliterated when we try to draw a sharp distinction between the cognitive and affective aspects of memoric experiences. Trying to dissect out a cognitive or emotional dimension can be false to everyday life. I will discuss only one example of the inseparableness of cognition and affect in memoric phenomena, but one that is pervasive, namely, the feeling of nostalgia (which can at times occur as a free-floating emotion that is only obscurely tied to specific personal memories). Undoubtedly there are other frequently occurring memory-based sentiments, but I have been unable to find any other that has produced equivalent intriguing theoretical commentary. In current usage the gamut covered by "nostalgia" reaches from sorrow and mourning to a kind of reflective pleasure in the mulling over of memories, although the etymology of the word is all on the side of sadness. *Nostalgia* has a Greek derivation meaning "homesickness," hence the word came to be applied to any longing for places or persons. But nowadays nostalgia frequently expresses a positive sense of enjoyment, a pleasant "wallowing in the past." Thus we speak of nostalgia for the Old West, old movies, old books, old records, old athletic contests, and just plain "old times." Generally any hint of sadness is barely discernible in our nostalgic reference to these items or in our frequent denomination of various "Golden Ages" (say, baseball in the 1920s, Hollywood in the 1930s, etc.). It could be argued that many of these nostalgic claims are commercially inspired and therefore embody a fake nostalgia rather than a true one. But it would appear that whatever its origins, nostalgia, like other experienced emotions, can never be false, no matter how deceptive the inspiration. So too it has been pointed out that to claim a nostalgia-provoking souvenir as "spurious" is beside the point.

The psychoanalytic point of view emphasizes the sorrow in memories, as well expressed by Hans Loewald, an essentially orthodox psychoanalyst.

> Memory, for the psychoanalyst, is not just a faculty or function of the intellect by virtue of which the mind registers, retains, and may remember experiences, events and objects. For him [the psychoanalyst], memory also has something to do with separation, loss, mourning, and restitution, and often carries with it a sense of nostalgia, especially as we get older. The words commemoration and memorial remind us of such connotations. (Loewald, 1976, p. 298)[2]

In giving an account of memory development Loewald adds that "memory is the child of both satisfaction and frustration." In early infancy there is simply an undifferentiated life-performance functioning, since "memory, as registration or recording, and perception are identical for the infant." Satiety in feeding and maternal stimulation are cited as important satisfying experiences, but it is evident that frustration is formatively dominant.

> Loss or separation from a love object appears to be a most powerful stimulus for the activation of memorial processes. . . . Although memorial processes often appear to be motivated by object loss, there would be no loss but only emptiness if the object were not already remembered in some form. . . . On the basis of retention, that is, of the internal, continuous, though unconscious, reproduction of interactional experiences, what otherwise would be inner emptiness or rage due to disruption, may become a longing that produces the experience of missing or realizing the absence of something, under the impact of renewed instinctual pressures" (p. 311).

Longing is put on a more permanent basis by "the resolution of the Oedipus complex, with its relinquishments and the internalization-repressions of Oedipal object relations."

Whatever the origins of the encumbered memories of longing, neither psychoanalysis nor psychology is very rich in descriptions of what nostalgia, as distinct from a mourning-related sentiment, can entail. The sociolinguist and folklore theorist Susan Stewart takes a long step toward remedying this need in her book *On Longing: Narratives of the Miniature, the Gigantic, the Souvenir, the Collection* (1984). From the wealth of examples in her book I will present brief commentary pertaining only to the souvenir, "an environmental object which serves both to provoke and satisfy nostalgia."

> We might say that this capacity of objects to serve as traces of authentic experience is, in fact, exemplified by the souvenir. The souvenir distinguishes experiences. We do not need or desire souvenirs of events that are repeatable. Rather we need and desire souvenirs of events that are reportable, events whose materiality has escaped us, events that exist only through the invention of narrative. (1984, p. 135)

Stewart emphasizes that the souvenir must have some material connection to a location. Thus we order postage stamp "first-day covers," and we feel disappointment if we receive a picture postcard from the sender's home rather than from the depicted sight. "The souvenir speaks to a context of origin through a language of longing, for it is not an object arising out of need or use value; it is an object arising out of the necessarily insatiable demands of nostalgia." Furthermore, the souvenir is not a model but an allusion since it comes after and not before the fact, and "it will not function without the supplementary narrative discourse that both attaches it to its origins and creates a myth with regard to those origins" (p. 136). But it should be made clear that it is the possessor's narrative not the object's. The importance of possessiveness shows in the fact that "the wide availability of high-quality photographs of various tourist sights does not cancel the attraction of taking one's own pictures of public sights."

Consonant with the claims of Halbwachs, there are familial souvenirs or heirlooms whose function, according to Stewart, is "to weave, quite literally by means of narrative, a significance of blood relation at the expense of a larger view of history and causality" (p. 137). Stewart adds, in line with Halbwachs's view of memories structuring time:

> Temporally, the souvenir moves history into private time. Hence, the absolute appropriateness of the souvenir as *calendar*. Such a souvenir might mark the privatization of a public symbol (say, the Liberty Bell miniaturized), the juxtaposition of history with a personalized present (say, the year 1776 posited against today's date with its concurrent private "dates"), and the concomitant transformation of a generally purchasable, mass-produced object (the material souvenir) into private possession (the referent being "my trip to Philadelphia"). (p. 138)

Stewart speaks of the *postcard* as "that remarkable souvenir" which also "repeats this transformation of public into private." But the personal *photograph* can possess even wider scope, although to be meaningful it must be individualized.

> The photograph as souvenir is a logical extension of the pressed flower, the preservation of an instant in time through a reduction of physical dimensions and a corresponding increase in significance supplied by means of narra-

tive. . . . For the narration of the photograph will itself become an object of nostalgia. Without marking, all ancestors become abstractions, losing their proper names; all family trips become the same trip—the formal garden, the waterfall, the picnic site, and the undifferentiated sea become attributes of every country. (p. 138)

An important dichotomy can be made. We can distinguish between souvenirs of well-known sights, in which the souvenir is most often some form of representation, and souvenirs of individual experiences. The former are generally purchasable while the latter, including personal photographs, are not. Stewart points out that children have many fewer personal souvenirs so that this adds to their eagerness to purchase commercial souvenirs as "a sign of their own life histories." Typically, personal souvenirs are not merely isolated mementos but are organized into autobiographical patterns. Individual items deal with rites of passage and status transformations (births, graduations, marriages, initiations), and they are often further compounded into scrapbooks, baby books, memory quilts, and photo albums. Such items are almost always of little material value but are of great worth to the possessor. "Because of its connection to biography and its place in constituting the notion of the individual life, the memento becomes emblematic of the worth of that life and of the self's capacity to generate worthiness" (p. 139).

Theoretically it could be said that although Halbwachs speaks of "collective time" and Stewart of "private time," there is no real contradiction. My personal time chronology registers a temporal immobilization that allows private calendrical dating established by my souvenir; this stoppage and chronological dating is stabilized within the coordinates of collective time. Not the least interesting aspect of souvenirs, according to Stewart, is that if through some historical circumstance or sudden economic demand they acquire a high monetary value, they can no longer remain predominately souvenirs; they are upgraded into collectors' trophies. The reason for this change is not that souvenirs must be meretricious or that an individualizing narrative connected with souvenir acquisition is necessarily lacking, but rather that with a large rise in intrinsic value nostalgia is inevitably subordinated to other emotions.

It is often the case that a nostalgic stimulus, though it is embodied in a material object, is knowingly fictional. A melding of fact and fiction can occur that is not unlike those early memories of the infant that combine actual happenings with wishful fantasies. A major difference, however, is that the fictive element in early memories is harder to discern. Sometimes nostalgia takes a more global form and is less attached to specific objects than to past periods in one's life, e.g., the era of the high school athlete or beauty queen. In these cases the "homesickness" aspect of nostalgia has a more temporal than geographical locus. When the penchant for nostalgia is carried to an extreme, one can become an antiquarian of one's own life well before the onset of the reminiscences of old age. An inventory of our real and imagined objects of nostalgia might, as the pioneer psychologist Francis Galton first stated about free associations, tell us more about ourselves than we would want to know.

In sum, it is obvious that nostalgia does not imply any concerted attempt to recover veridical memories. Accordingly, accurate recall is often deemphasized, while on the affective side nostalgia is not so much an attempt to recall experienced emotions as to engender them. (With sorrowful personal events, this engendering is often more peremptory than intentional, but there is also pleasure to be wrung from so-called "bittersweet" memories.) Fantasy embellishment is quite often desirable if it can be kept in character. On some occasions a nostalgia-like emotion concerns other than personally experienced events, as in contemplating the various Golden Ages that have occurred prior to one's birth or in connection with wholly fictional happenings. Insofar as we can describe them, emotions are not as specialized as the cognitive distinctions we can make. Can there be instant nostalgia? It seems unlikely, except in attenuated form. Although the souvenir and the instant snapshot give us a measure of immediate pleasure, we must wait through time and distance to gain full pleasure from contemplating the past and the absent. But certainly we are often aware, when we want to think about it, that we are collecting material for future nostalgic reminiscences. I would conclude that heterogeneous and slippery as the concept of nostalgia can be seen to be, it nonetheless constitutes an important category in the consumption economics of memory.[3] (Reunions, memorials, and media programming all cater to nostalgia-based motives in increasing numbers—a growth industry for aging populations!—yet nostalgia and its large family of related sentiments remain mostly unstudied.)

To close this sketch of how memory theory can be impinged on by social and historical considerations, it remains to point out that, to the extent that communications are necessarily social, problems of assessing social influence arise even for the psychologist who attempts to interrogate a single individual about his or her personal memories. A good example of the methodological difficulties one faces in "pinning down" memories that are uncontaminated by extraneous influences can be borrowed from the dream research field and applied to memory research in general. I cite psychologists Calvin Hall and Vernon Nordby in their popular book, *The Individual and His Dreams* (1972). They state that "a dream" can have three possible meanings. A dream can relate to what one experiences while he is asleep, or what one remembers when he awakens, or what one can report either orally or in writing; but "It is only the reported dream that has any objective existence." I would emphasize that these distinctions are not limited to dreams. All events have potential phases of being experienced as they happen, followed by being remembered and reported, with both remembering and reporting responsive to social considerations that are simultaneously facilitating and constraining. Some psychologists have maintained that even during the "being experienced" phase, remembering is concurrent with perception; but most psychologists ignore this possibility—which would add a continuity dimension to autobiographical memory—and instead insist that only *memory registration* occurs during the experience, followed by a potential *immediate memory* just after the experience. For those who theorize in this way the duration of spontaneous registration, which is unlikely to be sustained on an even keel indefinitely, or the extent to which registration and memory functions would or could tend to alternate during lengthy experiential sequences has not been asked, let alone answered. We only know that neither registration nor the immediate retention function that tracks ongoing experiences is wholly under volitional control.

A small postscript can be added. It has long been the hope of students of memory to move some *remembered* but not yet *reportable* memory contents a little nearer to "objective" status that to some degree short-circuits the reporting aspect. This goal of disclosing memories in a hermetic state has been attempted by use of the most diverse means, ranging from introspection and psychoanalytic interpretation to the study of hypnosis, reaction time, and physiological measurement. It is only the first two approaches that have been the focus of the preceding chapters. Nonetheless, it can be maintained that all of these methods of revealing personal memories ultimately have a socially shaped component, even when there is no overt intention of social communication.

Conceptual Summary

A distinction can be drawn between oral history and oral tradition. *Oral history* can be considered as dealing with oral transmissions within the same generation, whereas *oral tradition* deals with cross-generational transmissions. Anthropologist Jan Vansina believes that Halbwachs's concept of "collective memory" is borne out by the study of oral traditions. When separate but similar descriptions pertaining to the same event are obtained from oral tradition sources, Vansina reasons that these corroborating multiple descriptions usually have a common source, while similar multiple descriptions in oral history are probably of independent origin and therefore are confirming of each other. A frequent phenomenon in relation to cross-generational dating of events is the existence of both historically distant and relatively recent accounts of events with a lack of temporally intermediate accounts. Over time, the earliest accounts that are continuous with recent events shift toward the present, resulting in an altered forgetting gap, with formerly remembered events now forgotten. The label "floating gap" has been given to this characteristic shift in the chronology of accessible memories. A "floating gap" analogue in autobiographical memory may obtain when people recall repetitive events such as successive Thanksgiving celebrations. Oral traditions are frequently carried by means of a dramatic performance; therefore it has been claimed that an oral message cannot be well understood without assessment of its performance setting and the likely degree of textual distortion superimposed for dramatic effect. Whether the expertise exists to make such distinctions is a debated point. Some oral historians, like some psychotherapists, find a greater interest in respondents' mode of expression and their error-prone subjective beliefs as to what happened than in determining the veridicality of recalled events.

In an analysis of memoric aspects present in oral culture, ideas from three classical and literary scholars, Alfred Lord, Berkeley Peabody, and Walter Ong, have been cited. In studying the actual performances of epics by bardic poets—the modern counterparts of Homer and Hesiod—it was discovered that performances proceeded by producing patterns of schematic formulas and traditional themes rather than by memorization. For any specific epic there was no fixed model or original version of the epic. This differential sampling of formulas and themes leads to multiple versions. Because memories refer to an original version, i.e., an actual occurrence, they are open to accuracy assessments which are not relevant for bardic performances. Unlike preferences with rote memorization, the preference of skilled bards was for a temporal lag of a day or more between hearing and performing an epic. Limitations in the chain of associative choices, redundancy, and the regularization of structures can, to a considerable extent, simulate the results that are achieved by direct memorization through repetitions. Peabody even argues that bardic performance, where the bard is immersed in a performance tradition with few options, is akin to conditioned operant behavior.

Ong suggests that a separation should be made between the *primary orality* of ancient societies and the *secondary orality* found in contemporary, largely literate societies. Independent of this distinction, the early life of the child is, from the child's standpoint, carried on in an oral culture in every society. The concept of a freestanding "list" is unknown in primary oral cultures. Since the bare juxtapositions found in list-like material would be mnemonically difficult, narrative connectives are invariably present to serve as transitional links. Lists have always been the staple diet for the experimental study of memory, with a consequent narrowing of the usefulness of results obtained from such "list-learning" experiments. Only in literate cultures is emphasis placed on the narration of events in chronological order. Accurate absolute dating is impossible in an oral culture as calendrical benchmarks are mostly unknown. Oral presentations of any length produce digressions and flashbacks, which are handled by oral bards with varying degrees of skill. All verbal expression is dialogic. Even when alone one must anticipate what the self-as-audience expects, since the individual is both sender and receiver of the same communication. Going beyond what Ong stated, an extension of this idea is to consider memory communications that one makes to oneself as at least partially social in the same way as other self-communications.

A categorical distinction has been made in the experimental study of memory between multiple recalls by the same individual (*repeated* reproductions) and successive recalls of the same material by different individuals (*serial* reproductions). The laboratory finding has been that repeated reproductions tend to stabilize while serial reproductions quickly produce drastic and eccentric changes. A commentator on the retention of personal memories from the perspective of oral history has taken issue with the repeated-reproduction conclusion, even going so far as to propose that sometimes an individual is not the best authority on his own memories if emotion-laden memories are frequently repeated. One small empirical study also bears out the fallibility of *repeated* reproductions, insofar as it was demonstrated that the anecdotal recounting of "war stories" by veterans encouraged an increased number of factual errors. On the other hand, there are indications that some *serial* reproductions can be quite stable. Orally transmitted anecdotes reputed to have happened to a "friend of a friend" (called "urban legends" by folklorist Jan Harold Brunvand) have widespread dissemination in recent times. These out-of-the-ordinary but feasible, transmitted anecdotes are believed to be communicated in surprisingly stable form. It is hypothesized that, in a fashion analogous to the retention of jokes with punchlines, and unlike rumors and gossip, the *bizarreness* of these anecdotes (which is their "point") is the key to their accurate conservation.

Nostalgia possesses a distinctive theoretical interest because it offers an inextricable mixture of the emotional and the cognitive. Although personal memories are usually involved and a concept of the past is a prerequisite, there can also be instances of nostalgia induced by events that were not personally experienced. From the psychoanalytic standpoint, Hans Loewald claims that nostalgia derives from both satisfactions and frustrations experienced in infancy, but frustrations, actuated by the sorrows of separation, loss, mourning, and restitution, are the stronger influence. The resolution of the Oedipus complex with its repressions and relinquishments establishes a permanent foundation of unfulfilled longing. Stewart argues that nostalgia as a positive experience can be related to souvenirs in diverse ways. Although souvenirs are material artifacts, their function is to furnish opportunities for personal narratives that satisfy the insatiable demands of nostalgia. For example, the narrative possibilities of personal snapshots account for a popularity that is superior to commercial photographs of the identical scene, and with the passage of time the narration pertaining to one's personal snapshots will itself become an object of nostalgia. Souvenirs also assist in structuring personal time and memorializing familial events to enhance one's sense of worth. Events that are repeatable do not need souvenirs. Children, who have few personal souvenirs, are for that reason especially eager for commercial souvenirs. Once past childhood, previous temporal eras of one's life and even fabled "golden eras" that one never experienced are sometimes more serviceable for nostalgia than souvenirs.

Memories, like dreams, can be considered from three standpoints: the experience at the time of event occurrence, the memory as personally known, and the reportable memory content. Whether remembering is concurrent with ongoing event occurrence and the perception of the event remains open as a theoretical possibility for autobiographical experiential sequences. The discovery of methods of tapping the contents of memories other than by personal reporting is a persistent goal of experimental memory research. It is unlikely, however, that short-circuiting the reporting phase and sampling memories by means other than subjective reports will eliminate the intrinsic contributions made by social shaping.

10

Conclusions
and Possibilities

The three approaches taken to autobiographical memory—subjective, developmental, and social—have many cross-relationships, though no single discipline combines them satisfactorily. This state of affairs can be taken more as a challenge than a reproach. No exact and comprehensive definition of autobiographical memory has been proposed, but a number of phenomena have been described and will be discussed further that strengthen the case for considering autobiographical memory as possessing unique characteristics. In this chapter I extend consideration of previously described topics with only passing attention paid to origin or authorship. Some definite and possibly opinionated judgments and suggestions are expressed, and some new supporting material is introduced.

Before reviewing selected theoretical concepts, a generalization can be made about each approach. (1) The subjective acknowledgment of past occurrences as part of one's life history is always only a fraction of what can justifiably be included in the autobiographical memory category. This is so, regardless of whether an explicit unconscious dimension is assumed. (2) The period of infancy and early school life is critical for autobiographical memory because during this period, certainly by age 8 or 9, more formative and abrupt changes have occurred in memoric *processes* (not necessarily memoric content) than will occur in all of later life. (3) Personal memories can always be construed as occurring within a social framework. Social frameworks range from implicit dialogues and group identifications to explicit interrogations and intergenerational cultural transmissions.

Intentionality

Volition tends to be much less focused for personal memories than it is for many other forms of retention. Most personal events are not intentionally remembered and many events are recovered spontaneously. There is considerable evidence that "intention" is counterproductive. I have grouped several of these admonitions against undue effort together under the heading of the "effort paradox," since they have in common that there is an inverse relation between effort expended and effective retention. As prominent examples of this paradox, Frederic Bartlett asserted that in his experimental results "determination to remember was constantly correlated with actual forgetting." Knight Dunlap went considerably further in stating not only that a prolonged effort to remember (even if successful) prejudiced later recall but also that a "negative method" was desirable so that an item to be well retained should be actively "put out" of attention after it had been only briefly attended to.

The objection can be made that Bartlett and Dunlap were not particularly concerned with autobiographical memory. In rebuttal, it can be noted that it is particularly with autobiographical memory that a lack of noticeable effort both in memory registration and reinstatement is the usual state of affairs. According to the paradox, then, just this failure to summon special effort can be more optimal for success in remembering than common sense or most psychological theories suspect. Indeed, Freud, in seeking for diagnostic personal memories, early gave up on laborious direct recovery methods such as hypnosis and the pressure method, wherein patients attempted a concentrated attack on their specific problems. After disappointing results, Freud focused exclusively on indirect procedures such as analysis of the transference. And free assocations were no longer focused on presumed critical situations but dealt with whatever was occupying the patient's mind at the moment. Thus Freud joins those who find hard memoric effort counter-productive.

All theories of personal memory acknowledge the existence of contents that are unintentionally registered and retained. Theorists of widely different persuasions have discussed several types of inadvertent retention that they link to unintended or covert perception. Early theorizing in this vein involved explanations of *déjà vu* in terms of perceptions without awareness mediated by the so-called minor senses such as smell, taste, and kinesthesis. According to the French literary critic Georges Poulet, affective memory has been described as instigated by the minor senses not only by Proust but also by Hawthorne, Baudelaire, and Flaubert. Among psychoanalysts, Ernest Schactel, in particular, expatiated on the prominent role of odor and odor memories for young children who would have no means of representing these memories. Freud himself claimed that comparisons important in cognizing esthetic experiences were often mediated outside of awareness by motoric ideational mimetics that were the residue of past experiences. Some other covert perceptual phenomena tied to memory have little if any involvement with emotional experiences, thus avoiding the charge that emotions, which by their nature tend to be nonvolitional, supply the reason for perceptions being covert. Examples related to memory recovery include Solomon Asch's concept of recognition preceding recall in focusing memory recovery and psychologist Endel Tulving's concept of "encoding specificity," the idea that context that is encoded together with an item to be retained is a crucial influence in subsequent recall.

Without doubt, it is helpful for conceptual clarity that perception in some form be identified as the registration mechanism for retention that is incidental at best. Thus we have claims put forward for unaware registration of perceptions that cannot be strictly delimited, peripheral awareness of so-called minor senses, and direct physiognomic perceptions. Perhaps if we knew more about the retention of thoughts, dreams, and earlier memories, theories of incidental retention would not be so exclusively limited to perceptual explanations. An example of a nonvolitional, developmental memory concept without specific perceptual links is the Freudian concept of "deferred action." Piaget indicated a possible means of non-perceptual memory change in accounting for the mechanism of deferred action through the acquisition of more advanced cognitive schemes during the retention period. Partial empirical attacks have been made in investigating consciousness and intentionality in relation to memory. As detailed in Chapter 2, a current area of investigation is *automaticity* in retention, dealing with the implicit registration and accurate subsequent recall of delimited aspects of objects and events, with frequency of occurrence the most investigated topic. Depending on the theorist, conscious awareness in automatic retention is presumed to be either absent or irrelevant.

In the 1980s a renewed interest in *prospective memory,* or memory for carrying out plans, emphasized another aspect of intentionality in memory. (See Meacham, 1988.) It would not be wise, however to consider the resulting investigations *direct* measures of "memory for intentions," as is sometimes claimed. Difficulties arise in that intentions are compound since an *intention exists both as a description and as an associated performance.* This dual nature of intention leads to uncertainty in establishing criteria of correctness. For example, an associated performance can be carried out without recall of the intention, and the recalled intention will not always entail the associated performance. The prospective-memory format is widespread in human endeavors, since many habitual performances have the structure of a prospective memory, although the intentional description is no longer overtly expressed. Another complication is that most associated performances have temporal limits as to when they can be appropriately performed. Such temporal constraints are not always made explicit in the intentional descriptions, nor can they always be known ahead of time. On the other hand, a case can be made that future recall *at any time* of an intentional description by itself could constitute a valid though often useless memory. It is apparent that complications are easy to generate, and results obtained from prospective memory tasks are hard to interpret. Notwithstanding possible conceptual difficulties, many prospective tasks are well worth investigating for the purpose of furthering theoretical knowledge.

The Coding Analogy

Central to much recent academic theorizing about memory functioning is the seemingly innocuous *coding analogy,* which states that discrete memory "items" are "encoded" to be retained and "decoded" to be recalled. (I have, in fact, on several occasions used this analogy myself in the preceding chapters.) As a descriptive analogy, however, it is a close fit only for the restricted field of intentional memorization. As just described, in a variety of ways many autobiographical memories are in no sense either "encoded" or "decoded" within the usual meaning of these terms. Since repetitive memorization trials focusing on specific content do not occur, much of the content of personal retention remains unknown, perhaps a sizable fraction more or less permanently. Rote memorization also seems to be implicit in the coding analogy, because the understanding of meaning is usually judged to be irrelevant in estimating retention accuracy. But in real life rote memorization is rare. In all art forms, even where repetitive performances are ostensibly involved, structured variations and improvisations rather than rote repetition is what is valued. For example, with bardic performances of epic narratives and with musical improvisations, themes are retained but exact words and notes are not.

On a more down-to-earth level, the timely production of expressive variations on a recalled theme is a desideratum of our more banal personal remembrances, usually because we seek to avoid boredom and social ineptitudes. If the coding analogy is applied to these performances with the possibility of a different outcome at each reproduction, the analogy lacks any explanatory usefulness. More tempting is an application of the Piagetian concept of scheme as embodying the theme and the schema as representing enacted performance variations. A major deficiency in this description, however, is that schemes and schemas fail to link the narrative and sequential aspects found in artistic performances.

A factor that is completely omitted in the coding model is any acknowledgment of a social dimension. In mathematical information theory, which initially popularized the coding analogy in psychology, the encoder and the decoder were different individuals, but consideration that there could be something social in communication was ignored in memory theorizing by permitting only one-way transmission. The important influence of membership in social institutions on communication is part of the bread and butter of sociology, but it was noted in the academic study of memory only by acknowledging that accurate retention was often distorted by social biases and prejudices. Contrastingly, a more thoroughly social viewpoint, such as the long-ignored writings of Halbwachs, asserts that social influences are not so much biasing as foundational.

Lately the pendulum has begun to swing toward a more social emphasis. The primacy of communication has been a recent, much-emphasized social dimension, with importance given to dialogic construction of memories; efforts made in this direction extend from literary studies and folklore to oral history and anthropology. In this regard, theorists from several disciplines have suggested that self-communications are more akin to dialogues than to monologues. I have further suggested that dialogues in this sense can sometimes take place in communicating with one's personal memories. It is worth emphasizing, however, that although some memories and *attempts at memory recovery* can be cast in dialogue form, just as with dialogues between persons, many of the interactions are in the form of nonverbal exchanges, e.g., imagery alterations and changes in emotional tone. Perhaps this concept of a conversing with memory is already partially encompassed by the concept of "memory elaboration," with the acknowledgment that possibly unfortunate consequences can ensue when elaborations are persistent and peremptory, but that more melioristic outcomes can result when elaboration amplifies incomplete memories and makes them more consequential.

Affective and Conative Memories

How, or even whether, emotions and motivations are retained remains a problem on which little sure progress has been made. The dominant assumption has been that it is somehow more likely that memories are embodied in cognitions (say as memory traces) than in emotions or anything else that partakes of affect. Perhaps the undoubted fact that the majority of memories are neutral or lacking in strong affect has suggested this view. Or, alternatively, one can take Freud's logical perspective that the essence of an emotion is "to be expressed" so that affective "action at a temporal distance" is not possible. Hence no purely affective memory can exist. Postponing consideration of this controversy for the moment, I have noted that although the psychoanalytic case is weak for exact retention of early cognitions and Freud was negative in regard to retention of affects, a stronger argument can be made that conations, although not tied to exact cognitive representations, are formed very early and are retained. The claim by both Freud and Piaget that early in life there are multiple memoric registrations of the same event in different guises in fact precludes early cognitive coherency. It is therefore in respect to retention of early motivations that I would suggest psychoanalysts and other theorists are most justified in speaking of memories that have become "lost" by their incorporation into character and personality structures. Freud mentions such a conative perspective, the adult's search for the mood of childish pleasure; such a *search* can only be guided by some sort of memory, however amorphous its representation. Obviously, as with the examples of the retention of incidental perceptions already cited, conative retentions are mostly reinstated without full awareness. It must be admitted that in this formulation there is not a clear distinction between the retention of motivations and emotions, particularly when the latter give rise to long-lasting feelings or moods.

Traditionally, for practical reasons, cognition and affect have been separated, giving rise to the pseudo-problem of putting them back together again. The ease of subjugating affect by administering routine and mildly boring memorization tasks means that we have a one-sided view of memory, the view from tedium. Consideration of *nostalgia* was undertaken as an exemplary case to illustrate that such a separation is sometimes impossible. Nostalgia is an indissoluble compound of both thought and sentiment, since the cognitive framework lacks interest without affective content. Cognitions themselves can sometimes incorporate statements about affects that contribute to nostalgia and related feelings ("that was a happier time").

In this regard, the Freudian theory of happiness (not a strong point in psychoanalysis) might itself, in part, be classed as one of nostalgia for childhood. Freud's theory has been commonly characterized as "pessimistic," in large part because pleasure seems chiefly to consist in the avoidance of pain ("unpleasure"). But he proposed at least one direct road to happiness. At the very end of his book on humor, Freud, who several times stated that the feelings of infants are invariably much stronger than those of adults, asserted that humor techniques are not needed by the young child since he is capable of a spontaneous mood of happiness. "For the euphoria which we endeavor to reach by these means [i.e., economy of effort in the comic, jokes, and humor] is nothing other than the mood of a period of life in which we were accustomed to deal with our psychical work in general with a small expenditure of energy—the mood of our childhood, when we were ignorant of the comic, when we were incapable of jokes and when we had no need of humor to make us feel happy in our life" (p. 236). Thus, disturbing incidents on the minus side of life might sometimes be balanced by the reinstatement of positive childlike affect. With the artful effort that deliberate humor instigation such as jokes involves, I submit that Freud's description of the manufacture by adults of a state of satisfaction akin to childhood euphoria is closer to the intentional cultivation of nostalgia than it is to unconscious emotional regression.[1]

Childhood Memories

Freud's account of children's inability to recall early life events, which he termed *childhood amnesia,* is less clear-cut in scope and origin than is usually claimed. The most striking equivocation pertains to whether the presumed repression causing amnesia is social in nature (Oedipal conflict) or a product of biological maturation (organic repression). It has often been pointed out that analysts have not been concerned with the memories of pre-Oedipal infants but only with memories of occurrences from this time that are recalled much later. What is much less remarked is that, during the childhood period (approximately ages 6 to 12), when personal memories are readily available, psychoanalysis continues to evince little interest in memory recovery. This is, of course, unlike the situation with adult patients. Anna Freud (Sandler, Kennedy, and Tyson, 1980) has given a quite recent statement of this position, which emphasizes that the uses of the past are only of secondary interest in therapeutic work with children.

> Reconstructions of the past do not bring about a catharsis or abreaction in the case of children, with a massive release of emotion, as occurs in the treatment of traumatic neuroses in adults through the recovery, by means of interpretation or reconstruction, of the memory of the traumatic experience. Reconstructions of the past have other functions in child analysis, and these do not include the immediate lifting of repressions in the child.

Certainly the child may benefit from the reconstruction, but at best the benefit seems to be due to his receiving a license to bring up material which he might not otherwise mention. If the child is provided with a temporal dimension for the frame of reference in which he can understand himself, something in the present may not seem to be so serious because he can now refer it back, in some way, to the past. The emphasis on current conscious and preconscious preoccupations should be strong indeed, for they serve the therapist as gates through which to enter the past of the child, especially when they take the form of present transference derivatives of the past. The dynamic importance of current pressures and conflicts, as compared to the persisting influence of the past, is particularly great for children. (1980, p. 239)

Memories are not claimed to be unavailable, but "current pressures and conflicts" largely deprive them of interest, because memory recovery does not serve any major theoretical purpose. Presumably some of the same memories that are uninteresting to the child will come to be important in adulthood, both for the patient and the therapist.

Why current pressures and conflicts should be especially dominant in childhood is not explained theoretically by Anna Freud. Rather, it can be noted that she gives the assent of psychoanalysis to a long-observed developmental phenomenon. In Victorian times children's lack of interest in their personal memories was every bit as evident as it is today. In that era this indifference to the past was acknowledged with the proverbial wisdom that children are "future oriented," symmetrical with the elderly who are "past oriented." Children can recall numerous personal memories, but they do not choose to do so the way older people do. If we accept this description as generally valid, there is a kind of *tunnel effect* for many autobiographical memories in that they burrow out of sight for some years only to appear long afterward like seventeen-year locusts. And like locusts, they are numerous and surprisingly intact without needing intermediate exercise. A peculiarity of many of these long-term memories, though we have available only cross-sectional evidence and not the more pertinent longitudinal data, is that they tend to be recalled in adulthood with more descriptive fidelity than the child himself can muster soon after event occurrence. In the retention realm, only autobiographical memories seem to show such a long period of quiescence, followed years later by active and at times surprisingly accurate efflorescence.

Memory as Social

Chapters 8 and 9 discussed various social aspects of memory. In previous theorizing social points of view have been neglected, but a recent trend toward emphasizing social constructions in several fields of psychology should not lead us to claim too much for the social perspective, which is in fact a blanket term that covers different forms of interactions. At least five ways in which social factors relate to personal memories have already been presented:

(1) social interaction, (2) social identification, (3) social stereotype, (4) social transmission, and (5) social validation.

1. With *social interaction* by means of dialogue, memory retrieval is emphasized with little interest in memory registration. Sometimes, it is claimed, there is no memory registration as such, since initial remembrances are being constructed that have never before been expressed. Psychotherapists, in particular, view the conversational mode as advantageous, because it is more natural and less subject to blocking than self-reflection. Direct questions are avoided, as with free assocation, so that the memory information obtained can be inferential. At least initially, this procedure usually results in memory meanings being better understood by the therapist than by the client.

2. *Social identification* is theorized as shaping memories by the individual's membership in large and small, formal and informal social groups. Group affiliation from family to nation (perhaps species?) colors the form and content of remembering at all ages and across generations. Halbwachs has gone the furthest in claiming that there is no such thing as individually formulated memory content. With group identification intrinsic in every recall, there is no neutral ground; every personal memory has an aspect of affiliation bias.

3. A concept related to memory recall and recognition by Bartlett and an older generation of social psychologists is that of *social stereotypes*. How do we fill in memories that have faded, memories that are near the threshold of recall? And how do we complete anecdotal narratives that contain gaps? The answer is we replace actual memories by the normally expectable, the banally commonplace—the stereotype. A line of investigation pioneered by John Bransford and Jeffrey Franks in the 1970s indicates that these memory stereotypes can often be representations brought about by the implicit inferences that arise when we attempt recall. This interpretation suggests an interesting hypothesis: What is given as a memory is sometimes merely the most probably alternative drawn from a group of likely occurrences. This interplay among "reasonable" alternatives may be more continuous, particularly in narrative recall, than theorists have hitherto thought possible, for a consistent characteristic of narrative recall is that it has a few overt gaps. This continuity is in contrast to many laboratory studies, where rememberers are much more likely to omit items than to make substitutions. Doubtless this laboratory result is a function of using as an experimental task a memorization structure with few degrees of freedom—the recall of *lists*.

4. The *social transmission* of memories emphasizes the importance of societal frameworks as the basis for retaining memories in a specific society, particularly across generations. We especially acknowledge the potency of social frameworks when memory losses are correlated with societal changes. Thus we speak of social forgetting and social amnesia. (In Chapter 8 I cited as an example of a surprisingly rapid social transmission loss the historical forgetting of the Civil War's famous Confederate "rebel yell.") In a positive vein, Shils pointed out that we must constantly reenact traditions through the support given by memories in order to maintain the fabric of society. Members of

wholly oral societies have devised various means of limiting memory losses that are uncommon in literate societies.

5. *Social validation* of memories begins with the child turning to his parents to try to determine what is valid in what he knows. For the child it is not a self-evident task to separate the products of memory from those of imagination. Also, the child must validate many of his social identifications in conformity to the society in which he lives. A question about the nature of what is real is sometimes at stake, and even adults admit that, for short periods, they sometimes confuse dreams with memories. Since the determination of memory veridicality is a recurrent question, social validation often occurs together with other social factors that pertain to memories.

These five social categories are not exhaustive.[2] There are also social conventions agreed upon by in-groups that are used in framing concepts. As an example in the field of psychology, in the final section of this chapter I argue that how "memory" is defined rests in part on socially arrived at conventions that investigators have tacitly agreed encompass retention phenomena. What is social in memory is not always explicit, and obviously social influences need not necessarily be valid. Often social pressure must be disregarded to preserve a unique or eccentric memory content. Not infrequently there are simultaneous social factors that conflict with each other. Particularly in his later sociological writings, Freud often expanded his repression concept to refer to societal repressions. I would suggest, however, that with societal repressions there is seldom the nearly complete inability to recall disturbing content that is found when material is repressed by the individual. In a social context what is "unconscious" and leads to the disappearance of content is more frequently change in the supporting social fabric rather than the direct antagonism of moral censorship to unacceptable content.

In laboratory situations where tight control is maintained, social influences are to some extent minimized, but the claim that social factors are weak can also be made at the other end of the spectrum of volitional control, where memories occur involuntarily. A good example of lack of control is *déjà vu*. The mysterious arbitrariness of the occurrence of *déjà vu* was very much part of its fascination when it came into vogue at the turn of the century. Of course, *déjà vu* is not a valid memory at all but only a misplaced emotional experience posing as a memory. (Several theories suggest, however, that there are misrecognized memoric aspects.) It is a good example, nevertheless, of the generalization that when emotions figure strongly in retention, immediate social factors are often overridden. Psychoanalysis is particularly rich in involuntary memory phenomena that start at a very young age, such as multiple memory registration, transference, and repetition compulsion.[3] These mechanisms are asserted to be so inevitable that social influences do not go much beyond supplying the occasions that permit them to be enacted. The strongest argument against the influence of social factors on memories, and also the most frequently challenged, is Freud's claim that many early childhood memories can later be recalled in meaningful form. More impervious still to social factors are the archaic, hereditarily transmitted memories that Freud postulated. But the concept of archaic memories is an acceptable premise today only to orthodox Jungians.

Memory as History and Chronology

History nowadays includes generating new data about the past from the living. Specialists in current history, as well as oral historians, anthropologists, and folklorists, like psychologists and psychotherapists, obtain information and verification from interviews. Some practitioners in each of these disciplines have theorized that sophistication resides not only in ascertaining the factuality of what is recalled but also in the observation of attitudes, forms of expression, prosodic features, and even systematic recall errors. Here both historians and psychotherapists follow the general twentieth-century trend that *indirect* evidence is often of greatest value, since it is unlikely to have been deliberately distorted. The idea that, in dealing with memories, one acts as a personal historian has been put forth by a number of theorists, including Freud and Piaget. (Thus is fulfilled in the autobiographical realm the possibility prophesied by American historian Carl Becker—"every man his own historian.") Others, particularly later psychoanalysts, claim that it is the psychologist or therapist who is the historian, rather than the individual. Therefore, the question becomes, who is recounting the better historical narrative, the autobiographer or the biographer. Both inescapably are editors establishing patterns of meaning derived from events that are too detailed to be retained precisely. As time passes, revisions take place, so that distorted and mistakenly remembered events can be corrected by overlays of consistent interpretations. In psychotherapy another contemporary point of view is that the historical story line is best established dialogically through fruitful interchanges between therapist and patient. (According to some commentators, this has been the way that successful "talking therapies" have always operated.) But does a committee, even a committee of two, succeed in producing other than a compromise between truth and fiction? The pragmatic aims of therapy and the accuracy of life-history sometimes diverge.

Not to be overlooked is the difference between *real* history and *personal* history in regard to what use is made of obtained results. Psychotherapists want case histories that include personal memories for present understanding, but even more for extrapolations into the future. The lofty tone taken by historians that history is worthwhile in its own right and has nothing to do with forecasting or predicting the future cannot be taken by therapists. Historical evaluations, in contrast, are not considered definitive while events and lives are still in progress. Nonetheless, rationales given by therapists more and more resemble those given by historians: the goal to be worked for is a pattern of meanings. Thus any individual occurrence can be considered as less than crucial when taken by itself. Although the psychodynamic concept is still intact, for most therapists the single causal "traumatic incident" is today seldom invoked as more than a contributory factor. The recovery and verification of personal memories are among the past happenings that can often be adequately interpreted by approximations, redundancies, cross-referencing, and fitting events into a coherent pattern. But I would emphasize that whatever interpretive and diagnostic mode is in vogue, personal history as carried by personal memories is continuous and *not optional* for the individual. In this respect it is like history in the broader sense but unlike many other psychological functions where a degree of disengagement is periodically possible.

When all is said and done, similarities notwithstanding, there are two important contrasts between personal memory narratives and the narratives constructed by historians. An obvious contrast is that the historian frequently traces continuity across generations. Personal memory is confined to a single generation, but every individual must deal with obscurities arising from the radically different mental capabilities a person possesses in growing from infancy to adulthood. We may no longer believe that "man is a constant" across the centuries, but generational changes are much less drastic than those found in ontogeny. The second contrast lies in the duality that occurs because recall is displaced in time from the actual occurrence of events. In remembering, we may know the *explanatory interpretation* we subsequently give to certain remembered events, although we are likely to have lost access to our memory of the "experiential truth"—the feel of how events were known at the time of occurrence. Much more frequently the historian can come close to knowing the historical equivalent of both truths, the way an event was publicly received at the time of its occurrence and its later interpretation. For both the individual and the historian, the later interpretation tends to be preferred. Why? In history, because the meaning of what is true changes across time as additional information becomes available and new theories are formulated; in the lifetime of the individual, because more mature mental processes and comprehensive contexts accrue over time. But there are psychological contexts, such as psychotherapy, where the original experiential truth continues to have unacknowledged influence while the mature explanatory interpretation is so ineffectual as to constitute a mere rationalization.

History and autobiographical memory have in common the need for dating events and the construction of chronologies. Occasionally the two fields converge when the attribution of some historical date has depended on individual memory, and additional chronological verifications are sought in the autobiographies that interest historians. Unfortunately, in regard to dating personal memories, there appear to be no appropriate concepts that can be borrowed from the field of empirical memory study to formulate a theory of any generality. Even where a great deal of empirical data has been gathered, as in requesting earliest memories, no ideas of any consequence have emerged as to how a date is attributed or how "earliest" is determined. The dating process is too multiform to be limited to a few variables. One complexity is that the dating of personally experienced events usually involves two computational series, personal chronologies and public event chronologies. By definition, screen memories along with their other inaccuracies embody a permanent error in the dating of past events, but only the error in the personal chronology is usually considered important in psychoanalytic treatment, although misdating in reference to public event chronologies could be of some theoretical interest. As has been discussed, absolute chronologies such as are involved in knowing one's age and the calendrical year have become widespread accomplishments only in the last few centuries. They are arbitrary yardsticks set up by our culture. Relative chronologies are idiosyncratic in that they relate closely to personal, familial, and current events. A personal protocol was cited in which the acute phenomenological expert Maurice Merleau-Ponty proceeded to date events only by bootstrapping matching operations between past personal and public events. The only discernible difference in his protocol from those of phenomenologically unsophisticated observers was in his awareness of the emotional tone of past eras.

In academic psychology in recent years a type of memory performance has been taken note of where there is a specific match between public and personal chronologies because of the importance and the newsworthiness of some single public event. Psychologists have formulated a category called *flashbulb* memories, which refers to the phenomenon that many people can pinpoint in recall their own personal situation and exactly what they were doing at the moment of hearing the news of an especially notable and emotional public event. Studied events include the assassinations of John F. Kennedy and Martin Luther King, Jr., and the surrender days of World Wars I and II. The major result is that the *same* public event generates widespread claims of recall of "what one was doing" when he or she heard the news. The private occasions of deep emotion that arise in any individual's life where one might assume there would also be well retained memories of one's external circumstances have not been systematically studied for possible "flashbulb" effects.[4]

Recent decades have seen a tremendous increase in the use of photography to replay and memorialize both public and personal events. Photographs, audio tapes, and videotapes are not only important sources to provoke nostalgia but serve also as nodal points in personal chronologies and as means for placing personal chronologies within larger familial chronologies that antedate the life of the individual. Because any artifacts, event matches and associations, bracketing, and other methods of approximation can be a means to establish event dating and chronologies, there appears to be no way of simplifying the performance of dating in order to design realistic experimental studies. Any clue can be utilized; restricted studies of event dating would be incapable of generalization. The unaided soliloquy in establishing event ordering is increasingly rare; numerous artifacts, both objective and social, are the landmarks of our chronologies.

Memory Mechanisms and Psychological Systems

The failure of psychologists and philosophers to find subjective distinguishing marks for memories has been documented in previous chapters. (Baldwin's thesis that, unlike fantasies, memory images can be manipulated to be more preceptual in appearance, while they are also under greater personal control than perceptions, was probably the most interesting failure.) Could a different approach be more successful? An obvious method is to look for a distinctive mental process or memory mechanism that differentiates the memory act from other mental actions. Such a distinctive process would presumably be outside the awareness of the individual rememberer. By isolating a memoric process that consistently functions outside of awareness, the difficulties that adhere to introspection and the range of individual differences found with subjective judgments could be avoided. There is just one difficulty: No such distinctive process has ever been put forward by any major theory. Every theoretical system of psychology, whatever the mental processes espoused, applies the same mechanisms to both thinking and memory operations.

The main cognitive mechanisms claimed to function in thought and memory are association, conditioning, and schema formulation and manipulation. (This is a tremendous oversimplification, but it doesn't subtract from the overall claim that one process does for both thinking and memory.) Association explanations of memory were dominant in the late nineteenth century among philosopher-psychologists and laboratory introspectionists. The early Freud, as has been described in detail, adopted many association principles in describing both rational and irrational thinking, as well as memory mechanisms. Behaviorists, by and large, sought conditioning explanations for both thought and memory, but other theorists have also made use of these concepts. Both classical and Skinnerian operant conditioning were implicated by theorists discussed in earlier chapters: classical conditioning for explaining retention in stressful states (Sargant, Chapter 6) and operant conditioning as descriptive of the bardic extemporizations that mimic "memorization by other means" (Peabody, Chapter 9). Schema theory for the description of thinking and retention has attracted contemporary psychologists with functional and developmental interests and some recent psychoanalytic theorists. More difficult to classify, Gestalt theorists combined schema formulations of a structural nature with an admixture of associations. Piaget's schema theory has been especially forthright in emphasizing the continuity of memory with thinking; retention consists, essentially, of turning the intelligence to consideration of past events. In fact, however, though other theories often ignored the thinking–memory nexus, they too assumed that memory mechanisms were just an application of those used for thought.

The last thirty years, however, have brought the realization that older conceptions of memory processes lacked important details; a series of processing steps is required. Thus, with an information-processing perspective flowcharts are used to diagram successive steps. Other theorists invoked the concept of a "memory strategy," in some ways analogous to, but usually simpler than the retention plans used by mnemonicists. In spite of increased complexity, neither of these ways of representing the memory process embodies any uniquely memoric mechanism. Commonly memory is characterized as including thinking (or learning) mechanisms *plus* some form of storage. As functional psychological theories elucidating storage categories have not been highly successful—e.g., association networks, hypothetical traces, levels of processing, and the like—the task of defining the nature of storage is now very often surrendered to the neuropsychologist or neurophysiologist, whose first priority is to determine the localization of memory activity, as indeed it was for pioneer neuropsychologist Karl Lashley 60 years ago.

Another way to consider the role of memory is to ignore possible processing intricacies and assume the adequacy of memory functioning. From the standpoint of one's mental economy, memory can be viewed as necessary, but performing only a subordinate or housekeeping function like digestion or respiration. In this view, memory malfunctioning can be theorized as resulting from emotional and motivational conflicts which, when activated, produce memory deficits and distortions. Much of Freud's discussion of personal memory through all his theorizing is squarely in this category, for, as has often been said, Freud was more concerned with a theory of forgetting than a theory of learning. He assumed that registration and subsequent recall is ordinarily accurate and unimpeded if conflicting motivations are not present.

The subordination of memory to other personality aspects was carried a good bit further by the interpersonal analyst Harry Stack Sullivan. He offered a unique metamemory hypothesis that did not concern itself with either memory functioning and its mechanisms or with memory accuracy. Rather, he viewed the characteristic degree of confidence expressed in one's memory by patients during the psychiatric interview as diagnostically valuable in assessing motivational structure. The basis of this hypothesis is that high confidence in one's memory performance must indicate a simple and therefore effective motivational structure, whereas motivational complications lead to confidence decrements. For it is Sullivan's view that memory assessment is more closely tied to conation than to cognition; thus actual cognitive proficiency in memory performance scarcely figures in confidence judgments.

> It is useful to note the patient's *habitual attitude toward his recall or memory.* Recall is a function of motivation, and the person's attitude toward his own recall—be it assurance, vague uncertainty, or emphatic pessimism—may be quite revealing. By an attitude of assurance, I do not mean that anyone knows that his memory will always work, for nobody's memory always works . . . It is not that recall is important in itself, but that the person's *attitude* toward recall gives a valuable clue to the simplicity of his motivation. If his recall is relatively useful to him, he has probably been proceeding toward more or less clearly foreseen goals for a long time, and having some success at getting near them; and his motivational system is relatively simple. In trying to trace some unhappy people's motivational history, one may get into quagmires which take hours to wallow through, whereas one could have found a useful and immediate clue to much the same thing by noticing to what extent they could depend on their memories. (1956, pp. 116–117*n*)

Sullivan's "habitual attitude" toward one's memory can be construed as a global "sense of conviction" rather than the piecemeal confidence attached to specific memories discussed by the psychoanalysts described in Chapter 5. Who can deny, however, that faith in one's overall memory can often carry over to individual memories. In contrast to the Freudian approach, what is striking is Sullivan's acceptance of the rationality of the patient's attitude toward his own memory. If the patient distrusts his memory, it is for good and sufficent reason; his motives are so confused that his memory functioning is inevitably assessed as being in disarray. (Here, to be sure, memory other than life-historical events can be involved.) The possibility is not entertained that the patient's concern about his memory is unfounded or that his confidence in it is overblown.

If there is no difference in mechanism between thinking and memory, it is not inappropriate or illogical to consider that there is no need to distinguish a separate memory category. "Behavior" is a wide-varying category that includes thinking and memory and much more; this is the viewpoint of contemporary radical behaviorism just as it was for the founder of behaviorism, John B. Watson, in the 1920s. As for investigating "memories" by asking people about memory content, this is too subjective to allow any reliable theory to be formulated, even under the ostensibly scientific guise of studying information processing. According to B. F. Skinner, questions about memories—which are asked as one of the "practical exigencies of the helping professions"—are only short-cut probes, a poor substitute for the analysis of actual behavior.

> Psychotherapists must ask people what has happened to them and how they feel because the confidential relationship of therapist and client prevents direct inquiry. (It is sometimes argued that what a person remembers may be more important than what actually happened, but that is true only if something else has happened, of which it would also be better to have independent evidence.) But although the use of reports of feelings and states of mind can be justified on practical grounds, there is no justification for their use in theory making. The temptation, however, is great. Psychoanalysts, for example, specialize in feelings. Instead of investigating the early lives of their patients or watching them with their families, friends, or business associates, they ask them what has happened and how they feel about it. It is not surprising that they should then construct theories in terms of memories, feelings, and states of mind or that they should say that an analysis of behavior in terms of environmental events lacks "depth." (1987, p. 283)

Ironically, these warnings of the antiscientific bent of dealing in *memories* did not prevent Skinner from authoring by far the longest and most detailed autobiography ever produced by a psychologist (a 3-volume work of over 1,000 pages). In the volume *Particulars of my Life,* Skinner even admits that he is a bit of a dab hand at analyzing personal memories. "Proust was practicing a kind of psychology when he sought to explain strange recollections, and I myself began to analyze a few instances of Proustian recall in my own experience" (1984, p. 296). It is the case, then, that autobiographical memories are not without interest for behaviorists, even if taboo for behaviorism. A somewhat opposite point of view has been emphasized in the present work. It is not that the study of autobiographical memories is unscientific but, rather, that behaviorism, introspective and information-processing psychology, and psychotherapeutic endeavors are each by themselves too constrained to encompass with any adequacy all the desirable perspectives useful in studying personal memories.[5]

Psychotherapy, including psychoanalysis, in spite of Skinner's statement, has for a long time been less and less concerned with the study of autobiographical memories. Indeed, the psychoanalytic therapy dependent on recall of accurate early-life memories already was considered a failure by many analysts in the early 1920s. Thus Sandor Ferenczi and Otto Rank wrote in 1923:

> The requirements of the Breuer-Freud catharsis that the affects, displaced upon symptoms, should be led back directly to the pathologic memory-traces, and at the same time brought to a discharge and bound again proved to be unrealizable, that is, it succeeds only in the case of incompletely repressed, mostly preconscious memory-material as in the case of certain derivatives of the actual unconscious. (p. 37)

Many analysts now emphasize (as partially detailed in Chapter 5) that underlying wishes, desires, and fantasies rather than memories are what the analyst is after. Like Ferenczi and Rank, these analysts are quick to point out that since these dynamic properties were never experienced they can never be remembered. In the psychoanalytic literature of today, an interest in memory "reconstruction" often seems a bit old-fashioned. Theoretical justification can, if needed, be found in Freud's theory: Small children's personal memories have fallen prey to infantile amnesia; older children's memories, as Anna Freud tells us, are of little consequence in therapy; and what adults readily remember is considered either irrelevant or inappropriate, because such memories are too accessible to consciousness to be diagnostic of deep-seated conflicts.

The Self and Memory: Present, Absent, Dissociated?

The present survey of theories of autobiographical memory is obviously incomplete as it ends short of proposing a theory of the self. A satisfactory theory of self in relation to personal memories remains for the future even in the limited form of an "executive function" or volitional ego. The complexities that nonvolitional and unconscious memories bring to the formulation of a theory of self preclude any sketch of the self after the fashion of such pioneer self theorists as William James and James Mark Baldwin. It is often facilely asserted without memories we lack any personal identity, but the self is more than a constellation of memories and less than the full range of autobiographical memories, and neither learning nor forgetting can be said to augment or diminish the self in any demonstrable fashion. The need for distinguishing between self-related memories and others has long been recognized as a theoretical necessity. As early as 1911 Piaget's teacher Edouard Claparède wrote:

> We can distinguish between two sorts of mental calculations: those established *mentally between representations* and those established between *repre-*

sentations and the me, the personality. In the case of purely passive associations or idea-reflexes, solely the first kind of connection operates; in the case
of voluntary recall and recognition where the me plays a role, the second
kind of connection enters. (1911/1951)

With the caveat that self-related memories cannot be limited to voluntary
remembering and the notion of "idea-reflexes" is long outmoded, Claparède's
statement still seems descriptively pertinent. Theoretically, it can be noted,
there is a two-way street in that a theory of personal memory must necessarily
influence our interpretation of the idea of the self, as well as the way we
construe the self influencing the disposition of memories.

There is a far more radical stance that can be taken toward the construct of
the self; namely, that a concept of self is unnecessary and can be omitted from
theoretical consideration. Roy Schafer (1981) has argued forcefully in his 1980
Heinz Werner lectures on *Narrative Actions in Psychoanalysis* for dispensing
with a concept of self and similar terms insofar as they purport to function by
supplying personal continuity.

> In conventional discourse, personal continuity over linear time is usually
> assumed to require the existence of some entity or entity-like process or
> state of affairs that guarantees it. The way in which words like *trait, habit,
> character, state, self, identity,* and *disposition* are used in everyday speech
> shows this to be so. These words are used as explanatory terms that specify
> something a person *has,* some sort of possession or organ-like thing that
> guarantees his or her going on being the same. (1981, p. 30)

The prevalence of these concepts is not, however, an argument for their
necessity. Schafer claims that a better procedure is to follow historians in using
metatheoretical strategies that postulate no superfluous continuity term.

> It will be worthwhile to take a moment to consider whether some guaran-
> tee of continuity is required in world-historical accounts. The modern con-
> sensus would seem to be that it is not required. Historical continuity may
> be satisfactorily described from one or more vantage points, and in each
> case it may be attributed to, and described in terms of, the continued
> influence of certain factors of a technological, military, economic, political,
> or philsophical nature. (p. 32)

Thus, along with a strong appeal for the use of action language in psychoanalytic narrative and its substitution for the "blatant, question-begging, an-
thropomorphic, and mechanistic metaphors in both the received and the
newly proposed versions of psychoanalytic theory," Schafer challenges the
traditional assumption that "we must postulate mental entities that guarantee
personal continuity over time."

A related question is whether there is just one or more than one self, or,
if the concept of self be omitted, is there more than one agentic center that is
capable of retaining personal memories? In Piaget's commentary on Freud, it
can be recalled, a major objection to Freud's theory was that there were two
centers of mental activity because the unconscious was seen as an indepen-

dent source of action with its own memory contents. For Piaget, much that Freud attributed to the agentic manifestations of the unconscious could more appropriately be considered as way stations to maturity. There are other theoretical possibilities of separate centers of mental activity besides the psychoanalytical unconscious. Perhaps the most exotic manifestation is the phenomenon of multiple personality where some personalities, in part or in whole, lack awareness of the activities of the other personalities manifested by a single individual. In recent years the diagnosis of multiple personality, though still uncommon, has experienced a considerable increase. Literature on this topic has been summarized by Ernest Hilgard (1977), who also experimentally demonstrated *divided consciousness* (less drastic than multiple personality) for some hypnotized subjects, with a partial lack of awareness and hence unequal recall capability between the two divisions of consciousness. Theorizing concerning multiple personality and divided consciousness depends heavily on Pierre Janet's concept of dissociation, a distinctly non-Freudian concept that does not invoke the mechanism of repression. (Although such possible self-multiplications and self-divisions can importantly complicate personal memory considerations, they will not be pursued further here, because psychopathology and hypnosis are outside the boundaries of this theoretical survey.)

It is also pertinent to consider the possible dissociation of ongoing events from one's self (or self-surrogate) in a milder form. Have any such mechanisms been described? Certainly one example is Sullivan's concept of "selective inattention" in which environmental events that represent partially disowned "integrating tendencies" are permitted to impinge only weakly on the consciousness of the individual. "Weakly" means that there can be *recognition* of events if they are brought to one's attention, but there can rarely be *spontaneous recall* of events and, in particular, obvious inferences and elaborations that follow from these events will be kept out of awareness.

> But so far as the self-system is concerned, this identification of events without any development of their personal implications is all that happens, and the events pass by rapid transit into memory. They are available for recall, but not very easily available because a great deal of our recall is done by the facile flow of what we call association, which really means the aspects of a momentary pattern convenient for the recall of past events. . . . So while the experience that impinged on you, which you noticed and hurled into history, can be recalled, it is not anywhere near as handy as it might be, because it is not well tied into the general tissue of your life. (1956, p. 58)

Sullivan substitutes the dissociation of selective inattention for the repression concept.

> I very much prefer to speak of dissociation of major integrative tendencies rather than what is sometimes called the repression of such tendencies, for I do not think that repression actually describes what happens . . . All of us have some dissociated integrative tendencies; all of us have certain impulses which have not been provided with any reasonable channel for development

by the culture. In other words, Western culture does not use part of our impulse equipment, if you please, part of our adjustive potentialities. It is because there are such things that Freud was led into what I feel is the flat mistake of assuming that the unconscious is largely the habitation of the primitive, the infantile, the undeveloped, and so on. (1956, pp. 65–66)

It is not the clash of theoretical viewpoints that should receive major emphasis here. It is quite possible that both repression and selective inattention can be accommodated under the same theoretical tent. Rather, I would stress that, insofar as personal memory is at issue, Sullivan has introduced a "medium strength" concept rather than a strong concept, such as repression, to every situation whether appropriate or not. Doubtless selective inattention could be transformed to incomplete memory repression, but at the expense of losing important nuances. It is my contention that more of these mid-level concepts are needed to describe the topography of autobiographical memory with some adequacy. Other suggestions in this vein are presented in the next section. Ernst Kris should be acknowledged as an important innovator; in his emphasis on such mechanisms as *isolation* and *denial* (or *disavowal*), he illustrated several ways, other than repression, in which memory links with conscious realization were severed.

Interpretations and Suggestions

As no mechanisms or psychological principles have been found that deal uniquely with memoric activity, distinctions among types of memories are usually made in terms of modality (motor, odor, visual, or auditory memories) or representation category (symbolic, verbal, or nonverbal memories). Sometimes a memory category is classified by the material involved (pictorial or prose memory) and at other times by the temporal interval or presumed psychological procedure involved (immediate or rote memory). Whether material is easy or difficult to remember can also play a role. Consider a thought experiment in which items or events are so difficult to remember that no one remembers anything. Although remembering was attempted, if nothing was retained, we would not ordinarily consider that memory was involved. (This is quite different from the situation in which something was once known but is now completely forgotten.) But the converse occurs more frequently where for all practical purposes nothing has been forgotten. If content has been newly mastered, there is perhaps a short period during which we relate the content to memory functioning. Soon, however, the memory aspects fail to interest anyone. Instead we speak of habits, skills, automatic responding, and the like. The point is that degree of accuracy enters into what we are willing to label "memory." The extremes of either close to zero percent or 100 percent retention accuracy are commonly considered from perspectives other than memory. Over lengthy time-spans other activities have been noted in which retention occurs, but the memory aspect disappears, such as the absorption of memories into the character structure and the Piagetian incorporation of actions into permanent schemes that are not forgotten.

A denial of memory jurisdiction also occurs in the phenomenological claim that physiognomic perception rather than memory retention accounts for much that passes for memory recognition. The physiognomic hypothesis returns us to consideration of affective memory because, putting claims of validity to one side, it contradicts the view that emotions are dependent on prior cognitions and occur only after the fact. For in physiognomic perception we detect feelings of "happiness" and "sadness" as part of the total perceptual experience. The old idea that the bodily means by which emotions are expressed is the locus of emotional retention (just as we speak of "muscle" memory) probably plays a role in the assumption, often implicit, that emotional aspects of memories must lag behind cognitive aspects. Unexpressed emotions are also invariably denied the status conferred on unexpressed cognitions, namely, that they are able to exist in latent form. (The Freudian preconscious is a well-known cognitive rendezvous for latent thoughts, but emotions find no haven there. The same bias exists in many non-Freudian psychologists and philosophers, who, however, express themselves less forthrightly.) One attempt to rationalize cognition as fundamental is Piaget's view that cognitions are permanent subsisting structures, whereas affects are mere focused energies. But it does not logically follow that pristine latent cognitions are any more comprehensible than latent emotions. The turn-of-the-century psychoanalytic technical term "complex" possessed some holistic virtue in that idea clusters, partly or totally unconscious, were constituted by strong shared emotions. No attempt was made to consider ideas and affects separately. The term is now generally in abeyance in psychoanalytic usage; early disfavor came from distortions brought about by excessive public popularity and the term's intimate associations with the theories of Jung and Adler.

Almost all innovations in psychotherapy in the last half-century have in common a discounting of the importance of autobiographical memories. Certainly this is not surprising with behavior therapies or any variety of short-term therapy. More unexpectedly, it has also been true of mainstream psychoanalysis. It seems a safe prediction that future summaries of developments in the study of autobiographical memory will devote a proportionally smaller amount of exposition to concepts concerning memory stemming from psychotherapy, but at the same time the range of academic fields contributing theoretical ideas will be enlarged well beyond the number that I have mentioned.

Today there are major limitations that handicap therapists in studying personal memories. One limitation is the lack of emphasis put on memory veridicality. A "sense of conviction" about one's memory correctness is often considered an adequate attainment; after all, it is argued, there are no wholly accurate memories. What many would assume to be the central problem of memory study, memory accuracy, is thus of little concern. Within psychoanalysis an example of this disregard of verification is the historical fact that it has ultimately made little theoretical difference whether Freud's interpretation of the "seduction hypothesis" was based on actual occurrences or on fantasies.

Some few therapists have insisted on the importance of the distinction, but in the recent past they have been a small minority. It is ironic that past and present biographers of Freud have viewed his shift from a belief in actual seductions to fantasies as crucial, yet the major theoretical effect has been to devalue the unique importance of valid memories so that facts and fantasies can be equated. Thus, if a patient should too strongly grow to doubt the truth of false recollections pivotal to an autobiographical narrative, this lack of confidence might well be judged to be a therapeutic handicap. In some instances a memoric revelation of "what really happened" could be considered of primary importance, but therapeutically its usual status is that of a fortunate coincidence.

The question of memory veridicality did not arise in quite the same way for Freud himself since he believed that repressions could be overcome and, through reconstructions, valid memories could be determined. Yet Freud's few *obiter dicta* as to methodological procedures were generally negative regarding whether proof of verification should even be sought. Obviously this attitude helped discourage later analysts from serious investigation of autobiographical memories. I quote from the group discussion of the Kris Study Group (Fine, Joseph, and Waldhorn).

> The question was raised as to verification of a reconstruction by means of collateral material from another source, such as the report of the mother or other relatives. In this connection Lowenstein recalled a personal communication from Freud on the subject. Freud advised against seeking outside help to reconstruct what actually happened. He felt that it betrayed to the patient a lack of confidence in what can be accomplished through analysis. The opinions and memories of others usually do not count, and frequently will only cause confusion because of their own distortions. Freud believed that if the analyst worked carefully and bided his time, he would be able to reconstruct what is essential. (1971, p. 73)

The second major limitation of psychotherapy in obtaining useful data concerning personal memories is the restricted settings where therapy is conducted and its exclusive dependence on verbal interchanges. Recommendations such as those made by Samuel Novey have not been influential. He proposed incorporating into analysis actual visits and trips to locations or milieus where past personal happenings took place and, in general, considering the need people have for linking their reminiscences to their original settings. Also enlarging the experiential beyond the verbal, Freud himself took an active interest in manifestations of sensory imagery and motor phenomena that he claimed were partial memory representations, but there is little interest in these areas today. These investigations reported by Novey and Freud are simply two approaches among others that therapists have suggested as aids in the stimulation and interpretation of personal memories. Perhaps the verbal elucidation of memories must always be paramount, but much is omitted if memory production and content is restricted to the analysis of dialogues, narratives, and verbal free associations.

It is sometimes stated that the complications surrounding autobiographical memories make them almost impossible to study. Others in addition to therapists point this out. One claim of this sort is that, for all of us, but especially for children, autobiographical memories are undergoing *continuous* reorganization and restructuring. (This assertion is one strand in Piaget's argument for disregarding the data from autobiographical memories, and it was used by Ernst Kris in claiming that patterns such as the "personal myth" were relatively constant while more veridical memory contents were in flux.) I do not believe that this assertion is valid to nearly the extent that is claimed, but it would be a valuable finding if it could be shown to be the case. Surely there are, at a minimum, differential rates of memory reorganization depending on which subject matter category is involved.

Criticisms of theoretical approaches for not doing what they were never intended to do can be informing but not wholly satisfying. I conclude on the positive but personal note of indicating which areas are most susceptible in some productive way to theoretical and research endeavors. My suggestions as to useful and feasible areas for future investigation are limited to half a dozen topical areas drawn from the previous chapters, with emphasis placed on topics that are generally neglected despite some theoretical awareness. The first is the role of intentionality in retention, in particular the provocative claim that I have several times reiterated that too intense effort handicaps retention and recall. Here investigation of customary or habitual volitional attitudes is needed, not just coercive instructions either to remember or to forget.

A second area that remains largely undeveloped is that of *children's autobiographical memory.* I have pointed out some reasons for this neglect, but they do not curtail the theoretical interest of the topic. All veridical adult memories of early childhood have been retained during the intermediate eras of later childhood and adolescence. Or have they? Undoubtedly not *all* of them were accessible then. Perhaps some are reconstructed only in adulthood. In any case, children's remembrances of themselves when younger are worth investigating, even those that do not survive to adulthood.

A third area pertaining to social aspects of memory is that of the societal *simulation of memorization.* What are the ways in which general societal knowledge or certain subject matter genres curtail possibilities so that retention is performed more by limiting forced choices and inferences than by intentional memorization? This topic was raised in regard to the performance of traditional bardic epics; but, in less systematic ways, implicit mnemonic frameworks are pervasive in society. A related point emphasized by sociologist Maurice Halbwachs and psychoanalyst Anton Kris is that we can sometimes confuse our social attitudes with our memories. Thus we claim for ourselves remembrance of events that we have never experienced. (Once again I am asking the philosopher's question about where reasoning leaves off and memory begins.) It should also be noted that the plausibility that can often be obtained by purely circumstantial reasoning about the past is an important factor in allowing us to perpetrate with some success those interesting intentionally false recalls that fall under the heading of "success-ful lies."

A cluster of memory topics that have often been casually noted and have here received passing mention deserves more theoretical attention. These topics center on the concept of *suppression* of memories and the whole area of *intentional manipulation and control* of established memories. The acceptance of the importance of the mechanism of repression, with its emphasis on ab-sence of control over memory, appears to have led to a lack of interest in the extent to which people can control their memories or, at a minimum, believe they can exercise control. Repression is too strong a model to fit quotidian performance needs, even when melded with other defense mechanisms. Sulli-van opted for a less traditional mechanism to meet such needs with his con-cept of *selective inattention,* but there are certainly a number of other more volitional mechanisms. For example, many people claim they can, when they wish, terminate ongoing trains of unpleasant memories by shifting to pleasant topics, or at least topics that break up memory repetitions. Others mention the therapeutic benefit of memory repetitions that lead to the "dissipation" of unpleasantness and the realization of a less emotional outlook. This is an assertion closely analogous to the early Freud and Breuer claim of "wearing away" disturbing memories. Terminating bad memories on command and intentionally repeating unhappy memories to put them in realistic perspective appear on first consideration to be contradictory techniques, but both actions are aspects of memory control, even when only partly volitional. D. Ewen Cameron's theory has gone furthest in considering these and related tech-niques and in describing under what circumstances the exercise of these tech-niques, however brought about, can sometimes lead to undesirable outcomes. I would add that conceiving memory suppressions in the old-fashioned way as single "acts of will" tends to oversimplification; more complex, well-practiced *forgetting strategies* may be involved.

Another memory area in which a strong explanatory model holds too much sway, and thereby limits understanding, is the perfunctory application of the concept of *catharsis* to every form of memory telling. The notion that all benefits derived through communicating personal memories from exchanging confidences to describing traumatic experiences can be referenced under ca-tharsis is to ignore a range of striking differences. When Freud in his early theorizing included the concept of Aristotelian catharsis through abreaction as a major benefit from the lifting of repressions, the concept was, as Henri Ellenberger (1970) has documented, very much in vogue. And despite the superimposition of later theory and practice, orthodox psychoanalysis still reserves an important niche for catharsis and abreaction. Today, unfortu-nately, catharsis is an omnipresent concept. Journalists, philosophers, and a multitude of others allege that the emotional purging of catharsis extends from interviews (especially with journalists) to sporting events, movies, and vacations. The assumption seems to be that if only weak emotions are aroused, then the effect of catharsis is scaled down accordingly. Paying due homage to the historical longevity of the catharsis concept and its maid-of-all-work usefulness, it is nevertheless, a good example of a concept that has become so overextended that it is virtually meaningless. More precise concepts are needed, scaled to the levels of emotional arousal involved.

A final suggestion considers looking at another neglected area of memory study, that of *memory elaborations,* particularly those performed intentionally to give pleasure. This omission is related to a general lack of theoretical concern with the possible pleasures derived from memory manipulation other than the reputed satisfaction of ridding oneself of emotions through catharsis. In ordinary remembering, quite apart from indulgence in nostalgia, considerations of accuracy are often put aside in order to prolong and improve on past pleasurable moments. With college students, many fictional embellishments that "gild the lily," far from occurring as unconscious distortions, are readily acknowledged. With young people, pleasurable memories are also exaggerated because they are thought of as a springboard for the future and are mixed with the open-ended fantasies of expectations. It is only the psychologist, therapist, historian, or other memory investigator who customarily entertains the often gratuitous assumption that the underlying goal of personal memory reinstatement is always precise accuracy. Here Pierre Janet and students of oral cultures have reminded us that the transmission of emotions and performance excitement often eclipses information exchange. Not everything classed as a memory error is so for the rememberer.

In conclusion, there is a point of view that previous chapters have ignored. It is a completely lucid theory—possibly the only one that could be so characterized—that we have it within ourselves to discern without error any distinctions we might wish to make about memory. As such, it is a straightforward refutation of all the analyses that have been presented and any other that could have been presented. This perspective is incorporated in the statement made near the end of the eighteenth century by Thomas Reid, leader of the Scottish realist or common-sense school of philosophy. Reid's confident manifesto gives a glimpse of the thought of the learned man in the premodern world—a preordained, suprarational world (most of all perhaps in explaining human behavior) that ignored the quibbling uncertainties over the role of memory that have intrigued many curious minds during the past century. It is conceivable that, even today, Reid speaks also for the mythical man-in-the-street, if and when he ever considers memory functions (other than memory accuracy) problematic.

> I conclude also, that sensation, memory, and imagination, even where they have the same object, are operations of a quite different nature, and perfectly distinguishable by those who are sound and sober. A man that is in danger of confounding them, is indeed to be pitied; but whatever relief he can find from another art, he can find none from logic or metaphysics. I conclude further, that it is no less a part of the human constitution, to believe the present existence or our sensations, and to believe the past existence of what we remember, than it is to believe that twice two make four. The evidence of sense, the evidence of memory, and the evidence of the necessary relation of things, are all distinct and original kinds of evi-

dence, equally grounded on our constitution: none of them depends upon, or can be resolved into another. To reason against any of these kinds of evidence, is absurd; nay, to reason for them, is absurd. They are first principles; and such fall not within the province of reason, but of common sense (Reid, 1785/1970, p. 30).

Today in thinking about the possible boundaries of memory, many people feel puzzled rather than "sound and sober." Furthermore, they are often skeptical about believing in the "past existence" of what they only seem to remember. But I would argue that considering the demonstrated multiplicity of memory concepts is meaningful in a way that has been overlooked. One of the lessons that psychology can teach is the existence of unexpectedly wide ranges of individual differences. Individual differences are most often described in terms of measured abilities, performance outcomes, and descriptive taxonomies. In theorizing about memory, tabular and graphic displays containing such entities are numerous, but they are insufficient. It is more satisfying to go a step further and describe the ways in which specific procedures embody retained personal memories. This book has been about such procedures. Arrays of qualitatively different memory procedures were found in each of the developmental, social, and subjective spheres. On this basis, the speculation can be advanced that it is as much the mix of procedures that we use in dealing with past actions as the type of content that serves to individualize every autobiographical assessment.

NOTES

Usage Note

Sometimes there is the need to refer to memory in adjectival terms rather than as a noun. The word *memoric,* which I adopted for this purpose as such a modifier, seemed adequately clear and unambiguous. But, surprisingly, I discovered that "memoric" cannot be found in English language dictionaries and therefore is not an English word. I have used it, notwithstanding. In researching this book I was pleased to find that I had been anticipated in this usage by psychologist Knight Dunlap, who expressed the same preference some 60 years ago. He wrote: "We deliberately introduce the new word *memoric* here, because there is in English no established word which signifies *pertaining or related to memory.* The pedantic term *mnemonic* is sometimes used as we have used 'memoric,' but the usage is inaccurate, since 'mnemonic' strictly means 'assisting the memory,' or more generally, pertaining to methods or devices for improving or aiding remembering" (Dunlap, 1932/1972, fn. p. 149). (Strachey in his English translation of Freud used the adjective *mnemic,* a novel if somewhat unclear word that has also been used to refer to the organic memory conceptions of Richard Semon. But like *memoric* it is not found in the OED.) I would only add that the commoner adjective nowadays is *memorial,* also obviously unsuitable since it is much more frequently a noun than an adjective, and even as an adjective has as a first meaning "serving as a remembrance of a person or event; commemorative." Is Dunlap's suggestion too sensible to be generally adopted?

Chapter 1

1. I do not use the term *episodic memory,* popular in academic psychology, as synonymous with *autobiographical memory.* As a technical term, *episodic memory* does not coincide either with my use or the customary meaning of *autobiographical memory,* both for reasons of what is included and what is excluded. Brewer (1986) pointed out that "episodic memory" has included the performance of rote verbal memory, and Fitzgerald (1986) noted that the label "episodic memory" never refers to involuntary memory.

2. That memory should be dealt with in its unconscious aspects is not a discovery of Freud building upon daring speculative leaps of a few prescient forerunners. David Kay in his 1888 *Memory: What is it and how to improve it* (D. Appleton) devotes an entire chapter to "Mind, Conscious and Unconscious" presenting copious quotations from authorities such as Hering, Maudsley, Taine, Hamilton, Spencer, Ribot, Reid, and Stewart, among others. G. H. Lewes states in an epigraph: "The teaching of most modern psychologists is that consciousness forms but a small item in the total of psychical processes. Unconscious sensations, ideas and judgments are made to play a great part in their explanations. It is very certain that in every conscious volition— every act that is so characterized—the larger part of it is quite unconscious. It is equally certain that in every perception there are unconscious processes of reproduc-

tion and inference—there is . . . a middle distance of sub-consciousness, and a 'background' of unconsciousness." Consciousness, in fact, may be regarded as an evolutionary fault, since a Prof. Drummond notes that, "Many besides Schopenhauer have secretly regarded consciousness as the hideous mistake and malady of nature."

3. A lively field of memory research since the middle 1970s is that of "metamemory," pioneered by psychologist John Flavell. Metamemory research, however, has been concerned with *knowledge about memory* (need for memorization, difficulty in remembering, memorization tactics, etc.) rather than the *experience of remembering*. Metamemory topics are of most theoretical interest when children are interrogated, but children, even when the older introspective psychology was in vogue, have never been considered capable or reliable subjects where experiential descriptions are wanted. Perhaps experimental ingenuity could alter this viewpoint and devise meaningful ways to explore children's subjective memory experiences.

4. Ernest Jones's conclusion that Freud was "ill-informed in the field of contemporary psychology and seems to have derived from hearsay any knowledge he had of it" has been the authoritative statement regarding Freud's alleged lack of psychological knowledge (*Life and Work*, vol. I, p. 371). This false generalization appears not to have been challenged even in the recent flurry of publications exploring Freud's intellectual antecedents, hidden motivations, and immediate environmental milieu. In a curious backhanded way, Philip Reiff attempted to soften Jones's exaggeration: "Although his knowledge was vague, Freud's bibliomania probably supplemented to some extent mere hearsay. . . . Like most bibliophiles, he probably did not read anywhere near all he bought or was given, but it is worth noting that Ebbinghaus and two editions of that early and esoteric psychologist of the unconscious, Carl-Gustav Carus, were on Freud's shelves" (Reiff, *The Mind of a Moralist*, 1959, pp. 5–6).

Jones's short discussion of the limitations of Freud's psychological knowledge (vol. I, pp. 371–374) deals chiefly with the possible influence on Freud of J. F. Herbart (a psychologist who died 15 years before Freud was born and G. T. Fechner, who in Jones's very inaccurate view constructed a psychology "altogether built on Herbart's." Although Herbart can be considered an orienting influence, it cannot be denied, even by Jones that Freud in several places paid explicit and appreciative tribute to Fechner rather than to Herbart. Jones concludes his summary of Freud's psychological knowledge: "Freud who had studied his [Fechner's] writings at first hand, also [i.e., in addition to Breuer, who admired Fechner greatly] spoke highly of him. He said, 'I was always open to the ideas of G. T. Fechner and have followed that thinker on many important points' " (vol. I, p. 374; quotation from Freud (1925) *An Autobiographical Study*).

As J. Strachey's index of Freud's citations makes clear, Freud cited Fechner more than 15 times, drawing from four different works, including the two-volume tomes on psychophysics and esthetics. In addition, the other founder of academic experimental psychology, Wilhelm Wundt, was cited more than 20 times with references to three different volumes of Wilhelm Wundt's folk psychology (*Völkerpsychologie*) and the largest number of references to Wundt's famous physiological psychology text. More conclusively, in the preface to his *Totem and Taboo* (1912–1913) Freud wrote that this volume was inspired chiefly by Wundt and Carl Jung. Freud stated that his approach to social psychology through psychoanalysis offered a "methodological contrast on the one hand to Wilhelm Wundt's extensive work which applies the hypothesis and working methods of *non*-analytic psychology to the same purposes. . . ." Although Herbart was cited by Freud only once and Carus not at all, writings of many prominent psychologists were cited at a time when those who were primarily identified as psychologists were few in number. Psychologists cited in this group included Alfred Binet and Victor Henri in France, Edouard Claparède in Switzerland, Alexander Bain and Havelock Ellis in Britain, and Mary Calkins and G. Stanley Hall in America, with several of these citations specifically to psychology journal articles. Finally, as I point out in Chapter 4, Freud cited the Russian physiologist Ivan Pavlov for his psychological conditioning experiments at the early date of 1905. So much for Freud's *hearsay* knowledge of psychology!

If Freud knew nothing about psychology, it frequently encourages today's psychoanalytic authorities to do likewise, with sometimes a little disparagement thrown in to reinforce the tradition. A contemporary sample: "As distinct from psychoanalysis, which emphasizes the unconscious, repression, sexuality and the Oedipus complex, psychology deals with mental processes such as consciousness, ideation, sensation, and memory. Experimental psychology aspires to accreditation as a 'hard science' but often gropes about in a shadowy realm of elementary statistics and applied physics" (p. 51*n*, J. Spector, 1988, "The State of Psychoanalytic Research in Art History," *The Art Bulletin*, 70, 49–76). The irony of this assessment is that it was Freud's strong source of influence, G. T. Fechner, who more than any other individual was responsible for importing the "shadowy realm" into experimental psychology.

Chapter 2

1. Rudolph Arnheim, the foremost psychologist of the visual arts, has noted the schematic nature of Titchener's own imaginative images and seen in them an expression of the avant garde artistic *Zeitgeist* circa 1910. "The reckless and artistically gifted imagery of one great psychologist, Edward B. Titchener, suggested around 1909 that images need not be mechanically complete. In fact, some of his introspective reports read as though he described the abstract or semi-abstract paintings which were to be produced just then. For example, Titchener visualized the concept 'meaning' as follows: 'I see meaning as the blue-grey tip of a kind of scoop, which has a bit of yellow above it (probably a part of the handle), and which is just digging into a dark mass of what appears to be plastic material.' This description may be said to anticipate the Kandinskys of about 1912" ("Vision and Thought," in *Perspective on Education*, Columbia University, Fall 1968).

2. The primacy of memory-constructed reality over visual reality has been discussed for a long time in describing children's drawings of familiar scenes and objects performed from memory. Well-known examples are so called x-ray drawings, where the inside and outside of objects are illustrated simultaneously and side perspectives of animals show four legs, though not more than two or three could be visible at one time. Owing to these and like phenomena, for a time the catch phrase was applied to children's drawings that "they draw what they know rather than what they see." The important theorist in this domain was psychologist G-H. Luquet (especially for *Le Dessin Enfantin*, 1927, reprinted Neuchâtel: Delachaux et Nièstlé, 1967). The aspects of drawings that indicate "knowing" in the drawings of Luquet's children can be equated with the "imagination" component in the Piaget and Inhelder quotation.

My colleagues and I reasoned that if a drawing shows an obvious "condition contrary to fact" as a slight aberration from a realistic depiction, then imagination might well supply the appropriate realistic correction. A drawing of a house was shown to children in a classroom setting for one minute, after which it was removed from view and the children were requested to draw the house from memory. A chimney with a wisp of smoke was the key feature in the drawing as it was set at a right angle, perpendicular to the house's slanted roof, a chimney representation often seen in illustrated books for young children. Results somewhat exceeded our expectations since the tendency to reproduce the chimney realistically increased *directly* with an increase in age; that is to say, as age increased the children's memory drawings were *increasingly less accurate.* But this decreasing accuracy in terms of the originally displayed drawing indicated that more and more children were imaginatively altering the chimney position to an upright position so that their memory drawings were realistic. Actual mean *correct percentages* were kindergartners 100 percent, first graders 81 percent, second graders 75 percent, third graders not tested, fourth graders 54 percent. (There were between 25 and 30 children who performed memory drawings at each grade. Results are taken from "Operant understanding in reproductions of drawings" (Furth, H. G., Ross, B. M., & Youniss, J. (1974). *Child Development, 45,* 63–70).

3. The leading functional psychologist Robert Woodworth in his 1921 textbook *Psychology: A Study of Mental Life* accepted both types of recognition by pointing out the spread of difficulty involved in the two different definitions of recognition. "We recognize faces that we could not recall, and names that we could not recall. In short, recognition is easier than recall. Consequently any theory of recognition that makes it depend on recall can scarcely be correct." But at the end of his discussion on *recognition,* Woodworth states: "Complete recognition or 'placing' the object involves something more than these feelings [of familiarity] and rudimentary reactions. It involves the recall of a context or scheme of events, and a fitting of the object into the scheme."

More subtle is Woodworth's subjective analysis of the feeling of familiarity, including an account of the fact that *we do not have feelings of familiarity toward people or things that are the most familiar.* Three possibilities are considered. (1) "When we see the same person time after time in the same setting, as when we go into the same store every morning and buy a paper from the same man, we cease to have any strong feeling of familiarity at sight of him, the reason being that we are always responding to him in the same setting, and consequently have no feeling of responding to something that is not there. (2) But if we see this same individual in a totally different place, he may give us a queer feeling of familiarity. (3) When we see the same person time after time in various settings, we end by separating him from his surroundings and responding to him alone, and therefore the familiar feeling disappears" (my numeration).

Woodworth enlarges on situation (2), which he finds the most explanatory: "Now, the response we made to the object [or person] in its original setting was a response to the whole situation, object *plus* setting; our response to the object was colored by its setting. When we now recognize the object, we make the same response to the object in a different setting; the response originally called out by the object *plus* its setting is now aroused by the object alone. Consequently we have an uneasy feeling of responding to a situation that is not present. This uneasy feeling is the feeling of familiarity in its more haunting and 'intriguing' form."

In terms of contemporary theory, Woodworth's description is the complement of the idea of *encoding specificity,* that context encoded together with an object will assist subsequent remembering of that object. Encoding specificity is an additive function of context; Woodworth, however, is concerned with the often more frequent situation of the subtraction of original context on a later occasion.

4. Obviously I have only attempted to sample the philosophical literature in a few places to illustrate specific approaches. A considerable philosophical literature now exists commenting on psychoanalytic concepts; this literature will not be referred to except for a brief critique of philosopher Paul Ricoeur's treatment of memory at the

end of Chapter 5. Phenomenological descriptions of memory with memory as the central focus have been surprisingly sparse, but this gap has been partially rectified by a book-length phenomenological analysis of memory by philosopher Edward S. Casey. (*Remembering: A phenomenological study.* 1987, Indiana University Press.)

5. Philosophers generally prefer not to make dependence on human memory too important, as this would mean that much knowledge must be a function of a *contingent psychological attribute* of uncertain validity. After all, even to state "I remember such-and-such" is to admit the possibility of error. One solution to strengthen the validity of at least some statements about the past was given by philosopher J. O. Nelson (1963) in a paper in which he drew a distinction between contingent memory statements and "past-tense ground statements," which did not admit the possibility or error. A seemingly unassailable example, proffered by Nelson, of an absolute past-tense ground statement is, "I was alive last year."

Philosopher Don Locke attempted a refutation of this assertion by pointing out that "whether or not my knowledge that I was alive last year could naturally be expressed in a memory-statement, this knowledge is, surely, memory knowledge. It might be equally odd to suggest that this knowledge depends on personal memory, in that I know that I was alive last year only because I remember being alive then. But it is, nevertheless, factual-memory knowledge, knowledge I have acquired from past experience and since retained. If I could not remember in this sense, i.e., could not retain information, then I would not know that I was alive last year. So it is not true that my knowledge of past-tense ground-statements is independent of memory, the most we can claim is that it is independent of personal memory, and we have already seen that not all memory-knowledge rests on personal memory. But until we can establish the reliability of factual memory, unless we can show that such retained information is on the whole accurate, I cannot be entitled to rely on my conviction that I was alive last year—no matter how astonished I would be if that conviction proved mistaken" (Locke, 1971, pp. 118–119).

I would comment that perhaps one does tend to grow overconfident and carelessly believe that he or she was alive last year without adequate logical warrant. Putting personal superstitions to one side, an interesting point is made. Not all memory of the past, even of our own past, relates to autobiographical memory. Some retention of the past pertains to retained factual knowledge, which often interacts with memory content that is purely personal. It would be a complex and usually impossible task to disentangle the contributions of factual memory from autobiographical memory. But at least one important and inescapable example of this intermixing is discussed in Chapter 8. There consideration is given to the universal occurrence that as small children we are all early indoctrinated as to family, racial, religious, economic, and other identifications, and maintain these identifications as we grow older in a form not unlike a memory for facts whose specific sources have been forgotten.

Chapter 3

1. That Freud should theorize not only about imagery but also imagery types is a legacy from his revered teacher the French psychiatrist J. M. Charcot. Most English and American textbooks leave the mistaken impression that the "Victorian genius" Francis Galton was the first to institute psychological investigations of imagery. This is an error; Charcot's investigations not only preceded Galton's but were much more extensive. (Charcot, *Leçons sur les maladies du système nerveux*, Paris, 1873. Galton

first published an article on composite photography which produced what he termed "generic imagery" in 1879, and the next year published the results from his well-known imagery questionnaire in the British journal *Mind.*) Charcot was interested in what he called "ideational types" in thinking and retention. He categorized his patients according to whether they thought directly in imagery—visual, auditory, motor, and the like—or thought almost exclusively in words. But he also claimed that the use of words can demonstrate sensory preferences; some individuals prefer to image words visually, others auditorily, and some have a motor preference expressed in sub rosa vocalizing. Considerably predating behaviorist J. B. Watson's claim for covert speech as tantamount to thinking, Charcot considered this typology under the heading "internal speech." Classification of this sort was developed furthest by Charcot's assistant G. Ballet (*Le langage interieur*, Paris, 1888). I have not found that Freud went so far as to make use of the imagery distinctions Charcot attached to internal speech. Nonetheless, my main point is that it was natural for Freud to theorize about imagery representations in memory processes quite independently of his intense interest in dreams.

2. A wider ranging summary of theories concerning childhood amnesia has been presented by Sheldon White and David Pillemer (1979). In addition to the discussed theories, other possibilities are surveyed, including neurological and physical changes in early childhood, animal experimental analogues, and children's information-processing, with greatest space devoted to Juan Pascual-Leone's neo-Piagetian model of development, which stresses age-increasing cognitive capacity.

3. That repression was fundamentally an organic phenomenon, hence only in part an educational, social or individual phenomenon, had been broached by Freud much earlier without any evolutionary causal explanation in *Three Essays on the Theory of Sexuality* (1905). Biological build-up of repression with a possible assist from education was conceived as a somewhat drawn-out affair that occurred during the period of sexual latency. "It is during the period of total or only partial latency that are built up the mental forces which are later to impede the course of the sexual instinct and, like dams, restrict its flow—disgust, feelings of shame and the claims of aesthetic and moral ideals. One gets an impression from civilized children that the construction of these dams is a product of education, and no doubt education has much to do with it. But in reality this development is organically determined and fixed by heredity, and it can occasionally occur without any help at all from education. Education will not be trespassing beyond its appropriate domain if it limits itself to following the lines which have already been laid down organically and to impressing them somewhat more clearly and deeply" (pp. 178–179).

4. A pre-Darwinian, Victorian comment reverses the child-sympathy emphasis of Anna Freud and pridefully classifies odor disgust as an achievement which separates man from the brutes. "Of all animals, he [man] can best distinguish the various degrees of sound, and he appears to be the only creature whose sense of smell is sufficiently delicate to be affected by unpleasant odors" (1849, *The Naturalist's Library*. A. A. Gould, Ed., Boston: Phillips, Sampson).

Chapter 4

1. For an earlier use of the "tip-of-the-tongue" term where the feeling of imminent accessibility was mistaken see the Otto Fenichel quotation on repression in the previous chapter. Brown and McNeil took their use of the term from an example by William James.

2. Freud at this point was a little theoretically laggard. Titchener had written in 1898 that "We may note, in pasing, that the innervation sensation, while it remains a theoretical possibility, has been generally given up by the experimental school" (The Postulates of a Structural Psychology, *Philosophical Review,* 1898, 7, 449–465).

3. The presentday Charing Cross that Freud refers to could in several respects be taken as a physical model of the vicissitudes that happen to many individual memories of long standing. A current London guidebook (*Nicholson*) states: "The Charing Cross was the last of the stone crosses set up by Edward I to mark the funeral resting places of Queen Eleanor's body on its way to Westminster Abbey. Originally placed where Trafalgar Square now is, it was demolished in 1647 and the statue of Charles I now stands in its place. The stone cross in the station courtyard is a replica." In other words, both the cross itself and its location are fake, but for all that, the larger meaning is yet retained despite gross falsification.

4. "Repetition compulsion" only increased in theoretical importance for Freud after 1920, notably in its incorporation into Thanatos, the death instinct, a theoretical concept accepted by relatively few other analysts. An interesting biographical application of the concept occurs in a 1982 article by Edwin Wallace ("The Repetition Compulsion," *Psychoanalytic Review,* 69(4), 455–469), who tried to show that the concept arose from Freud's life experiences. "My thesis is that the primary determinants of the repetition compulsion are psychodynamic. The interest in unpleasurable repetitive phenomena which ultimately led Freud to the repetition compulsion was motivated by recurrent neurotic phenomena (most notably death anxiety and difficulties with friends) in his own life. These repetitive phenomena were manifestations of Freud's father conflict. . . . The idea of a compulsion to repeat reflects Freud's partial awareness of his own dynamic—that he must reenact the father conflict and suffer the guilt. But hypothesizing an overriding regulatory principle similar to Fate also allowed Freud to disown responsibility for these recurrent phenomena" (p. 468). My speculation in this chapter that Freud's views on memory were partially dictated by the excellence of his own memory is rather tame in comparison to Wallace's depiction of Freud abstracting major theoretical concepts from his own neurosis.

Chapter 5

1. The small selection of contemporary psychoanalytic theorists whose views are presented is meant to be representative of recent psychoanalytic theorizing only in regard to the problems encountered in obtaining and interpreting autobiographical memories. Thus theorists speaking for Kleinian (Melanie Klein) developmental psychology, Mahlerian (Margaret Mahler) object relations, Kohutian (Heinz Kohut) self psychology, and several other important psychoanalytic persuasions are omitted because personal memory considerations are of limited concern to their theoretical uniqueness.

I have omitted explicit discussion of the Lacanian (Jacques Lacan) viewpoint from a more theoretical prejudice. The notion that the unconscious is primarily verbally structured seems to me to be mistaken and psychologically limiting in a way that Freud's theories with their strong emphasis on imagery were not. My outlook in this regard has been strongly influenced by the intensive empirical work conducted by my colleagues and me some years ago with young profoundly deaf children who had not acquired English and who were forbidden to learn sign language. This is a situation that, happily, no longer exists to any great extent in American schools for deaf children. Although I am not much concerned with claims to theoretical priority, it should, nevertheless, be noted that it is widely recognized that it was Lacan who made Freud's memoric concept of "deferred action" much more consequential than it had been previously. I, like others, have in several places indicated the theoretically pivotal position of this now broadly applied concept. Perhaps the Lacanian exponents, of whom there are now several varieties, will be able to point out other important advances Lacan contributed to memory theorizing.

Chapter 6

1. The distinctive autobiographical theories of analytical psychologist Carl Jung have not been described, as well might have been expected, since the ramifications of a "collective unconscious" exceed usual memory bounds—and my competence. It can be noted in passing that in his autobiographical memoir *Memories, Dreams, Reflections* Jung attributed more personal significance to childhood memories in his own adult life than did either Freud or Adler, though both made ample use of their memories as representative specimens, usually without mention of the true source. One complication that a collective unconscious fosters is that regression can be carried back to unearth archaic memories in ways that other theorists would not claim. Not only is this point made by the Jungian Elie Humbert (1988, The Well-Springs of Memory, *Journal of Analytical Psychology, 33,* 3–20), but also the assertion is put forward that Jung's exceptional theoretical insights stemmed, in part, from the "protracted regression" that Jung experienced from 1913 to 1916.

2. The "Mystic Writing-Pad" refers to the children's toy where one can make a mark on a transparent sheet with a plastic backing and then lift the sheet to erase the mark, yet the mark remains as a slight permanent trace on the backing. Freud suggested that the Mystic Pad furnishes a rough model of the system Pcpt.-Cs. (perception–consciousness) in its relation to memory. Pcpt.-Cs. registers temporary traces, but is devoid of lasting memories. Freud can be considered as perspicacious in advocating a double memory system and in attempting to deal with the perception–memory interface. When the information-processing point of view entered academic psychology in the 1960s, psychoanalytic theorists were quick to point out that Freud's postulation of two separate but interrelated memory systems had anticipated the short-term and long-term memory classification then so prevalent. Though as the information-processing field advanced, some theorists saw a better match with the dual concepts of "working memory" and the "permanent memory store."

In a more speculative vein, Freud also suggested that perception functions by sending out rapid periodic impulses of cathectic innervations. "Thus I attributed the interruptions, which with the Mystic Pad have an external origin, to the discontinuity in the current of innervation; and the place of an actual breaking of contact was taken in my hypothesis by the periodic non-excitability of the perceptual system. I further suspected that this discontinuous method of functioning of the system Pcpt.-Cs. lies at the bottom of the origin of the concept of time." Setting aside the possibility of cathectic innervations, whatever they may be, there is much later evidence for the discontinuous nature of the perceptual system, e.g., the retinal "stopped image" phenomenon, which illustrates that when eye movements are disallowed by appropriate compensations in an optical viewing system, the image of a consciously attended to visible line disappears. But even David Rapaport (1951, *Organization and Pathology of Thought*), Freud's learned and faithful metapsychological acolyte, could not fathom the speculation about the origin of the concept of time. "The evidence on which this last consideration is based is not presented, nor is it obvious" (p. 337).

3. In his autobiography, written near the end of his life, G. Stanley Hall (*Life and Confessions of a Psychologist,* 1923) stated that the orthodox explanation given for the Freudian theory of therapy was mistaken. Instead, "it is the motives of shame and shocked modesty which I believe are the chief curative agents in many if not most of the interesting cases on record . . . the [patients] are cured by the very modesty which the analyst would destroy and not by the confession which the doctor can secure only by combatting this instinct of concealment that they call prudery or resistance" (pp. 72–73).

Chapter 7

1. In an earlier discussion of developmental memory theories (Ross and Kerst, 1978) an extended comparison was made between Baldwin and Piaget. Concern there was not limited to autobiographical memory as it is here. Instead, Piaget's major memory concepts were presented in greater detail, with emphasis on the extent to which Piaget applied and altered theoretical concepts previously formulated by Baldwin.

2. Piaget frequently expressed skepticism concerning the data worthiness of childhood autobiographical memories. To clinch this point he on several occasions described a "memory" of his own that turned out to be imaginary, with the implicit implication that all personal memories were therefore useless as data sources. "I myself, for example, have a very precise, very detailed and very lively memory of having been the object of a kidnapping when I was still a child strapped to my carriage. I recall a series of precise details of the site of this adventure, the struggle between my nanny and the thief, the arrival of a passerby, the policemen, etc. When I was fifteen, the nanny wrote to my parents that she had invented the whole story and that she herself had been responsible for the scratches on her forehead, etc. In other words, about the age of five or six, I must have heard the story of this kidnapping, which my parents then believed and, using this story, I invented a visual memory which today still remains" (Piaget, 1944, pp. 43–44).

Piaget claimed that this anecdote vividly illustrates two conclusions he had arrived at theoretically—indeed they are in agreement with many other memory theorists also. One conclusion is that an individual can't introspectively arrive at the truth or falsity of a memory, and the other "that every operation of the memory of evocation includes a reorganization; in other words memory works in the manner of a historian who, studying some incomplete documents, in part deductively reconstructs the past." This second point is claimed to stand as a argument against Freud who believed, simplistically according to Piaget, that memories were stocked in the unconscious "where evocation would remove them at will without modification or reorganization."

Philosopher Adolf Grünbaum, in his 1984 *Foundations of Psychoanalysis,* cites this "poignant illustration" of a pseudomemory from Piaget's early life twice (p. 33 and p. 243)—false memories attested to by authoritative sources apparently being hard to find—and uses it as a stick with which to beat Freud regarding his failure to take into account "the malleability of memory by suggestion to generate pseudomemories that never occurred." This frequently reiterated anecdote is, in my opinion, not very theoretically freighted. At age 5 or 6, a peak period of memory suggestibility according to such theorists a Ernst Kris and Baldwin, a child is told on several occasions of an occurrence that happened to him when he was less than two years old and subsequently comes to believe he remembers the occurrence himself. As discussed in Chapter 3, Freud admitted (after some prodding from Havelock Ellis) that a similar indoctrination might have been the origin of Leonardo da Vinci's belief that he remembered a vulture opening his mouth with its tail. In both cases a personal memory from childhood is engendered by indoctrination with the aid of manufactured imagery rather than by the registration of lived-through events. Such a concession to repeated indoctrination hardly undercuts either the tenacity or the theoretical importance of youthful autobiographical memories. At a minimum, Piaget did strongly and with great detail retain the memory of a childhood belief concerning himself into late adulthood and, of some theoretical interest, apparently continued to retain it even after he knew it to be fiction.

3. In spite of wide theoretical differences elsewhere, Piaget and Freud are in considerable agreement regarding when the onset of an organized autobiographical memory could occur. In his screen memory paper Freud wrote, "It is only from the sixth or seventh year onwards—in many cases only after the tenth year—that our lives can be reproduced in memory as a connected chain of events" (1899). Assuming this age for the organization of connected memories suggests that early and possibly traumatic happenings must be registered as isolated events that are not easily recallable in original context at an older age, whether or not repression has taken place. Organization of life-events into "narrative" may have its therapeutic uses, but it is not an important point in Freud's theorizing about retention or recovery of early traumatic events.

A good deal of effective event-ordering is, nonetheless, possible before serial understanding is mastered. Much useful temporal ordering is performed with before-event versus after-event bracketing and the use of associative matching, say linking particular events with specific people, as occurs when family photo albums are perused. When adults search for items in their own past chronologies, their protocols indicate that they use the same limited techniques rather than reason from any neatly ordered life-text.

4. Children's symbol production is seen by Hans Furth as providing a unifying common factor in the disparate theories of Piaget and Freud. Since pervasive symbol formation begins early in life, according to both theorists, this commonality offers a key linkage for developing further syntheses and complementarities between the two theories as development progress toward adulthood. Furth undertook this theoretical coupling in his 1987 book *Knowledge as Desire* (Columbia University Press).

5. Freud's overdependence on principles of association has been a continuing criticism across several generations. An early assessment was given by Titchener after Freud's lectures at Clark University in 1909 on his only trip to America. "His [Freud's] psychology is, basically, the psychology of associationism. The fundamental fallacy of that psychology is that it looks upon "ideas" not psychologically as very fluid existences, but logically, as hard static meanings. The idea of the associationists is always a meaning, a symbol, even when it is not termed by them a "symbolic" idea . . . Freud's *Affektbetrag* is really only *another meaning,* another symbol, mechanically transferred from idea symbol to idea symbol—I offered to attempt a translation out of this psychology of association into modern psychological terms, and Freud laughed at me, and said that if I came to him for half a year I should see that modern psychology needed to be 'revolutionized' in his way" (Titchener letter to Adolf Meyer, September 19, 1909, letter excerpt reprinted in *Edward Bradford Titchener—a sketch,* brochure prepared by Rand B. Evans for the American Psychological Association, 1972). Ironically, Titchener criticized Freud for his old-fashioned dominantly cognitive approach,

whereas some psychologists of the 1960s praised Freud for his modernity in casting so much of his theory in cognitive terms.

6. Preliminary experiments performed by some of my students indicate that age $3\frac{1}{2}$ for stated age of earliest memory holds as a good mean approximation from age 10 to early adulthood. But children younger than age 10 begin to lower their estimates.

Chapter 8

1. Both Halbwachs and Bloch were French academicians of Jewish descent who were executed by the Nazis, which accounts for the fact that the books I cite were left unfinished and were completed by others. This chapter was drafted before I also became aware that their theoretical views, so complementary to each other and well adapted to the perspectives of this book, were likely due in some measure to collegiality. They were both professors at the University of Strasbourg for an overlapping period of more than 15 years following World War I. (I learned of this relationship through the typescript of a talk by historian Carole Fink, "Marc Bloch: Historian, Soldier, Patriot," delivered at the Woodrow Wilson International Center for Scholars, October 13, 1987.)

2. The arguments on behalf of the "original intent" doctrine were most fully made by Judge Robert Bork in his 1987 failed attempt to be confirmed by the Senate as a Supreme Court justice. In reply to the questioning of Senator Arlen Specter, Judge Bork offered his approach to the United States Constitution from the "original intent" perspective. "In the case of the Constitution, I referred to the fact that we can't know their [the Framers'] specific intentions; I think you read that in one of those pieces [submitted writings of Judge Bork]. We can't know their specific intentions and indeed we can't, and indeed their specific intentions wouldn't help us a great deal because *our* task is to apply their general understanding, their public understanding of what they were protecting to modern circumstances as to which they could have no specific intentions.

But when I talk about the original understanding what a judge needs from the Constitution is a major premise, what it is he's supposed to protect. And then he has to protect it" (*New York Times,* September 20, 1987).

"Original intention" when translated into "general understanding" appears as an even more unknowable historical goal to some commentators. One riposte to Judge Bork was: "Even if we can find out what individual Framers intended, how can we find out the "group intention" of the Framers as a collective body? There is no such thing as a group mind, and we may suspect that there is no such thing as a group intention either. . . . To construct a group intention out of information about individual intentions we will need some rule of combination. Do we count the intentions of Framers who opposed a measure? What of those who supported it but only as a regrettable compromise?" (Report from the Center for Philosophy & Public Policy, Vol. 7, No. 4, Fall 1987, University of Maryland, College Park, MD).

3. The question about the true nature of the "rebel yell" (or "yells," as some claim it had regional variations) is still under investigation. The largest trove of material bearing on these sounds, including a recording, is at the Library of Congress, Washington, D.C. The recording is not convincing, since the "yell" vocalist utters two alternative verions within a period of a few seconds and then confesses that neither version is necessarily valid.

4. The only psychological theoretical viewpoint that comes close to Halbwachs's in

emphasizing the primacy of the "social" for all human mental functions is that of the Marxist-grounded Russian psychologist Lev Vygotsky. "We might, furthermore, say that all the higher functions have formed not in biology, not in the history of pure phylogenesis, and that the very mechanism underlying the higher mental functions is a copy of the social. All the higher mental functions are interiorised relations of a social order, the basis of the social structure of the personality. Their composition, genetic structure and mode of action, in a word, all of their nature is social; even when transformed into mental processes it remains quasi-social. Even when alone man retains the functions of communication" (p. 45, L. S. Vygotsky, Development of the Higher Mental Functions. In A. Leontyev, A. Luria, and A. Smirnov (Eds.), *Psychological Research in the U.S.S.R., Vol. 1,* 1966, Moscow: Progress Publishers. Abridged from original publication in 1930–1931).

Chapter 9

1. Folklorists around the world, acknowledging Brunvand's initiative, have collected urban legends arising in their own cultures. A good example is *The Gucci Kangaroo & Other Australian Urban Legends* by Amanda Bishop (1988, Australasian Publishing Company). In the title story Italian tourists accidentally kill a kangaroo with their rented car. Taking advantage of the fatality, they dress the kangaroo in the Gucci blazer and take snapshots of themselves with their new companion. "They had taken only a few photographs when the kangaroo, which had been merely stunned by the impact, came to and hopped back into the bush, taking with it the Gucci blazer and, in its pockets, two hundred dollars in cash, a passport and a membership card in an Italian nightclub" (p. 27). (A more recent Brunvand collection is *The Mexican Pet,* Norton, 1986.)

2. Much of interest in social terms concerning memory in relation to memorials, mourning, and commemoration is presented in Philip Ariès's 1974 short book *Western attitudes toward DEATH: From the middle ages to the present* (Johns Hopkins Press). Two brief selections illustrate Ariès's descriptive presentation in terms of once slowly moving but now relatively more rapidly changing "waves of public sentiment" (a possibly depersonalized substitute for the taboo concept of "group mind"?) First, Ariès points out the marked change in attitude in France in the second half of the eighteenth century after a millennium of little concern for the place of burial of immediate family members. "It was at this time that the burial concession became a certain form of property, protected from commerce, but assured in perpetuity. This was a very significant innovation. People went to visit the tomb of a dear one as one would go to a relative's home, or into one's own home, full of memories. Memory conferred upon the dead a sort of immortality which was initially foreign to Christianity. From the end of the eighteenth century and even at the height of the nineteenth and twentieth centuries in anticlerical and agnostic France, unbelievers would be the most assiduous visitors to the tombs of their relatives. The visit to the cemetery in France and Italy became, and still is, the great continuing religious act. Those who no longer go to church still go to the cemetery, where they have become accustomed to place flowers on the tombs. They meditate there, that is to say they evoke the dead person and cultivate his memory.

"Thus, it is a private cult, but also from its very origins a public one. The cult of memory immediately spread as a result of one and the same wave of sensibility" (pp. 72–73).

A second selection from Ariès shows his keen eye for the unique memorialization represented by presentday Washington, D.C. "It is in America, in Washington, D.C., even more than in the Panthéon of Paris, that we find the first major manifestations of the funeral cult of the hero. In a city filled with commemorative monuments, such as those to George Washington, Thomas Jefferson, and Abraham Lincoln—which are 'tombs' without sepulchers—a twentieth-century European encounters an even stronger phenomenon: Arlington Cemetery. Here, despite its public and national character, the garden of the Lee-Custis House has preserved its appearance of a private estate.

"Although astonishing to a European of today, the civic and funerary landscape at Arlington and along the Mall sprang from the same sentiment that caused a multiplicity of monuments to the war dead in the France of the 1920s, monuments which are doubtlessly today quite incomprehensible to the descendants of those who created Arlington and the Center of Washington.

"Thus, regardless of religious differences, simplicity and the romantic, hero cults formed the common denominator throughout Western civilization in the late eighteenth and early nineteenth centuries" (pp. 78–79). (Ariès's points are mostly well taken, but he has not characterized Arlington Cemetery precisely. The Lee-Custis House was seized during the Civil War, and the grounds were turned into a cemetery as an act of retribution for the defection, from the Union standpoint, of General Robert E. Lee to the Confederacy. A Supreme Court decision returned the mansion to the Lee family in 1882, and they sold it to the U.S. government in 1883—a problem-avoiding decision as there were already 16,000 graves located on the Lee estate grounds. As an act of restitution, the house and garden were later restored as well as was possible to their antebellum state—in part to serve as a "tomb without sepulcher" for the Lost Cause. Official recognition of the House as a permanent memorial to General Lee came by act of Congress only in 1925.)

3. One would not want to altogether rule out the possibility of *instant* nostalgia, since some have even envisioned *future* nostalgia. The late, long-time mayor of Chicago, Richard Daley, is alleged to have remarked at a civic ceremony, "We look forward to this event with nostalgia."

Chapter 10

1. I would like to clarify somewhat further the idea put forward here and earlier in Chapter 5 that *conative memory* can be active very early in human development. This conception differs from the well-known hypothesis of psychoanalytic psychologist David Rapaport (1951), who proposed that there are dual types of memory organization: very early there is solely a drive organizational basis, which is increasingly supplanted by a conceptual basis, with adult memories partaking of both drive and conceptual organization. The present proposal of a conative memory, although also dealing with motivation, is different from Rapaport's conception and is, in principle, close to the ideas of Ernst Schactel in that an actual remembering or re-experiencing of a drive or motivation-related state is involved rather than just a reason for remembering.

Schactel proposed that the infant has a type of memory he termed *passive resensing*—"when the global situation 'happens' to him [the infant] notices that the feeling is a familiar one." Voluntary recall is a later achievement, with adult remembering a mixture of both passive and voluntary remembering. What Schactel wrote to differentiate his theory from Rapaport's also holds for the present conception of early conative memory. "While Rapaport, consistent with orthodox Freudian thought, ties the primitive organization of memory to need tension, believing that memories arise originally only with mounting need tension, I am inclined to assume that they can also arise, and perhaps more often do, from the feeling of familiarity in re-experiencing a complex, global sensory-motor affective state, without particular need tension in the sense of striving for relief from tension" (Schactel, 1951, p. 151n). The notion that actual remembering of feelings is important in conative formation and persistence is as consistent with Freud's formulations as, in Rapaport's words, "cathexes freely displaceable to any of the representations organized around the drive."

2. Another social category is memory storage. Artist Andy Warhol reminded us that one function of our friends is to serve as memory repositories. Alternatively, we may use a machine for the same purpose—although most interactions of this sort fall short of man–machine matrimony. "I have no memory. Everyday is a new day because I don't remember the day before. Every minute is like the first minute of my life. I try to remember but I can't. That's why I got married—to my tape recorder. That's why I seek out people with minds like tape recorders to be with. My mind is like a tape recorder with one button—Erase" (*The Philosophy of Andy Warhol,* 1975, p. 199).

3. In Breuer's case of Anna O., which in many respects Freud considered the founding case of psychoanalysis, a type of repetition recall took place that remains theoretically unexplained, that of "anniversary repetitions" in which there were no external cues to use as a guide for the repetitions. With the 22-year-old Anna O. possessing an alternating "normal" and "sick" personality, the remarkable feature was that the sick personality lived 365 days earlier than the healthy one. Apparently Anna O. had no access to any written record, but thanks to the diary her mother had kept about her illness, Breuer was able to check that the events she hallucinated had occurred, day by day, exactly one year earlier. This was but the beginning of her exceptional memory performance. During psychotherapy, she told Breuer in reverse chronological order each appearance of a given symptom, often with exact dates, until she reached the original manifestation and initial event, and then the symptom disappeared. For the symptom "not hearing when someone came in" there were 108 separate detailed instances.

Breuer (*Studies on Hysteria*) wrote, that these instances were so clearly differentiated in the patient's memory "that if she happened to make a mistake in their sequence she would be obliged to correct herself and put them in the right order; if this was not done her report came to a standstill. The events she described were so lacking in interest and significance and were told in such detail that there could be no suspicion of their having been invented. Many of these incidents consisted of purely internal experiences and so could not be verified; others of them (or circumstnaces attending them) were within the recollection of people in her environment." Remembering was often of a near-hallucinatory type rather than simple verbal: "the particular symptom emerged with greater force while she was discussing it. Thus during the analysis of her not being able to hear she was so deaf that I [Breuer] was obliged to communicate with her in writing."

Henri Ellenberger (1972, "The Story of 'Anna O.': A critical review with new data," *Journal of History of the Behavioral Sciences, 8,* 267–279) garnered new facts concerning the Anna O. case and traced the case chronology with such exactitude that it is unlikely further verifiable evidence of any importance will ever be found. He noted that though the case is still often cited, the peculiar and indeed amazing features of Anna O.'s performances are downplayed. Whereas in his 1970 book Ellenberger seemed hopeful that the Anna O. case could be explained, he concluded his later investigation with doubt and a tribute to the case's uniqueness. "Anna O.'s illness was not a 'classical case of hysteria' but a unique case of which to the author's knowledge, no other instance is known, either before or after her."

4. American culture has, unfortunately, been amply supplied with "flashbulb" events for a long time. In a pioneering study F. W. Colegrove (1899, *American Journal of Psychology*) reported a number of responses to the question: "Do you recall where you were when you heard Lincoln was shot?" Results from the question when posed to respondents in 1898: "Of the 179 persons interviewed, 127 replied in the affirmative, and were able to give particulars; 52 replied in the negative. A few who gave a negative reply recalled where they were when they heard of [James A.] Garfield's death" [1881]. To remember learning of Garfield's death but not Lincoln's can be considered a triumph of recency over fame—17 vs. 33 years had elapsed. (William McKinley, the president in office when the question about Lincoln's death was asked, soon became a candidate for presidential-assassination recall in his own right when he was killed by an assassin in 1901.)

It is possible to think of the incidence of "flashbulb memories" as yielding a measure of the affective importance of events on public consciousness. In recent years the *Challenger* space shuttle disaster has been cited as a prime candidate. Because of wide recent publicity given the *flashbulb* phenomenon, it may be that a considerable segment of the public will not be quite as un-self-conscious in registering time and place when they hear news about future shocking public events.

Claims of the past occurrence of flashbulb remembering are sometimes put forward to demonstrate that a biographical subject had achieved full-blown "celebrityhood." In their 1989 book *Will Rogers' World* (M. Evans & Co.), authors B. B. and F. N. Sterling claim that actor and homespun commentator Rogers was such a familiar personage in depression-era American that his death in a 1935 plane crash had the same effect on the public as the death of President Kennedy in 1963. "For decades afterward people would remember where they were and what they were doing at the moment they heard the news." This claim seems a typical biographical exaggeration (except that I can attest to its truth from my own experience).

5. Skinner himself, through his autobiographical writing, has become a method-ological example of the ambiguities inherent in personal recall. In a short autobiogra-phy included in a 1967 collection of autobiographies by prominent psychologists, *A History of Psychology in Autobiography* (E. G. Boring & G. Lindzey, Eds.), Skinner described a graduate student existence in which he "saw no movie or plays, seldom went to concerts, had scarcely any dates and read nothing but psychology and physiol-ogy" (p. 398). But in the 1979 autobiographical volume *The Shaping of a Behaviorist* he wrote, "I was recalling a pose rather than the life I actually led." Duane and Sydney Schultz (1987) comment in *A History of Modern Psychology (4th ed.)*, "Although Skinner's school days may be of minor importance in the history of psychology, the two versions in print, both written by the participant, indicate something of the difficulties historians face. Which set of data, which version of this incident is the more accurate? Which characterization comes closer to reality? Which is based on the vagaries or the self-serving nature of memory, and how are we to know?" (pp. 8–9).

An obvious earlier parallel in American moral autobiography is one of the best known, that of Benjamin Franklin. As Peter Shaw says in the introduction to a 1982 Franklin *Autobiography* reprint (Bantam), "The protagonist of the book, it has often been pointed out, is not precisely Franklin himself, but a personal, or invented self. By canny omissions and changes of emphasis, Franklin adjusted the details of his career so as to produce an impression of moral probity and success through striving." Thus Skinner, on a small scale, was only following an established American literary tradition of didactic teaching through the recounting of an exemplary life.

REFERENCES

Adler, A. (1929). *The science of living*. New York: Greenberg. [Excerpts reprinted in H. L. Ansbacher and R. R. Ansbacher (Eds.) (1964), *The individual psychology of Alfred Adler*. New York: Harper & Row.]

Adler, A. (1937). Significance of early recollections. *International Journal of Individual Psychology, 3* (4), 283–287. [Reprinted in H. A. Olson, (Ed.) (1979), *Early recollections*]

Allen, B. (1984). Review of *Oral historiography* by D. Henige. In *Journal of American Folklore, 97,* 241–243.

Allen, B., & L. Montell. (1981). *From memory to history: Using oral sources for historical research*. Nashville, Tennessee: American Assocation for State and Local History.

Allport, G. & L. Postman. (1947). *Psychology of rumor*. New York: Holt.

Angell, J. R. (1908). *Psychology (4th ed.)*. New York: Holt.

Asch, S. E. (1969). A reformation of the problem of associations. *American Psychologist, 24,* 92–102.

Ansbacher, H. L. (1947). Adler's place today in the psychology of memory. *Journal of Personality, 15,* 197–207. [Reprinted in H. A. Olson, (1979), *Early recollections*]

Ayer, A. J. (1956). *The problem of knowledge*. London: Penguin.

Baldwin, J. M. (1913). *History of psychology: A sketch and interpretation (Vol. 2)*. New York: G. P. Putnam's Sons.

Baldwin, J. M. (1920). *Mental development in the child and the race (3rd ed. rev.)* New York: Macmillan. (Original publication 1906)

Bartlett, F. C. (1961). *Remembering: A study in experimental and social psychology*. Cambridge: Cambridge University Press. (Original publication 1932)

Bergson, H. (1908). Le souvenir du présent et la fausse reconnaissance. *Revue Philosophique*. December.

Brenner, C. (1973). *An elementary textbook of psychoanalysis, (2nd ed.)* New York: International Universities Press.

Brewer, W. F. (1986). What is autobiographical memory? In D. Rubin (Ed.), *Autobiographical memory* (pp. 25–49). Cambridge: Cambridge University Press.

Bloch, M. (1953). *The historian's craft. New York: Random House*.

Bransford, J. D., R. Barclay, & J. V. Franks. (1972). Sentence memory—a constructive versus interpretative approach. *Cognitive Psychology, 3,* 193–209.

Bransford, J. D., & J. J. Franks. (1971). The abstractions of linguistic ideas. *Cognitive Psychology, 2,* 331–350.

Brown, R. & D. McNeill. (1966). The "tip-of-the-tongue" phenomenon. *Journal of Verbal Learning and Verbal Behavior, 5,* 325–337.

Brunvand, J. H. (1981). *The vanishing hitchhiker*. New York: Norton.

Brunvand, J. H. (1984). *The choking doberman*. New York: Norton.

Burnham, W. H. (1889). Memory, historically and experimentally considered. *American Journal of Psychology, 2,* 39–90.

Cameron, D. E. (1947). *Remembering*. Nervous and Mental Disease Monographs. New York: Coolidge Foundation.

Casey, E. S. (1980). Piaget and Freud on childhood memory. In H. J. Silverman (Ed.), *Piaget, philosophy and the human sciences*. Atlantic Highlands, New Jersey: Humanities Press.

Casey, E. S. (1987). *Remembering: A phenomenological study*. Bloomington, Indiana: Indiana University Press.

Claparède, E. (1911). Recognition and "me-ness." In D. Rapaport (Ed.) (1951), *Organization and pathology of thought*. New York: Columbia University Press.

Craik, F. I. M. (1979). Levels of processing: Overview and closing comments. In L. S. Cermak and F. I. M. Craik (Eds.), *Levels of processing in human memory*. Hillsdale, New Jersey: Erlbaum.

Craik, F. I. M. & Lockhart, R. S. (1972). Levels of processing: A framework for memory research. *Journal of Verbal Learning and Verbal Behavior, 11*, 671–684.

Darwin, C. (1888). *The expression of emotions in man and animals*. New York: D. Appleton. (Original publication 1872)

Dunaway, D. K., & W. K. Baum (Eds.) (1984). *Oral history: An interdisciplinary anthology*. Nashville, Tennessee: American Association for State and Local History.

Dunlap, K. (1972). *Habits: Their making and unmaking*. New York: Liveright. (Original publication 1932)

Ellenberger, H. F. (1970). *The discovery of the unconscious*. New York: Basic Books.

Ellis, H. (1922). *The world of dreams*. Boston: Houghton Mifflin.

Engen, T. (1982). *The perception of odors*. New York: Academic Press.

Erikson, E. H. (1975). *Life history and the historical moment*. New York: Norton.

Fenichel, O. (1945). *The psychoanalytic theory of neurosis*. New York: Norton.

Ferenczi, S. G. & O. Rank. (1925). *The development of psychoanalysis*. New York: Nervous and Mental Disease Publishing Company.

Fine, B. D., E. D. Joseph, & H. F. Waldhorn (Eds.) (1971). *Recollection and reconstruction* and *Reconstruction in psychoanalysis* (Monograph IV: The Kris Study Group of the New York Psychoanalytic Institute). New York: International Universities Press.

Fitzgerald, J. M. (1986). Autobiographical memory: A developmental perspective. In D. Rubin (Ed.), *Autobiographical Memory* (pp. 122–136.) Cambridge: Cambridge University Press.

Freud, A. (1946). *The ego and the mechanisms of defense*. International Universities Press. (Original publication 1936)

Freud, A. (1979). *Psycho-analysis for teachers and parents*. New York: Norton. (Original publication 1935)

Freud, S. (1953–1974). *The Standard Edition of the Complete Psychological Works of Sigmund Freud, 24 Volumes*. London: Hogarth Press.

———. (1893). With Breuer, J. On the psychical mechanism of hysterical phenomena: Preliminary communication. *Standard Edition, vol. 3*, 25.

———. (1894). The neuro-psychoses of defence. *Standard Edition, vol. 3*, 43.

———. (1895). With Breuer, J. *Studies in hysteria. Standard Edition, vol. 2*, 1.

———. (1898). The psychical mechanism of forgetting. *Standard Edition, vol. 3*, 289.

———. (1899). Screen memories. *Standard Edition, vol. 3*, 301.

———. (1900). The interpretation of dreams. *Standard Edition, vols. 4 and 5*.

———. (1901). The psychopathology of everyday life. *Standard Edition, vol. 6*.

———. (1905a). Three essays on the theory of sexuality. *Standard Edition, vol. 7*, 125.

———. (1905b). Fragment of an analysis of a case of hysteria. *Standard Edition, vol. 7*, 3.

———. (1905c). Jokes and their relation to the unconscious. *Standard Edition, vol. 8.*

———. (1910a). Five lectures on psycho-analysis. *Standard Edition, vol. 11*, 3.

———. (1910b). Leonardo da Vinci and a memory of his childhood. *Standard Edition, vol. 11*, 59.

———. (1912). Recommendations to physicians practicing psychoanalysis. *Standard Edition, vol. 12*, 109.

———. (1912–1913). Totem and taboo. *Standard Edition, vol. 13*, 1.

———. (1914a). Remembering, repeating and working-through. *Standard Edition, vol. 12*, 145.

———. (1914b). Fausse reconnaissance (*déjà raconté*) in psychoanalytic treatment. *Standard Edition, vol. 13*, 201.

———. (1914c). On the history of the psycho-analytic movement. *Standard Edition, vol. 14*, 7.

———. (1915a). Repression. *Standard Edition, vol. 14*, 146.

———. (1915b). The unconscious. *Standard Edition, vol. 14*, 159.

———. (1916–1917). Introductory lectures on psychoanalysis. *Standard Edition, vols. 15 and 16.*

———. (1917). A childhood recollection from 'Dichtung und Wahrheit.' *vol. 17*, 145.

———. (1918). From the history of an infantile neurosis. *Standard Edition, vol. 17*, 3.

———. (1920). Beyond the pleasure principle. *Standard Edition, vol. 18*, 3.

———. (1921). Group psychology and the analysis of the ego. *Standard Edition, vol. 18*, 67.

———. (1923). The ego and the id. *Standard Edition, vol. 19*, 3.

———. (1924). The dissolution of the Oedipus complex. *Standard Edition, vol. 19*, 173.

———. (1925a). A note upon the 'Mystic writing-pad.' *Standard Edition, vol. 19*, 227.

———. (1925b). An autobiographical study. *Standard Edition, vol. 20*, 7.

———. (1926a). Inhibitions, symptoms and anxiety. *Standard Edition, vol. 20*, 77.

———. (1926b). The question of lay analysis. *Standard Edition, vol. 20*, 177.

———. (1930). Civilization and its discontents. *Standard Edition, vol. 21*, 59.

———. (1933a). New introductory lectures on psychoanalysis. *Standard Edition, vol. 22*, 3.

———. (1933b). Letter from Freud. [Reply to letter from Einstein]. *Standard Edition, vol. 22*, 203.

———. (1937a). Analysis terminable and interminable. *Standard Edition, vol. 23*, 209.

———. (1937b). Constructions in analysis. *Standard Edition, vol. 23*, 255.

———. (1939). Moses and monotheism: Three essays. *Standard Edition, vol. 23*, 7.

———. (1940). An outline of psycho-analysis. *Standard Edition, vol. 23*, 144.

———. (1941). Findings, ideas, problems. *Standard Edition, vol. 23*, 299.

Furth, H. G. (1987). *Knowledge as desire: An essay on Freud and Piaget.* New York: Columbia University Press.

Gage, D. F., & M. A. Safer. (1985). Hemisphere differences in the mood-state dependent effect for recognition of emotional faces. *Journal of Experimental Psychology: Learning, Memory, and Cognition, 11*, 752–763.

Gibson, J. J. (1941). A critical review of the concept of set in contemporary psychology. *Psychological Bulletin, 38*, 781–877.

Gill, M. M. (1976). Metapsychology is not psychology. in M. M. Gill & P. S. Holzman (Eds.), Psychology versus metapsychology: Psychoanalytic essays in memory of George S. Klein. *Psychological Issues*, vol. V, no. 4 (Monograph 36).

Greene, R. L. (1986). Effects of intentionality and strategy on memory for frequency. *Journal of Experimental Psychology: Learning, Memory, and Cognition, 12,* 489–495.

Grünbaum, A. (1984). *The foundations of psychoanalysis.* Berkeley: University of California Press.

Habermas, J. (1971). *Knowledge and human interests.* Boston: Beacon Press.

Hall, C. S., & V. J. Nordby. (1972). *The individual and his dreams.* New York: New American Library.

Halbwachs, M. (1980). *The collective memory.* New York: Harper & Row. (Original publication 1950)

Hasher, L. G., & R. T. Zacks. (1979). Automatic and effortful processes in memory. *Journal of Experimental Psychology: General, 108,* 356–388.

Hasher, L. G., & R. T. Zacks. (1984). Automatic processing of fundamental information: The case of frequency of occurrence. *American Psychologist, 39,* 1372–1388.

Hebb, D. O. (1969). The mind's eye. *Psychology Today* (May), *2,* p. 54.

Henige, D. (1982). *Oral historiography.* London: Longman.

Hilgard, E. R. (1977). *Divided consciousness: Multiple controls in human thought and action.* New York: Wiley.

Humphrey, G. (1951). *Thinking: An introduction to its experimental psychology.* London: Methuen.

Inhelder, B. & J. Piaget. (1964). *The early growth of logic in the child.* New York: Norton.

James, W. (1950). *The Principles of Psychology* (two volumes). New York: Dover. (Original Publication 1890)

Janet, P. (1905). A propos du déjà vu. *Journal de psychologie normale et pathologique,* July–August.

Janet, P. (1928). *L'évolution de la mémoire et de le notion du temps, Vol. I.* Paris: Chahine.

Jenness, A. (1944). Hypnotism. In J. McV. Hunt (Ed.), *Personality and the behavior disorders, vol. I.* New York: Ronald Press.

Jones, E. (1953). *The life and work of Sigmund Freud: vol. 1. The formative years and the great discoveries.* New York: Basic Books.

Jung, C. G. (1973). *Memories, dreams, reflections (revised edition).* (Recorded and edited by A. Jaffé). New York: Random House.

Klein, G. S. (1976). *Psychoanalytic theory: An exploration of essentials.* New York: International Universities Press.

Koestler, A. (1967). *The act of creation.* New York: Dell.

Köhler, W. (1969). *The task of gestalt psychology.* Princeton, New Jersey: Princeton University Press.

Kosslyn, S. M. (1980). *Image and mind.* Cambridge, Massachusetts: Harvard University Press.

Kris, A. O. (1982). *Free association: Method and process.* New Haven: Yale University Press.

Kris, E. (1950). On preconscious mental processes. In *The selected papers of Ernst Kris.* 1975. New Haven: Yale University Press.

Kris, E. (1956a). The recovery of childhood memories in psychoanalytic technique. In *The selected papers of Ernst Kris.* 1975. New Haven: Yale University Press.

Kris, E. (1956b). The personal myth: A problem in psychoanalytic technique. In *The selected papers of Ernst Kris.* (1975). New Haven: Yale University Press.

Kris, E. (1975). *The selected papers of Ernst Kris.* New Haven: Yale University Press.

Ladd, G. T., & R. S. Woodworth. (1911). *Elements of physiological psychology* (rev. ed.). New York: Scribners.

Langer, S. K. (1967). *Mind: An essay on human feeling, Vol. I.* Baltimore: Johns Hopkins University Press.

Laplanche, J. & J.-B. Pontalis. (1973). *The language of psycho-analysis.* New York: Norton.

Leavy, S. A. (1980). *The psychoanalytic dialogue.* New Haven: Yale University Press.

Lewis, H. B. (1981). *Freud and modern psychology. Vol. 1: The emotional basis of mental illness.* New York: Plenum Press.

Locke, D. (1971). *Memory.* New York: Doubleday.

Loewald, H. W. (1976). Perspectives on memory. In M. M. Gill and P. S. Holzman (Eds.), *Psychology versus metapsychology: Psychoanalytic essays in memory of George S. Klein. Psychological Issues* (Monograph 36).

Loftus, E. F. (1979). *Eyewitness testimony.* Cambridge, Massachusetts: Harvard University Press.

Lord, A. B. (1960). *The singer of tales.* New York: Atheneum.

Madison, P. (1961). *Freud's concept of repression and defense, its theoretical and observational language.* Minneapolis, Minnesota: University of Minnesota Press.

Malcolm, N. (1977). *Memory and mind.* Ithaca, New York: Cornell University Press.

Masson, J. M. (1985). *The assault on truth: Freud's suppression of the seduction theory.* New York: Viking Penguin.

Mazlish, B. (Ed.) (1963). *Psychoanalysis and history.* Englewood Cliffs, New Jersey: Prentice-Hall.

McDougall, W. (1926). *Outline of psychology.* New York: Scribners.

McNeill, W. H. (1986). *Mythohistory and other essays.* Chicago: University of Chicago Press.

Meacham, J. A. (1988). Interpersonal relations and prospective remembering. In M. M. Gruneberg, P. Morris, and R. N. Sykes (Eds.), *Practical aspects of memory: Current research and issues, Vol. I.* London: Wiley

Merleau-Ponty, M. (1945). *Phenomenology of perception.* London: Routledge & Kegan Paul, 1962.

Mitchell, W. J. T. (1980) Editor's Note: On Narrative (entire issue, pp. 1–236), *Critical Inquiry, 7,* No. 1, Autumn.

Munroe, R. L. (1955). *Schools of psychoanalytic thought.* New York: Dryden.

Neisser, U. (1967). *Cognitive psychology.* New York: Appleton-Century-Crofts.

Neisser, V. (1982). *Memory observed: Remembering in natural contexts.* San Francisco: W. H. Freeman.

Nelson, J. O. (1963). The validation of memory and our conception of a past. *Philosophical Review, 72,* 35–47.

Neuenschwander, J. (1984). Oral historians and long-term memory. In D. K. Dunaway, & W. K. Baum (Eds.) *Oral history: An interdisciplinary anthology.* (p. 324–332). Nashville, Tennessee: American Association for State and Local History.

Novey, S. (1968). *The second look: The reconstruction of personal history in psychiatry and psychoanalysis.* Baltimore: Johns Hopkins University Press.

Olson, H. A. (Ed.). (1979). *Early recollections.* Springfield, Illinois: Charles C Thomas.

Ong, W. J. (1982). *Orality and literacy: The technologizing of the word.* New York: Methuen.

Paul, I. H. (1959). Studies in remembering: The reproduction of connected and extended verbal material. In *Psychological Issues, 1,* Monograph 2. New York: International Universities Press.

Paul, I. H. (1967). The concept of schema in memory theory. In R. R. Holt (Ed.), Motives and thought: Psychoanalytic essays in honor of David Rapaport. *Psychological Issues, vol. 5.* (Monograph 18/19)

Peabody, B. (1975). *The winged word: A study in the technique of ancient Greek oral composition as seen principally through Hesiod's works and days.* Albany, New York: State University of New York Press.

Peto, E. (1936). Contribution to the development of smell feeling. *British Journal of Medical Psychology, 15,* 314–330.

Piaget, J. (1951). *Play dreams and imitation in childhood.* London: Routledge & Kegan Paul.

Piaget, J. (1973). Affective unconscious and cognitive unconscious. *Monographs of the Journal of the American Psychoanalytic Association, 21* (2).

Piaget, J. (1974). *The child & reality: Problems of genetic psychology.* New York: Viking Press.

Piaget, J. (1981). *Intelligence and affectivity: Their relationship during child development.* Palo Alto, California: Annual Reviews.

Piaget, J. & B. Inhelder. (1971). *Mental imagery in the child.* New York: Basic Books.

Piaget, J., & B. Inhelder. (1973). *Memory and intelligence.* New York: Basic Books.

Pillsbury, W. B. (1908). *Attention.* London: Allen & Unwin.

Pillsbury, W. B. (1912). *The essentials of psychology.* New York: Macmillan.

Plewa, F. (1935). The meaning of childhood recollections. Excerpt from the *International Journal of Individual Psychology, 1* (1), 88–101. [Reprinted in H. A. Olson (Ed.) (1979), *Early recollections]*

Popper, K. R. (1976). *Unended quest.* Glasgow: Fontana/Collins. [Quoted in P. N. Johnson-Laird and P. C. Wason (Eds.) (1977). *Thinking: Readings in cognitive science.* Cambridge: Cambridge University Press]

Poulet, G. (1959). *Studies in human time.* New York: Harper.

Posner, M. I., & C. R. R. Snyder. (1975). Attention and cognitive control. In R. L. Solso (Ed.), *Information processing and cognition: The Loyola Symposium.* Hillsdale, New Jersey: Erlbaum.

Reid, T. (1970). *An inquiry into the human mind,* T. Duggan (Ed.). Chicago: University of Chicago Press. (Original publication 1785)

Ricoeur, P. (1970). *Freud and philosophy.* New Haven: Yale University Press.

Ricoeur, P. (1984). *Hermeneutics and the human sciences.* New York: Cambridge University Press.

Rieff, R. (1959). *Freud: The mind of the moralist.* New York: Viking.

Rom, P. (1965). Goethe's earliest recollection. *Journal of Individual Psychology, 21,* 189–193. [Reprinted in H. A. Olson (Ed.) (1979). *Early recollections]*

Ross, B. M., & S. M. Kerst. (1978). Developmental memory theories: Baldwin and Piaget. In H. W. Reese and L. P. Lipsitt (Eds.), *Advances in Child Development and Behavior, vol. 12.* New York: Academic Press.

Rubenstein, B. B. (1967). Explanation and mere description: A metascientific examination of certain aspects of the psychoanalytic theory of motivation. In R. R. Holt (Ed.), Motives and thought: Psychoanalytic essays in honor of David Rapaport. *Psychological Issues,* vol. V, No. 2–3 (Monographs 18/19).

Rubin, D. (1986). *Autobiographical memory.* New York: Cambridge University Press.

Russell, B. (1921). *The analysis of mind.* London: Allen & Unwin.

Russell, B. (1954). *The analysis of matter.* New York: Dover. (Original publication 1927)

Sandler, J., H. Kennedy, & R. L. Tyson. (1980). *The technique of child psychoanalysis: Discussions with Anna Freud.* Cambridge, Massachusetts: Harvard University Press.

Sanders, R. E., E. G. Gonzales, M. D. Murphy, C. L. Liddle, & J. R. Vitina. (1987). Frequency of occurrence and the criteria for automatic processing. *Journal of Experimental Psychology: Learning, Memory, and Cognition, 13,* 241–250.

Sargant, W. (1975). *The mind possessed: A physiology of possession, mysticism and faith healing.* New York: Penguin.

Sartre, J. P. (1961). *The psychology of imagination.* New York: Citadel. (Original publication 1940)

Schactel, E. G. (1959). *Metamorphosis: On the development of affect, perception, attention, and memory.* New York: Basic Books.

Schafer, R. (1976). *A new language for psychoanalysis.* New Haven: Yale University Press.

Schafer, R. (1978). *Language and insight.* New Haven: Yale University Press.

Schafer, R. (1981). *Narrative actions in psychoanalysis.* Worcester, Massachusetts: Clark University Press.

Schneider, W., & R. M. Shiffrin. (1977). Controlled and automatic human information processing: I. Detection, search and attention. *Psychological Review, 84,* 1–66.

Sherry, D. F., & D. L. Schacter. (1987). The evolution of multiple memory systems. *Psychological Review, 94,* 439–454.

Shiffrin, R. M., & W. Schneider. (1977). Controlled and automatic human information processing: II. Perceptual learning, automatic attending, and a general theory. *Psychological Review, 84,* 127–190.

Shils, E. A. (1981). *Tradition.* Chicago: University of Chicago Press.

Skinner, B. F. (1984). *Particulars of my life.* New York: New York University Press.

Skinner, B. F. (1987). Whatever happened to psychology and the science of behavior? *American Psychologist, 42,* 780–786.

Spector, J. J. (1972). *the aesthetics of Freud: A study in psychoanalysis and art.* New York: McGraw-Hill.

Spence, D. P. (1982). *Narrative truth and historical truth: Meaning and interpretation in psychoanalysis.* New York: Norton.

Stewart, S. (1984). *On longing: Narratives of the miniature, the gigantic, the souvenir, the collection.* Baltimore: Johns Hopkins University Press.

Straus, F. W. (1966). *Phenomenological psychology: Selected papers.* New York: Basic Books.

Sullivan, H. S. (1956). *Clinical studies in psychiatry.* In H. S. Perry, M. L. Gawel, & M. Gibbon (Eds.), *The collected works of Harry Stack Sullivan, M.D. vol. II.* New York: Norton.

Titchener, E. B. (1909). *Lectures on the experimental psychology of the thought-processes.* New York: Macmillan.

Titchener, E. B. (1926). *A text-book of psychology.* New York: Macmillan. (Original publication 1910)

Vansina, J. (1985). *Oral tradition as history.* Madison, Wisconsin: University of Wisconsin Press.

Wallace, E. R. (1982). The repetition compulsion. *Psychoanalytic Review, 69,* 455–467.

Warhol, A. (1977). *The philosophy of Andy Warhol.* New York: Harcourt, Brace, Jovanovich.

Werner, H. (1961). *Comparative psychology of mental development.* New York: Science Editions. (Original publication 1948)

White, S. H., & D. B. Pillemer. (1979). Childhood amnesia and the development of a socially accessible memory system. In J. F. Kihlstrom and F. J. Evans (Eds.), *Functional disorders of memory.* Hillsdale, New Jersey: Erlbaum.

Zacks, R. T., L. Hasher, J. W. Alba, H. Sanft, & K. C. Rose. (1984). Is temporal order coded automatically? *Memory and Cognition, 12,* 387–394.

Zajonc, R. B. (1984). On the primacy of affect. *American Psychologist, 39,* 117–123.

INDEX